Praise for *The Compassion~~~~*

"*The Compassionate Englishwom*~~~~
ical scholarship that combines a
British atrocities in the Boer Wa~~~~ ~~~~nt of
Emily Hobhouse's determination ~~~~uelty and deaths
associated with the notorious British concentration camps. At a
time when the history of humanitarianism is receiving increased
attention, Emily Hobhouse stands out as a passionate crusader,
who was prepared to travel around the world, enter war zones and
challenge authorities in both Britain and South Africa to bring
the suffering of women and children to an end.

Well connected, but without formal power, Emily Hobhouse
is a foremost example of all those courageous women who have
agitated for the rights of humanity and thus paved the way for
expanded conceptions of human rights."

*Marilyn Lake, Professor in History at the University of Melbourne and
Immediate Past-President of the Australian Historical Association.*

"A well-researched and readable account of the humanitarian
work of Emily Hobhouse, offering a too little aired perspective
on the atrocities of the British forces in the Anglo-Boer War. The
book is likely to attract a wide readership among those interested
in military history, imperialism, colonial affairs, women's lives,
South African history, and humanitarian concerns."

Dorothy Driver, Professor in English at Adelaide University.

"In following the work of Emily Hobhouse in South Africa in
the Anglo Boer War, Robert Eales provides a sensitive account of
the sufferings of the Boer women and children who risked death
rather than beg their husbands to surrender. On the part of Emily
Hobhouse it is a story of determination and persistence and we
see the human spirit at its best."

*Jennifer Hobhouse Balme, Author of books on Emily Hobhouse and
custodian of her papers.*

For Jane
and our children
With love

The COMPASSIONATE ENGLISHWOMAN

The COMPASSIONATE ENGLISHWOMAN

EMILY HOBHOUSE IN THE BOER WAR

ROBERT EALES

MH
PRESS

THE COMPASSIONATE ENGLISHWOMAN
Emily Hobhouse in the Boer War

Published by Middle Harbour Press Pty Ltd Australia
Email: middleharbourpress@bigpond.com
http://www.middleharbourpress.com

National Library of Australia Cataloguing-in-Publication entry

Creator: Eales, Robert, author.
Title: The Compassionate Englishwoman : Emily Hobhouse in the Boer war / Robert Eales.
ISBN: 9780992527624 (paperback)
             9780992527631 (ebook)

Notes: Includes bibliographical references and index.
Subjects: Hobhouse, Emily, 1860-1926
             Women philanthropists--Biography.
             South African War, 1899-1902--War work.
Dewey Number: 361.74092

Disclaimer:
This book is a work of history. All reasonable efforts have been made and care has been taken to verify the information contained herein. All reasonable efforts were made to obtain permission to use materials reproduced in this book, except where the copyright is believed to have expired. The publisher welcomes further information in this regard.

Contents

List of maps
and photographs

Map of Southern Africa In 1899

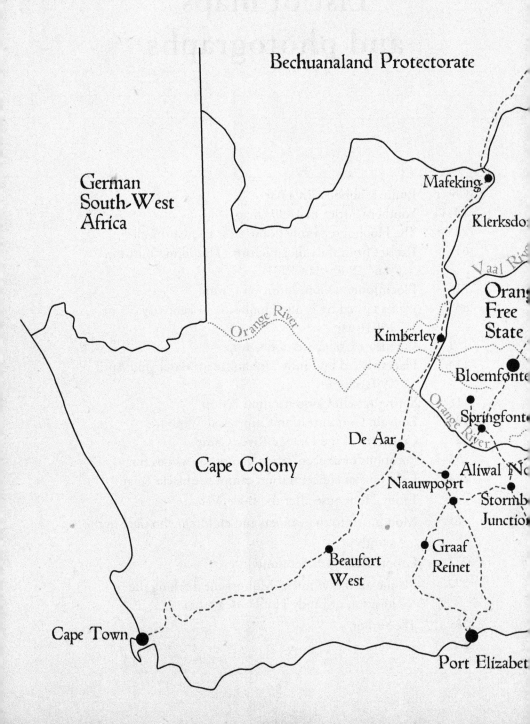

Bechuanaland Protectorate

German South-West Africa

Mafeking

Klerksdo

Vaal Riv

Orange River

Kimberley

Oran Free State

Bloemfonte

Springfont

Orange River

De Aar

Cape Colony

Aliwal No

Naauwpoort

Stormb Junctio

Graaf Reinet

Beaufort West

Cape Town

Port Elizabet

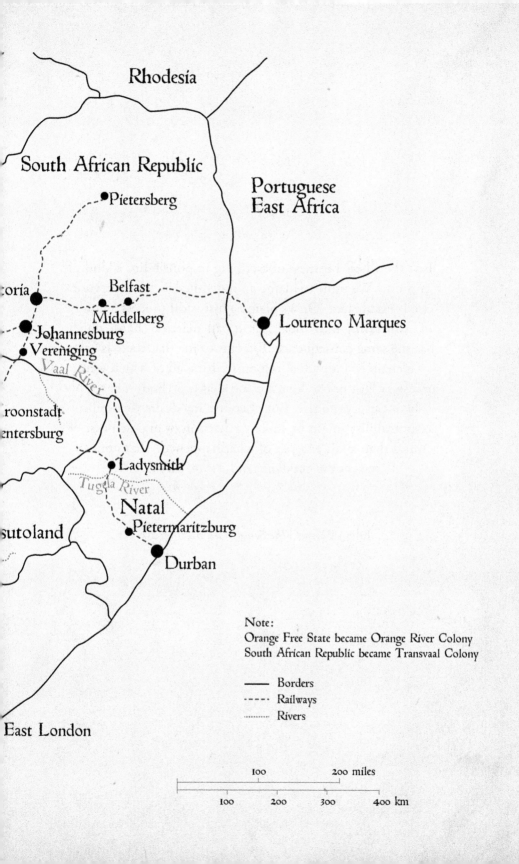

Isn't the whole business of ascribing responsibility a kind of cop-out? We want to blame an individual so that everyone else is exculpated. Or we blame a historical process as a way of exonerating individuals. Or it's all anarchic chaos, which has the same consequence. It seems to me that there is - was - a chain of individual responsibilities, all of which were necessary, but not so long a chain that everybody can simply blame everyone else. But of course my desire to ascribe responsibility might be more a reflection of my own cast of mind than a fair analysis of what happened. That's one of the central problems of history, isn't it, sir?

Julian Barnes, *The Sense of an Ending*, 2011

PART 1

In southern Africa

Chapter 1

The mission begins

Emily Hobhouse embarked at Southampton on 7 December 1900, bound for Cape Town. She was not a good sailor and did not enjoy the next two weeks at sea. It was not the motion of the ship that particularly troubled her but the enforced idleness. She did not know what to expect on arrival and was not confident that she would be able to accomplish what she had in mind. The sooner she arrived, the sooner she could make an assessment and begin preparations. She contented herself with asking her fellow passengers to tell her all they knew of southern Africa and studying the language of the people she would encounter. 'Boer Dutch' she called it.

Emily was heading for a land at war. She was concerned for the women and children caught in the fighting in the interior of southern Africa. She hoped to discover the nature and extent of their difficulties and to deliver assistance from the modest resources at her disposal.

When the ship arrived off Cape Town in the middle of the night, the small harbour was full and so they anchored in the bay. The next morning, Emily rose early. Excited, and driven by her sense of urgency, she talked her way onto the first support vessel that came alongside the ship and made her way to land, leaving her luggage on board. Passengers of her class were supposed to disembark later in the day.

Ashore, evidence of war abounded. The harbour was full of troopships and the docks were piled high with military supplies. Soldiers in khaki were everywhere. Idle locals hung about hoping for a chance to earn a quick shilling amid all the activity. Prices in the town were very high, some higher than in London.

When her fellow passengers landed, they found that accommodation was hardly obtainable and Emily assisted her friends, the Rowntrees, to find lodgings. She did not have to concern herself with this difficulty on her own account, for she was expected and arrangements had been made. Friendly faces came to meet her, her luggage was claimed, and they transported her around the foot of the mountain to a suburb of gracious colonial homes. By late afternoon, she was eating fresh figs and apricots on a spacious veranda and nursing a pet meerkat as if she had known it always.

It was high summer, and the weather contrasted greatly with the cold, wet and wintry conditions she had left behind. The great, moody mountain towered in the background, as it does over everything that happens in Cape Town. Emily had not given much thought to the scenery that would greet her on her arrival, and she was smitten from that first sunrise on the ship in the bay. *I was nearly knocked down by Table Mountain and its attendant Devil's Peak and Lion's Head*, she wrote to her brother, Leonard Hobhouse, a few days after coming ashore. *They are magnificent – but what pleases me still more are the Blue-Berg Mountains, a long range with jagged peaks which came as a surprise for I had never heard of them.*[1]

The war had started fourteen months earlier in October 1899. In this conflict, Britain was engaged in yet another colonial conquest. She was at the peak of her power and possessed an empire that circled the globe. But that was not enough. There were more opportunities in Africa and Cecil John Rhodes, that arch-imperialist, had articulated the vision a few years earlier: he wanted

Britain's control to stretch through Africa from south to north, unbroken from the Cape to Cairo.

Most of that vision had already been accomplished before this war. In the north, Egypt and the Sudan were effectively part of the Empire and so were Kenya and Uganda. Together they constituted a continuous chain of control from the Mediterranean to the equator. In the south of the continent, British power extended over a great deal, too. It encompassed the coastal colonies – the Cape Colony and Natal – Basutoland (now Lesotho), Bechuanaland (now Botswana), Rhodesia (now Zimbabwe and Zambia) and Nyasaland (today's Malawi). Only a comparatively small gap remained in Rhodes's vision where Tanzania sits today. In the west, Nigeria, the Gold Coast (Ghana) and Sierra Leone were also in the bag.

However, Britain did not possess the most valuable part of the southern interior – the territories of the two Boer republics, the South African Republic (SAR) and the Orange Free State (OFS). (See the map on pages 10–11). The SAR contained the largest gold deposits ever discovered and its rapidly growing mining industry meant that it would soon dominate the economy of the region. The OFS was less interesting, but it was closely allied with the SAR by culture, kinship and formal treaty, and it lay between the SAR and the existing coastal colonies. As these republics prospered, their neighbours would find markets in this emerging concentration of wealth and people, and Britain's influence over the region might wane. To avoid that prospect, Britain would, in this war, extend her hold over the whole of southern Africa and unify the region under the Crown.

The assessment was that seizing the republican territories would make them Britain's forever. They would be defensible against others who also had colonial ambitions and were envious of what Britain already possessed. The strategic risks were clear. Germany, France, Portugal and Belgium already had large African colonies, some adjacent to Britain's area of control, and also wished for more. Some of them, perhaps all of them, also had eyes on the two republics. Then there were the Dutch. They had been expelled from southern Africa at the beginning of the nineteenth century – by Britain – but had retained strong cultural and other ties with the Boers and might wish to reassert their influence if a suitable opportunity should appear.

However, it was not just a matter of Imperial ambition, global dominance and strategic control. Some of the most powerful entrepreneurs in the gold-mining industry were newcomers who had raised the capital for their ventures in London. They much preferred to operate under British rule and had played a significant part in fomenting the British invasion.

The ruling politicians and bureaucrats did not speak in these terms with the British people before or during the war. Suggestions that there were territorial objectives or an interest in the gold were strongly denied. Instead, they provided other reasons for invading the republics. Their aim was, they said, to defend the rights of the thousands of British citizens who had joined the gold rush and were now in the southern SAR; not the mine owners but the common man out to make his fortune. They said they would bring democracy and good government to these parts of the African continent and establish a more civilised society.

But deeds speak more truly than words, and for such noble words to have meaning they must be followed by noble deeds. Readers will soon form their own views as to whether the fine words were spoken in sincerity or for convenience.

Emily Hobhouse was one of the significant British minority who opposed the war. Soon after the conflict erupted, the prominent politician, lawyer and academic, Leonard Courtney, started an anti-war organisation in London called the South African Conciliation Committee (SACC). He invited Emily to become the secretary of the women's branch and she eagerly accepted the opportunity to work for a cause in which she believed. Similar organisations emerged elsewhere in the United Kingdom, too, sometimes as branches of the SACC.

She was thirty-nine years old, unmarried and at her age, in those times, unlikely ever to marry. She was, however, competent, industrious, articulate and committed and soon became involved in ceaseless activity, arranging events across Britain to promote the cause of conciliation. Sometimes she spoke herself at these events. The war had popular support during this period and persuading the British people to think differently was not easy.

As the war progressed, Emily learnt of the existence of camps in southern Africa that contained people who had been displaced by the hostilities. The camps were occupied mainly by Boer women and children, and she heard that they were having a difficult time. These camps also held the elderly and the disabled as well as men who were attempting to stand aside from the fighting. Most men were elsewhere. Some had died in the fighting, but many more were still on campaign opposing the British or had been captured and sent as prisoners of war to distant shores: St Helena Island, India, Ceylon, Bermuda and other faraway places.

Later there would be camps for black people, too.

As more information reached her, Emily became increasingly concerned for the people in the camps. After much hesitation, she established a new organisation to assist them, the South African Women and Children Distress Fund. It was independent of the SACC, and her fervent wish was that it should be seen as apolitical and in pursuit of purely humanitarian objectives. However, its supporters were mainly people who opposed the war, and over time it inevitably came to be associated with the anti-war movement.

She persuaded prominent and wealthy people to serve on the fund's committee and busied herself raising money. By the time the formal registration was complete, there was already enough to make a start in delivering aid. But what were the needs? No one had a clear view of the circumstances of the displaced people. No one seemed to know how many there were or even how many camps existed.

British military achievements were in the London papers the next day, thanks to the telegraph line from London that spread its dendritic tentacles across the southern veld, but it was hard to obtain news of the destruction of homes and of the consequences for women and children. Enquiries through official channels produced little information. So Emily proposed to her newly formed committee that she should go to southern Africa herself to investigate and begin the distribution of aid. The committee agreed, pledging to continue raising funds and collecting clothing in her absence.

On her arrival in Cape Town, Emily was greeted and accommodated by Caroline and Charles Murray. It was on their veranda that she ate figs and patted the meerkat on her first day ashore. Charles was a respected doctor while Caroline was the sister of Percy Molteno, a member of the Distress Fund's committee in London. Percy had introduced Emily to Caroline when Caroline had visited London.

Percy was married to a shipping heiress and they were well able to contribute to the fund. But for Emily, the value of the Molteno siblings went further than accommodation and money. Percy and Caroline's father had been the prime minister of the Cape Colony. Together the brother and sister provided a bridge between politically involved and wealthy individuals in London and influential people in Cape Town. It was a crucial connection in Emily's project.

Chapter 2

In Cape Town

After her arrival in Cape Town, Emily was accommodated by a succession of leading families in and around the city. After a week with Caroline and Charles Murray, she went to the Merrimans. He, John X Merriman, was a prominent member of the Cape Parliament and a future colonial prime minister. Next she accepted an invitation to stay with Mr and Mrs Harry Currey and wrote to her aunt about her time with them. *Their house is all amongst pine trees like Bournemouth but with the big mountains close behind. The grapes are just ripening and peaches, apricots and other fruits abound. The flowers and flowering shrubs are legion.*[2]

In this community of Cape English, Emily felt welcomed and supported. Her successive, influential hosts introduced her to other influential citizens. She found that people were interested in her mission and were willing to offer advice, share their views on the war and suggest where she could acquire more information or assistance.

The majority of the whites in the Cape Colony, it might be inferred, shared Emily's anti-war sentiments. The Dutch speakers, more numerous than the English, were overwhelmingly opposed to the war. So were some of the colonial Englishmen and women, as Emily discovered. They deplored the way the war had been fomented and were troubled by the morality of Britain's use of force to expand its colonial empire into the Boer republics. Some of the influential among them, Merriman included, had made personal efforts to defuse the tension, promote consultation and arbitration, and avoid bloodshed. They understood only too well how their peace-making efforts had been systematically undermined. Later, as stories of the manner in which the war was being fought reached Cape Town, their disquiet deepened.

In the Colony, the English and Dutch had come to terms with each other after a century of tension between them. The leading citizens feared that the war in the interior would polarise attitudes again, strain relationships anew and leave them with a difficult legacy. Neither Dutch nor English wanted this. For all of them it made sense to support an Englishwoman who was sympathetic to the mainly Dutch victims of the war and was preparing to make tangible, visible efforts to assist them.

Emily had not come to oppose the war, however. Her humanitarian mission was best served by keeping her attitude to the conflict to herself. The question was where to begin.

Before her departure from England, she became aware of a refugee camp at Port Elizabeth, a city on the south coast of the Cape Colony and far from the turmoil of the interior. Her intention was to go first to this place. However, the people she met at the Cape knew that the situation was more complex and troubling than she realised and they assisted her to become better informed, directing her to people who had relevant information.

In her first long letter from southern Africa to her Aunt Mary, Lady Hobhouse, she mentions meetings with Sir Henry de Villiers, Chief Justice of the Cape Colony, and CP Schultz, a leading citizen who served in a voluntary capacity as the secretary of two committees formed to assist widows and orphans in the republics. She also met Elizabeth Roos who, according to Rykie van Reenen, editor of Emily's letters, was one of Cape Town's most influential women. Mrs Roos later founded a Christian Women's Association that attracted country-wide membership.[3] Emily liked her; she secured her support and they hoped to work together.

Soon Emily began a round of meetings with people who had been displaced by the war and had succeeded in reaching Cape Town. She wrote of this to her brother, Leonard. *It is frightfully hard to find time to write when I have to go from place to place talking to people … The endless tales I am told are most confusing and to keep them clear at all I have to write down every woman's conversation when she is gone. The things I am told are humiliating and heartrending in the extreme and the effort to listen to it all sympathetically for a few hours exhausts one more than I had deemed possible.*[4]

She now realised, as her hosts knew she would, that the fate of women and children in the war-ravaged interior should be her primary concern. By comparison, the occupants of the camp at Port Elizabeth were few in number and were living under better conditions. To fulfil her mission, Emily had to go into the hinterland, into the former republics and into the war zone, and she began to make new plans. Others might have hesitated, but perhaps Emily had known all along that this was where she would have to go.

The mountain towered over all her encounters in and around Cape Town, ever present, ever changing, never changing. Sometimes its white table-cloth of cloud seems to fall endlessly down on the city, never reaching the bottom, never exhausting the length of ephemeral fabric from which it is magically drawn. On another face, the mountain obstructs the flow of sea air, forcing it to rise. The moisture in it condenses first to cloud, then to gentle rain and so, relieved of some of its burden, it scales the towering cliffs and disappears over the top. Sometimes the residents living high on these slopes can see that over there on the distant plain, the sun shines brilliantly while they have to unfold their umbrellas. On other days, the weather is kinder and allows all to enjoy the generous, warming, southern sun. Emily loved it all and wrote again to her aunt, *As for the scenery it is lovely; far more beautiful than I had been led to expect ...*[5]

Emily needed the permission of the High Commissioner for South Africa and Governor of the Cape Colony, Sir Alfred Milner, to visit the interior and she was not sure she would obtain it. The initial signs were not encouraging. She called at Government House with a letter of introduction from Lady Hobhouse and was asked the subject on which she desired an interview. When she replied 'the condition of women and children', she was told that it was not likely that Sir Alfred would see her on *that* topic.[6] Nevertheless, she received an invitation to lunch with the high commissioner a few days later.

I feel a little nervous about my coming interview with Milner, so much depends upon it[7], she wrote to her brother Leonard on 6 January 1901. Two days later she was able to report to Lady Hobhouse:

> *I have just come back from Cape Town and from lunching at Government House. It is such a relief that this meeting is over and I think I may say it was on the whole a satisfactory interview and thanks to your introduction so pleasant. I admit that I was in a 'blue funk' for twenty-four hours beforehand, not that I was afraid of His Excellency, but afraid that I should not plead my cause at all adequately. There were eight gentlemen at lunch and only me. Afterwards Sir Alfred took me alone to the drawing-room and we sat together on the sofa and went at it hammer and tongs for an hour. He admitted the farm burning* [British soldiers were selectively burning Boer farms] *was a mistake (how mild to put it like that) and he said he thought something should certainly be done to ameliorate the condition of the women and children, about whom he was evidently uneasy, for with his own eyes he had seen some truck-loads of women when he came down the line, and it had occurred to him that it was rather terrible. Finally,*

after I had told him many details (and I did not mince matters) and told him how uneasy the English conscience was growing and how desperately sore the Afrikanders [Afrikaners] *felt and how for the honour of England we ought to mend matters in the camps, then finally he said he would do all in his power to forward my going the round of the camps as representative of the English movement and with me a Dutch lady whoever I and the people here like to choose as representative of South Africa.*

Then I said I must be allowed to take two trucks with me, one with clothing and one with provisions, and this too he conceded, but – there is a 'but' and here it comes, he must refer it to Kitchener. He said he could do no more than recommend and urge Kitchener to allow us to go ... In a few days he will let me have Kitchener's reply, and meanwhile we are to settle on the Dutch woman ...

He struck me as amiable and weak, clear-headed and narrow. Everyone says he has no heart, but I think I hit on the atrophied remains of one. It might be developed if he had not, as he says he has, made up his mind to back up the Military in everything.

Now I wait on Kitchener ...[8]

Years later in her draft autobiography, Emily acknowledged that she had been far more worried about the interview than she had let on at the time: *I was well-nigh sick with terror lest I should prove incompetent for the ordeal. And as was (and is) usual with me in moments of mental or emotional strain my heart beat so violently I could hardly breathe.*[9] Milner, however, put her at her ease. *It was wonderful how, as we sat on the low couch in the coolness and quiet of that spacious room, with its windows opening upon the green sward and grand old oaks of the garden, my nervousness passed away and I was able to converse freely. This return of calm was undoubtedly due in large measure to Sir Alfred's singular charm and sympathetic manner so calculated to put one at ease.*[10]

General Herbert Horatio, Lord Kitchener, successor to Lord Roberts as the commander-in-chief of the Imperial forces in southern Africa, was based in Pretoria. He had served his early career in the Royal Engineers; he was systematic and hard-working and directed the war in considerable detail. He spent many hours each day at his desk sending telegrams to his field commanders in every corner of the theatre of war, responding to London's incessant demands for information and demanding more resources himself. He was a good judge of men, but, as a bachelor, he was said to be uncomfortable around women. It is unlikely that he welcomed the thought of one of them on the loose, by herself, unguarded, in the midst of his war.

There is no record of his thoughts on the request from Milner, and one can only speculate. He was probably in two minds about it. The war, and particularly the way that Roberts and then he had chosen to conduct it, was making women and children homeless. On the one hand, he might have thought, it would be good to have a woman review the well-being of these refugees and assist them where assistance might be needed. On the other hand, there was a risk that she would turn out to be a busybody who made political mischief out of the situation. But then she had declared her mission to be purely humanitarian and if Milner recommended her, if she had come with an introduction from her aunt, Lady Hobhouse, it meant she was one of them, an Englishwoman of social standing, a person who could be expected to say and do what was best for the establishment, best for England, best for the advancement of the Empire.

Chapter 3

Emily

Emily Hobhouse was indeed a product of the ruling nexus of church, politics, wealth and aristocracy. She was born on 9 April 1860, the fifth of six surviving children, in the Cornish village of St Ive (pronounced 'st eve'). It is a few kilometres east of Liskeard, just a dot on the map and not to be confused with the better known town of St Ives. Reginald Hobhouse, her Oxford-educated father, was the village rector and an archdeacon in the Anglican Church while her mother, Caroline, was a Trelawny, a prominent Cornish family. Despite her father's modest position, his inherited wealth, her mother's money and the income from the parish enabled them to build a new house across the road from the church. They did not regard it as large, and yet it had three sitting rooms and a school room, possessed two pianos and had accommodation for the family, governesses and servants.[11] Because the family's financial resources were ostensibly stretched by the need for her father – in poor health – to spend the worst of the English winters in the south of France, the four girls were educated at home by governesses and their mother. The two boys went to boarding school. Her mother could manage Latin, French, German and Italian in various degrees of fluency and spent as much time educating her girls as she could in a busy pastoral life.

The Hobhouse family home at St Ive, Cornwall

When the parents went to France, the children were either minded by the trustworthy housekeeper, her gardener husband and the governesses or placed with relatives. Thus Emily made regular and sometimes protracted visits to her uncle and aunt, Sir Arthur and Lady Mary Hobhouse, later Lord and Lady Hobhouse. They lived in Mayfair in London and were politically engaged. Arthur, a barrister, had served as the legal adviser to the governor-general of India and had been vice-chancellor of the University of Calcutta. He was a one-time unsuccessful parliamentary candidate but became a judge in the Privy Council instead. The Privy Council acted as the highest court of appeal for legal issues arising in Britain's dominions, colonies and other overseas possessions.

Emily

Affairs of the day were constantly discussed in their house. Around the dinner table, Emily learnt that national figures were mere people, even familiar people, whose inclinations could be identified, foibles recognised, utterances dissected, decisions criticised or supported and achievements deplored or praised. If there were policies, other policies also merited consideration, even opposing policies. Government decisions, once made, could be unmade. For a girl from the delightful Cornish countryside, these were insights she would not otherwise have received and she understood and absorbed them. Emily's aunt and uncle were key influences in her life. Arthur and Mary, in turn, recognised in her a remarkable child and a close and lifelong relationship developed.

Emily's mother died when she was nineteen. She and Maud, an older sister, now managed the house and cared for their ailing father. When Maud married and moved out, the task fell to Emily alone. The energetic, capable Emily did much more than attend to her father's needs. She believed that those who could had an obligation to assist the less fortunate in the community. She worked tirelessly in the parish, visiting the modest cottages of farm workers, miners and others where need existed – often covering considerable distances on foot in all weathers. Where she could not provide the necessary assistance herself, she arranged for others to help. The young Emily became accustomed to making a difference in people's lives, developed considerable organisational abilities and grew in capability and self-confidence.

These experiences seemed unremarkable at the time, especially to her. If a situation was not satisfactory, one considered how it might be changed for the better, marshalled the appropriate resources and set in train processes that would improve matters. It was just what a normal, moral, sensible person of standing in the community did.

She was thirty-five when her father died. Now free but homeless, she felt herself ill-equipped by education or experience to make her way in the world. It appears that her share of the family inheritance was sufficient to support a modest life, and she resolved to commit herself to the only thing she knew – caring for others.

She decided to work among Cornish miners who had emigrated to the United States of America, people with whom she shared a common origin. It seems a strange, if adventurous choice. With the assistance of the wife of the Archbishop of Canterbury, she obtained a posting to Minnesota. When she arrived, the bishop assigned her to the new, rapidly developing town of Virginia. Its growth was driven by logging and iron-ore mining, and it was a rough and ready place. There were disappointingly few Cornishmen among the miners, but it did have forty-two saloons (bars), four brothels and plenty of places to gamble. In summer, the unmade roads were quagmires and in winter two metres of snow fell. Adaptable and pragmatic, Emily bent her efforts to her assigned task and did her best to reduce the volume of alcohol consumed and get the men to church on Sundays. She managed to establish a library and was soon recognised and liked. People called her 'the English Lady' and meant it as a term of respect.

She became engaged to a local businessman and mayor of Virginia, JC Jackson, in what was to be the only romantic interest in her life. His business was not doing well in Minnesota and he suggested that they go to Mexico to make a fresh start. This part of her life is not well documented, but it seems that Emily travelled ahead and bought a farm at her own expense. While she waited for her fiancée to arrive, she made plans for the building of a house on the property. It never materialised. Jackson continually found business reasons for delaying his arrival and after two years of solitude and uncertainty, the engagement ended in 1898 and a poorer Emily returned to England.[12]

Her four years in the Americas reveal something of who she was. Those years were a time of emergence from a genteel and sheltered life in ancient, settled, rural England. The town of Virginia could hardly have been more different. The masculine culture and the severe weather of the Canadian border region could have held no appeal for her, yet she remained and worked there until romantic reasons drew her away. Was her persistence a product of emotional and physical resilience coupled with dedication to her appointed task, secure in the knowledge that this was not forever and that she could return to England whenever she wanted? Or did she stay because she felt that she belonged nowhere else and had nothing else to do in life? Did Jackson pack her off to Mexico as a means of extricating himself from an engagement he did not mean to honour? Were the two years there evidence of her patience, independence and ability to cope in a country where she did not speak the language? Or was she naïvely spending her money in the hope of securing a brighter future, clinging to a mirage that she should have realised would never materialise? Operating on her own and with no one to talk things over, she had not looked after her own best interests.

But she had taken to the wider world and once again demonstrated competence, adaptability, self-reliance and self-confidence under difficult conditions. She had displayed one of her enduring qualities: she saw life through the opportunities it offered her to be there for others. What she really needed was to be needed, by a man with whom to build a new future or by a cause that mattered to which she could devote her life, preferably both. In the Americas she had found neither. Yet her time there had been part of the essential preparation for the work that would be the hallmark of her life. After Virginia, Minnesota, no male-dominated society could intimidate her, no matter how masculine it was or how adverse the conditions might be.

Back in London, Emily bought an apartment in Chelsea and took in a lodger to help make ends meet. She now worked with the Women's Industrial Committee, an organisation concerned with the well-being of women and children at their places of work. Many factories then still employed children. In this role she had scope to address issues at the policy level, though she did not express it in those terms. She was there when the war broke out and Leonard Courtney approached her to become the secretary of the women's branch of the South African Conciliation Committee.

There is nothing in Emily's background that hints at the remarkable things she did later: she was an unmarried, middle-aged woman with little formal schooling though she was, in fact, well-educated by the standards of her time. She had lived most of her life in a small community in Cornwall, had spent two years doing social work in an out-of-the way mining town in the USA and then two years achieving nothing of significance in Mexico.

Yet, despite the ordinariness of her life before she went to southern Africa, she remained secure in her identity. One of her biographers, John Hall, writes: *Certainly she retained a sense of self-consequence throughout her life. ... She never forgot that uncle Arthur was a peer and privy councillor; or that other close relations included two members of parliament, a bishop, and baronets on both sides of the family; close kinsmen included John Cam Hobhouse, Lord Broughton, the intimate of Byron. The origins of the Hobhouses might not have been ancient, but marriages by the fast-rising family during the Georgian era linked the clan with the higher reaches of Britain's landed classes and aristocracy ...*[13] That sense of self-consequence, of importance, and the self-confidence that went with it, was the crucial ingredient in her make up that underpinned her adaptability, her capacity for handling difficult human situations and her readiness to speak forthrightly with people in authority on behalf of others.

In Cape Town, Emily busied herself with preparations for her journey to the interior, confident that she would get permission to go. Her knowledge of the camps improved steadily. Relatives of Capetonians in the former republics were anxious for the world to know what they were seeing and experiencing, and they wrote of it. Travellers and returning soldiers arrived daily bearing letters and had fresh tales to tell.

To Lady Hobhouse she wrote on 8 January: *A soldier fresh from Johannesburg, gave me a horrible description of the camp there. He, a rough man, was broken hearted over it. Johannesburg has about four thousand in this camp. I know already of at least 11 camps and there are more. I can't tell the exact numbers in these camps but they are large and growing.*[14]

She was acclimatising to the place, its people and their colonial culture. Her excellent connections and humanitarian mission gave her access to yet more prominent people. She had a meeting with Dr Andrew Murray, a church minister, theologian and founder of several girls' schools. He had progressive ideas on women's education and was a leading member of the Afrikaner community despite his Scottish roots.

Ellie Cronje was one of her informants who had reached Cape Town from the interior. She was the daughter of Commandant Piet Cronje, the Boer general defeated and captured by Lord Roberts in a crucial British victory on the Modder River. Ellie enthusiastically supported Emily's objectives and volunteered to accompany her on her journey to the interior. Very much liking this young woman, Emily wished to take her to assist with the language difficulties she expected to encounter.

Emily accompanied the chief justice, Sir Henry de Villiers, and Lady de Villiers on one of their weekly visits to the prisoner-of-war camp outside Cape Town. From newly captured burghers, she learnt of the defiant state of mind of those still in the field. She was told that they had no intention of laying down their arms and giving up the fight. The implication was that the war would not be over any time soon.

She met young Boer nurses, who had worked in military hospitals during a great outbreak of enteric (typhoid) in the north. Deeply committed to their calling, they explained to Emily that they had nursed British soldiers as diligently as Boer casualties.

Emily also met Mr JW Sauer, a cabinet minister in successive colonial governments, and was particularly taken with his wife, Mrs Mary Sauer. Just as she was impressed by many, so they, in turn, learnt of Emily's mission, wished her well and became her supporters. Later, this would matter.

There were practical arrangements to be made, too. Caroline Murray agreed to remain her point of contact in Cape Town and, with other volunteers, to handle the transmission of aid that would hopefully continue to arrive from Britain, both material and financial. In addition, Emily thought it would be sensible to establish a committee of influential people to oversight the affairs of the Distress Fund in southern Africa and intercede on its behalf with officialdom should that become necessary. Lady de Villiers and Dr Murray agreed to serve on this committee. Aiming high as ever, Emily hoped the third and final member would be Sir William Bisset Berry, Speaker of the Cape Parliament, but he was out of town and she could not ask him directly.

In her memoirs, Emily made an interesting comment about the people in Cape Town whom she met during this period in her mission. She wrote: *I was struck, for instance by the intense devotion to England, a devotion which had received a severe blow. This feeling differed entirely from our own natural love for our country which allows us to see her faults without abating our devotion. The Cape people had seen England through a veil of idealism which had small relation to the reality. The Tory Government's war policy had torn asunder this veil with disastrous results. The effects were deep. Something lifelong had snapped within them – their bearings were lost.*[15]

There were grounds for this reflection, but it was the impression of a newcomer. People like the Merrimans, the De Villiers, Dr Murray, Mr Schulz, Mrs Roos and the Sauers understood Britain's chequered involvement in this part of the world. They knew perfectly well that British engagement in southern Africa over almost a hundred years had not always been benign, constructive or well-considered. They knew of the attempts to suppress the Dutch language and the Cape Dutch culture, of the abolition of democratic institutions in favour of direct rule from London, of the annexation of lands occupied by the Boers across the Orange River, across the Vaal River and across the Drakensberg mountains in Natal, of the seizing of the Kimberley diamond fields from the Orange Free State, of the earlier struggles of the republicans to free themselves from those annexations and of the earlier, smaller war with the Transvaal Boers, a war that Britain did not pursue. They had seen at close range the boundless imperialism and unbridled ambition of Cecil John Rhodes and his unconscionable Jameson Raid just a few years earlier in which he attempted to seize the Transvaal by force with the tacit support of the Colonial Secretary, Joseph Chamberlain. They plainly understood Alfred Milner's war-mongering in the current conflict. It is unlikely that they were quite as starry-eyed about Britain as Emily supposed. But they were perfectly entitled to believe that the British nation – if not their representatives in southern Africa – had higher values and to hold her government to higher standards of conduct. In this respect they were indeed disappointed, as Emily's comment indicates.

The white people with whom she mixed in Cape Town were no longer English or French or Scottish or Dutch or German or Irish or Welsh expatriates. Rather, they were members of an educated and cultured Cape colonial society that had evolved from its mainly European roots over two and a half centuries to become something new and different. They were often underestimated. When it came to matters relating to southern Africa, Britain – in the guise of the Colonial Office, Milner and the governors before him – did not attribute sufficient weight to their views, indeed sometimes ignored their opinions entirely, and this irked them. In the lead-up to the war, Milner had again shown a steely deafness to their advice, suggestions or pleas.

Then, as Emily was continuing her discussions, Lord Kitchener's reply arrived.

Chapter 4

Journey to the interior

Kitchener's reply, when it came, was a calculated compromise.[16] He would allow Emily to visit the camps in the southern part of the war zone, but knowing what he had in mind in the north, he would keep her well away from there. Perhaps he was setting her a test: if she conducted herself satisfactorily, he would reconsider.

She wrote to her brother, Leonard, on 20 January 1901:

> *This week has been such a rush. After what seemed a long*
> *waiting, Kitchener's answer came and the Governor sent*
> *it to me with a letter from himself. I at once went up to*
> *Government House to talk it over with him and he kindly*
> *vouchsafed me another interview and he said he would do his*
> *best to secure me a comfortable journey. Then he offered his*
> *secretary to work out the details for me and we two saw the*
> *Military Head of the Lines, Colonel Cowie, and the Head of*
> *Permits (Major Moseley Leigh, I think).*
>
> *My truck is to start to-morrow night the 21st and I follow*
> *on Tuesday, 22nd. So far, so good. But alas, Kitchener only*
> *vouchsafes half of what I asked and which Milner himself*
> *'urged and recommended'. He forbids the Dutch companion or*

anyone but me and will not at present allow me further north than Bloemfontein ...

I thought it was wiser to accept such permission as was vouchsafed and work on from that rather than fly into a pet and say I must have all or nothing. This is what the more violent folk here advise but I can't see it in that light. I think, considering the state of the country, to be allowed within the war areas at all is a considerable concession. And much needs doing at Bloemfontein and at Kimberley and at camps south of Bloemfontein – notably Norvals Pont. Milner recommends me to visit them from that base. I explained to him that it would not satisfy me unless I got to Johannesburg and he replied that he thought Lord Kitchener was fairly well disposed towards the plan and that if I wrote to him direct from Bloemfontein no doubt he would let me proceed. Anyhow, now I can make a beginning ...

I hope it will be thought I have decided rightly in going thus far, but it is a great disappointment about Mrs Roos and will double my difficulties.[17]

After her first meeting with Sir Alfred Milner, it had been settled that Mrs Roos would be the Dutch woman to accompany Emily rather than the young Ellie Cronje. Emily would have liked to take both, but Kitchener's letter ruled both out. Besides depriving her of a companion, the ruling created a further, awkward difficulty for Emily. Milner asked her to say nothing of Kitchener's prohibition of the Dutch companion and Emily was left to indicate, without explanation, that she would not, after all, be taking the prominent Mrs Roos or anyone else. She later wrote in her memoir: *The Cape Dutch, too, had set their hearts upon it and took the prohibition badly. Some indeed really stirred up bad feeling, accusing me of 'keeping in with Milner' and wishing to keep everything in my own hands and also blaming the Governor himself. I was unable to make the matter clear ...*[18]

Milner had agreed to allow her two rail trucks to move aid to the interior, but she was given one large one instead. On 21 January 1901 she wrote to Lady Hobhouse:

All day I have been loading my big truck. I have taken great quantities of foodstuffs and all the clothing which had come from our English sources. The food came to nearly £200. It was such a pity not to have been able to cram the great truck full, as I have been allowed it carriage-free, and I want to make myself a big base of supplies in Bloemfontein and work up to Johannesburg from there as soon as I can wheedle Lord Kitchener into giving me a further permit. ...

I have been meeting Mr Fichardt, a charming young man, educated in England of course and lately Mayor of Bloemfontein. He was wounded and taken prisoner soon after [the battle of] Paardeberg ... He is here on parole. His family are people of position in Bloemfontein and he has asked his mother to put me up when I get there on Friday.[19]

In this letter, Emily added comments about the military situation:

My host has just returned from Kimberley and up-country and describes the British Army – sick, weary, worn, spiritless, fit for nothing. The Boers have seldom had a better chance than they have at this moment. ... I wish you could hear the accounts from eyewitnesses of some of the engagements lately fought.

After [the battle of] Nooitgedacht the other day 7,000 Boers raised another memorial. Each man brought a stone, put his mark on it and solemnly swore to fight for independence till death.

I think if you could see these people you would see their spirit is wholly unquenchable, while the spirit of our soldiers is gone out like a candle.[20]

These views were probably influenced by her contact with the Boers in the nearby prisoner-of-war camp. As it happens, Sir Alfred Milner had similar views about the soldiers fighting on their side. He wrote to the Colonial Secretary, Joseph Chamberlain, at about this time expressing annoyance and humiliation that they were unable to deal with the guerrillas. He attributed some of this to the extreme staleness of the British and Colonial troops.[21] So Emily had grounds for her views. But she was forgetting something: it was wartime and military censors read letters. With comments like these, her apolitical stance was placed at risk.

Moreover, the remarks were not entirely justified and the real situation was more complicated. Though the battle of Nooitgedacht in the Magaliesberg west of Pretoria on 13 December 1900 *was* an important Boer victory, it was against the run of play. For the most part, the Boers were on the defensive and moving constantly to avoid being cornered by the Imperial forces. In their ranks, too, the men sometimes felt demoralised and overwhelmed by the much greater troop strength and military resources ranged against them.

Milner was still unaware of the depth of Emily's anti-war views and generously wrote to General GT Pretyman, Military Governor of the Orange River Colony (formerly the Orange Free State), asking him to assist her when she arrived in Bloemfontein. Pretyman, despite his title, controlled the civil administration in the newly annexed colony. Sir Alfred gave Emily a copy of this letter and authorised her to use it to indicate that she had his and Lord Kitchener's approval to go as far as Bloemfontein and visit the camps.

At the time of her departure, several of her friends came to the station to see her off and wish her well. She wrote in her memoir:

*My kind Cape friends provided me with a box of foods such
as should more or less withstand the heat and a kettle lamp
for making tea and cocoa, and a few of them saw me off the
evening of the 22nd.*

*It was a glorious moonlight night. Their kindness had
been unceasing and I felt I had in them a solid background in
case of need. But as the train moved off towards the strange,
hot, war-stricken North with its accumulations of misery and
bloodshed, I must own that my heart sank a little and I faced
the unknown with great trepidation, in spite of the feeling
that the deep desire of months which had laid so urgent a call
upon me, was indeed finding accomplishment.*

*Young women of this generation could not, I think, credit
the state of miserable cowardice in which I found myself when
the train moved off – my friends were left behind and I had to
face alone not only the strange country and strange language
but the unknown and terrible strangeness of war ...* [22]

This admission came late in her life. At the time, she said nothing
of her trepidation to anyone. She was the only woman on the
train.

During that first night the train twisted through the mountains and by morning they had reached the arid plateau. *It was
wonderful to see the totally new world which greeted me at dawn and
to see the sun rise for the first time over the silent Karoo. The train
was very slow and stopped about a good deal for meals as there was
no food on the [train]. These station meals were very unappetizing
and as they were thronged by British Officers it was always difficult
for a mere woman, middle-aged, and somewhat dowdy at that, to
squeeze in. When there was time a relay was arranged which gave
me a chance of getting something. Oftener I fell back on my own supplies, which of course after the first day naturally failed in variety, the
butter particularly, in spite of damp cloths and tin, soon ran away.
But my great stand-by was a large tin of apricot jam – I recall it with*

40

gratitude for that tin served me through all my tedious journeys for months, moistening the inferior bread I could get here and there. For days, even weeks together, bread and apricot jam was my only food three times a day with a cup of cocoa.[23]

After the train had left the fertile valleys of the Western Cape, the first settlement of significance was the small town of Beaufort West, 500 kilometres from Cape Town. Two hundred and fifty kilometres later they reached De Aar, a rail junction and important military depot. Here Emily's journey took her at right angles to the east and 120 kilometres later, at Naauwpoort (now Noupoort), another rail junction, the train resumed its northerly direction for the final 350 kilometres to Bloemfontein. See map on pages 10–11.

To her aunt, Lady Hobhouse, she wrote: *I did not have a bad journey from Cape Town, though it was rather a lonely one. Going through the Karoo it was very hot and the second day there were horrible dust-storms varied by thunderstorms. The sand penetrated through the closed windows and doors, filled eyes and ears, turned my hair red, and covered everything like a table-cloth. As far as extent and sweep and sky go the Karoo is delightful, but it is a vast solitude and in many parts the very plants grow two or three yards apart as if they abhorred society.*[24]

Though the sparsely inhabited country had its faint charms for the resolute Emily, once she entered the war zone it was different. What struck her there was not what nature had wrought, but man. Here the rainfall is better and there should have been more human activity. But that is not what she found: *... from Colesberg on it was a desolate outlook. The land seemed dead and silent, absolutely without life as far as the eye could reach, only carcasses of horses, mules, and cattle with a sort of mute anguish in their look, and bleached bones and refuse of many kinds ... I saw a few burnt farms – but those unburnt seemed still and lifeless also ...*[25]

There had been considerable and serious fighting around Colesberg, a town on the Cape side of the border with the Orange

River Colony. From there onwards, the train was a target for the Boer guerrillas and, though the line was guarded and frequently patrolled, an attack could not be ruled out. Nevertheless, the three-day journey ended without misadventure. Emily had hoped it might be different: *The disappointment of the journey was that no Boer Commando swooped down and captured our train! It would have enlivened the journey and been immensely interesting.*[26] And very dangerous.

Bloemfontein station was crowded with soldiers – she was still the solitary female – and much showing of papers was required. She found it all an appalling experience. She had arrived nine months after Lord Roberts's army had departed on its long march to Pretoria, and the place had settled into an awkward, uncomfortable existence – the capital of a small country under military occupation. The town was safe enough under the protection of its garrison, but the British control extended only as far as their big guns could shoot. Beyond their reach, the guerrillas roamed largely at will and owned the countryside.

Emily spent the first night at an inn. The next day Mrs Fichardt, a widow, sent her carriage for Emily. When they met, Mrs Fichardt said she would like to welcome her to her house but did not dare do so without the written permission of General Pretyman. Emily went immediately to see Pretyman who, it turned out, came from south-west England and knew some of her relatives. He said that he and Mrs Pretyman had intended that Emily should stay with them, but they were regrettably overrun with doctors and nurses on account of the typhoid. Her response took Pretyman by surprise.

General Pretyman nearly jumped out of his skin when I said I wanted to stay with Mrs Fichardt ... 'Oh, but,' he said, 'she is very bitter.' 'Just so,' I replied, 'but my visit may have a softening effect upon her.' This was a new idea to him and he admitted there was something in it and I stood over him while he wrote me a permit, stating his approval. Rather against the grain, but nevertheless he did it.[27] Emily could have handled this better. Getting on the wrong side of the governor was not a good way to begin her visit.

Caroline Fichardt was under surveillance, suspected of transmitting information to the Boers during her regular visits to her husband's grave on their farm outside Bloemfontein. Sensitive to the implications, she was heard to say, 'That's the end of us' when she received her son's suggestion that Emily stay with her. But she accommodated and assisted Emily all the same.[28]

The Fichardts were self-made business people and ran one of the largest trading enterprises in the once fledgling republic. Their large and gracious home, Kya Lami, had simultaneously accommodated Sir Alfred Milner and Paul Kruger, President of the South African Republic, during the fruitless peace negotiations in the middle of 1899. In the months ahead it became a base and haven for Emily.

Caroline Fichardt was a friend of the Steyns, the first family of the former Orange Free State. President Marthinus Steyn was in the field, living with the republican commandos, and constantly on the move. A lawyer who had qualified in the Netherlands and England, he was a conciliator before the war and did everything he could to prevent bloodshed; he understood perfectly clearly that war would be a disaster for his republic and its people and wished to avert it at all costs. He hosted that peace conference between Milner and Kruger and when, to his dismay, it failed, he still tried hard to forestall conflict. He interceded directly with the British Government and restrained Kruger from taking pre-emptive action until virtually all Kruger's pre-emptive strategic advantages had been lost.

But now that Bloemfontein had been overrun by Roberts and he had been driven out of town, now that his seat of government had been usurped and his independent republic annexed as a British colony, now he was indomitably opposed to the British occupation. Wherever he went, at every opportunity, he breathed new life into the resistance. Right until the end of the war when his health deserted him, it was Steyn more than any other leader who kept alive the spirit of defiance and refused to settle or compromise. Capturing or killing him was one of the highest military priorities of the British.

Caroline Fichardt introduced Emily to the dignified Mrs Steyn, whose every move was shadowed by a soldier in uniform. After the war, this acquaintance grew into a friendship that lasted until the end of Emily's life.

Caroline Fichardt and Isabella 'Tibbie' Steyn came from English and Scottish stock respectively, the former a Beck, the latter a Fraser. When the deposed president wrote to his wife, he wrote in English, and some say the Steyns spoke English at home. Among these staunchly republican women, language was thus not the barrier Emily had feared. In her inimitable way, she had entered this new society at its highest level. But from the perspective of the British Army she had not chosen her friends wisely.

Emily's truck had left Cape Town ahead of her, but at De Aar it had been hitched to the train she was on and it arrived when she did. The Fichardts provided her with storage space and practical assistance and she spent a hot morning unloading and sorting everything.[29]

She was ready to visit her first camp. However, now the narrative must turn to events that occurred before Emily's arrival in southern Africa.

Chapter 5

Lord Roberts

The Boer republics belonged to no one but the people who lived in them. The white people who governed them had had enough of British interference for a hundred years and they were determined to resist the invasion.

They were literate, God-fearing Christians and they thought they were civilised enough, thank you, and had fine democracies already. The constitution of the Orange Free State, for example, was modelled on the constitution of the United States and they abided by it. As in other parts of the world in those times, only men, indeed only white men, could vote. The Englishmen who opposed them in this war did not intend to change that.

The republican burghers spoke a local version of Dutch. Over the centuries, their language had diverged from its origins in the Low Countries of the Rhine delta. It had absorbed words from all the peoples who came to live in the settlement or were there in the first place. The French, the Germans, the English, slaves from the Dutch East Indies (Indonesia) and Malaya and the local African nations had all made their contributions. This patois, with its own, emerging grammar and spelling, was forged into maturity by the war of this chronicle. Soon after the conflict it was proclaimed a new language, Afrikaans. For these people, this language was the hallmark of their now distinct culture and the bearer of their deeply held values.

They referred to themselves as 'Boers', farmers, for farmers they mostly were and farming is all that most ever wanted to do.

The term Boer had other connotations, too. A Boer was capable, independent and resilient; a Boer could get things done. To be a Boer was to be a real man. The foreigners who did not understand these implications used this name as a handy label for the war, the 'Boer War' or the 'Anglo-Boer War'. The Boers themselves called it the Second War of Independence. The name points to the earlier, smaller struggle in which they had successfully ended British occupation.

Nowadays, historians call it the South African War of 1899–1902 for it is recognised that it involved not only the Boers and the Imperial nations, but others too. Especially black people. All the same, as short hand, the term Boer War is used in this book. Everyone knows what it means.

Wars rarely turn out as the invaders expect, and this war was no different. Pre-war assessments had made victory seem easy. Britain – with its then world-leading manufacturing industries and an army that had conquered nation after nation in far-flung corners of the globe – was squaring off against two small countries with no industry to speak of and hardly any standing army. The total Boer population in the two republics numbered less than 200,000[30] – man, woman and child – roughly the population of a mid-sized English city of that time. There were many more indigenous people, of course, but both sides understood, initially at least, that involving them in the conflict would not be wise. This would be a white man's war, and the number of white men in the republics was small.

Sir Alfred Milner, British High Commissioner for South Africa, who was so charming to Emily, was not all he seemed to her. He had had more than a small part in fomenting the conflict. He conducted the pre-war negotiations with the republics on behalf of the government in London, and he was not helpful in avoiding bloodshed. At the peace conference that preceded the outbreak of hostilities, he abruptly terminated the discussions and walked out, fearing that the Boers would agree to his demands. If they agreed, there could be no war, and without war there would be no inclusion of the republics into the Empire. He would not be able to unify southern Africa on his watch, as Lord Carnarvon, a former Colonial Secretary had wished. The mining entrepreneurs would be left to run their enterprises under a Boer government.

If war was necessary to achieve his vision and the aims of others, so be it. The Boers were weak – on paper, at any rate. Not knowing of their resolve, he thought the war would be short and the expense low. More likely, if he called their bluff, they would crumble and concede before a shot was fired. In his assessment, the republican territories could be added to the Empire at reasonable cost.

Milner advised the British Cabinet that Imperial objectives would most likely be achieved by sending 10,000 troops to southern Africa, a number that would roughly double the size of the garrisons already there. When these troops arrived, they would be moved up to the borders of the republics. Faced with such a threat, he assured the cabinet, the Boers would most probably surrender their territories. They would realise that they could not resist the might of a determined and vastly more powerful British Empire.

Robert Cecil, Lord Salisbury, the prime minister, was unconvinced. But the majority in the cabinet believed Milner. Salisbury, old and infirm, did not have the energy to dig in his heels. The 10,000 embarked and Milner rejoiced. Britain was now committed. She would never withdraw, could never withdraw, if the Boers were intransigent. If 10,000 soldiers were not enough, well, there were many more.

The Boers were unimpressed. The embarkation of these soldiers precipitated the war and on 11 October 1899 the burghers pre-emptively crossed into colonial territory. They defeated and then surrounded and trapped 12,000 troops at Ladysmith in Natal and also besieged garrisons at Kimberley and Mafeking in the west. So much for 10,000 soldiers.

The cabinet now realised that the assessment Milner had presented was very wide of the mark. Somewhat alarmed, they authorised another 50,000 troops and dispatched General Sir Redvers Buller, Britain's most senior field general, to take charge as commander-in-chief of the forces in southern Africa. He had fought in southern Africa earlier in his career, ironically with the Boers against the Zulus, and with his local knowledge, broad experience and great authority, he seemed just the man to lead Britain to victory.

When the reinforcements were in place, Buller launched a three-pronged invasion with armies advancing on the republics from the east, south and west. But in December 1899, the Boers defeated all three advances in the space of one week: first General Gatacre on the southern front at Stormberg, then General Lord Methuen on the western front at Magersfontein, and, most alarmingly, General Buller himself on the eastern front at Colenso. All the defeats were on colonial soil. The enlarged invasion force had been stopped before any republican border had even been crossed.

It caused shock and consternation back home in England. Arthur Conan Doyle, the man who invented Sherlock Holmes, was a volunteer doctor with the British Army in southern Africa and he wrote one of the first histories of the war. He summed up the situation:

> The week which extended from December 10th to December 17th, 1899, was the blackest one known during our generation, and the most disastrous for British arms during the century. We had in the short space of seven days lost, beyond all extenuation or excuse, three separate actions. No single defeat was of vital importance in itself, but the cumulative

effect, occurring as they did to each of the main British forces in South Africa, was great. The total loss amounted to about three thousand men and twelve guns, while the indirect effects in the way of loss of prestige to ourselves and increased confidence and more numerous recruits to our enemy were incalculable.[31]

At this point in the conflict, the Boers were holding strong positions that the British could not penetrate except by incurring further large loss of life, something Buller was not prepared to countenance. He halted the advance and called for yet more reinforcements. This was to his credit, but London saw it differently and he got more than he bargained for. The cabinet agreed to send a further 55,000 men, and, to Buller's dismay, they also dispatched a new commander-in-chief, Field Marshall Lord Frederick Sleigh Roberts of Kandahar. Roberts was sixty-seven and came out of retirement for this purpose. He was an old rival and to become his subordinate was a bitter blow to Buller. In view of Roberts's age, the Secretary for War thought it wise to appoint another experienced general as Roberts's chief of staff. Lord Kitchener was chosen for this task.

Roberts concentrated the new reinforcements to the west of the Orange Free State at the Modder River, some 40 kilometres south of Kimberley. From there, beginning on 11 February 1900, he marched his army around the stalemated position at Magersfontein. A month later, with clashes along the way, he made an unopposed entry into Bloemfontein, the capital of the Orange Free State. Roberts was of the view that he had vanquished this republic. The Free State Boers did not see it that way.

The army had marched and fought across 160 kilometres of veld and they rested in Bloemfontein for six weeks, waiting for supplies to catch up. Bloemfontein was a modest town with a white population of about 5,000 and perhaps a similar number of blacks. The arrival of the great army completely overwhelmed its resources and typhoid broke out. It killed British soldiers much more effectively than the Boers had done. Nevertheless, Roberts then set his men on an even more arduous march to Pretoria, the capital of the South African Republic, 450 kilometres away. The Boers did not succeed in stopping him this time either, and on 5 June 1900 he occupied this city. Having taken possession of both republican capitals, Roberts thought the war was over and awaited the Boer surrender.

It did not come.

The Boers had long realised they could not defeat the overwhelming numbers ranged against them in conventional, head-to-head battles and had quietly settled on a guerrilla strategy. They would attack when and where they could, aim always to surprise, then vanish into the vastness of the veld. No one told Roberts and the penny did not drop. To his annoyance, he was obliged to fight on in places and at times of his enemy's choosing.

By late September 1900, he was satisfied that only mopping up remained and declared that the war had been won. He handed control to Kitchener on 28 November 1900 and sailed home to Britain.

After the early defeats, good news was needed and the diminutive, one-eyed, ageing Lord Roberts fitted the desire for a hero very well. On his arrival home, he received a huge welcome, was showered with honours and wealth, and succeeded Lord Wolseley as commander-in-chief of the British Army. He, after all, had turned the tide and now assured them that the enemy had been vanquished.

As it turned out, the war had not even reached the halfway mark. While the British occupied most of the larger towns and patrolled the railroads, the burghers still owned the veld. Across the wide land they moved at will and could sustain the war indefinitely.

Not only was the war not over, Lord Roberts had opened the door to a far darker side of the conflict. This is where we find the roots of Emily Hobhouse's mission.

When Roberts first marched into the Orange Free State from his base at the Modder River, he took a conciliatory policy towards the resident population. By way of a formal proclamation[32] issued in February 1900 he warned all burghers to desist from further hostility and said: *I undertake that any of them, who may so desist and who are found staying in their homes and quietly pursuing their ordinary occupations, will not be made to suffer in their persons or property on account of having taken up arms in obedience to the order of their Government.* The same proclamation concluded: *Orders have been issued by me, prohibiting soldiers from entering private houses, or molesting the civil population on any pretext whatever, and every precaution has been taken against injury to property on the part of any person belonging to, or connected with, the Army.*

After he had reached and occupied Bloemfontein, thousands of Free State burghers accepted these assurances, and, considering the war irretrievably lost, went home. They were mostly volunteers and there was nothing their commanders could do to stop them from abandoning the resistance.

But thousands of others did not. While Roberts was still at Bloemfontein, the Boer leaders gathered for a council of war at Kroonstad and formally adopted the guerrilla strategy. In a head-to-head battle, the British could muster far more men and heavy guns than they could and it made no sense to expose their men to inevitable slaughter. It was better to use brain than brawn, better to exploit their superior mobility, capitalise on their local knowledge and take advantage of the community support they had. They began to pick off smaller British detachments and make the land unsafe for the invaders. To impede progress, they destroyed railway lines, bridges and telegraph lines in front of and behind the Imperial advance.

While the Boers were destroying infrastructure, the Imperial forces were doing a bit of destroying, too. One of the first reports of this was a letter home from a Private Stanton from New South

Wales. It appeared first in the *Sydney Telegraph* and was reprinted in London in early May 1900. The young soldier wrote about his participation in the destruction of a farmhouse:

> *Within 800 yards of the farm we halted and the infantry blazed a volley into the house. Then we marched up to it and on arrival found it locked up and not a soul to be seen, so we broke open the place and went in. It was beautifully furnished, and the officers got several things they could make use of, such as bedding, etc. There was a lovely library – books of every description in Dutch and English. I secured a Bible, also a Mauser rifle … After getting all we wanted out of it, our men put a charge under the house and blew it up. It seemed such a pity. It was a lovely house with a nice garden around it.*[33]

This was no isolated event. Later in the same month, *The Morning Leader*, a London paper, reported that:

> *General French and General Pole-Carew, at the head of the Guards and 18th Brigade, are marching in, burning practically everything on the road. The brigade is followed by about 3,500 head of loot, cattle and sheep. Hundreds of tons of corn and forage have been destroyed. The troops engaged in the work are Roberts' Horse, the Canadians and Australians.*
>
> *I hear today that General Rundle burnt his way up to Dewetsdorp. At one farm only women were left. Still rifles were found under the mattress. Orders were inexorable. The woman threw her arms round the officer's neck pleading that the homestead be spared. When the flames burst from the doomed place, the poor woman threw herself on her knees, tore open her bodice, and bared her breasts, screaming 'Shoot me, shoot me! I have nothing more to live for, now my husband is gone, and our farm is burnt, and our cattle taken.*[34]

There were rifles on every farm in southern Africa in those days. Predatory animals still threatened humans and livestock; herds of game still afforded opportunities to feed the family without slaughtering your own farm animals.

When Lord Roberts entered the territory of the South African Republic on the march north to Pretoria, he issued a proclamation as conciliatory as his Free State statement but with a twist: *Subject to the terms of this Proclamation*, it read, *personal safety and freedom from molestation are guaranteed to the non-combatant population*. But it also read, *If, however, wanton damage is done to property, not only will the actual perpetrators of such acts and all directly or indirectly implicated in them be liable to the most severe punishment in person and property, but the property of all persons, whether in authority or otherwise, who have permitted or not done their utmost to prevent such wanton damage will be liable to be confiscated or destroyed.*[35]

This was a crucial development. The wanton damage he had in mind was not the destruction of homes and farms committed by his soldiers, it was the sabotage of infrastructure by the burghers resisting the invasion. In view of the seniority of the officers involved in the destruction of private property, it is inconceivable that he did not know what his men were up to. Perhaps he had ordered it. Yet he acted as if he did not know that the destruction of homes was already occurring in spite of his assurances and not necessarily in the circumstances suggested in this new proclamation.

The proclamation was puzzling. To protect their private property, the residents were now expected to do 'their utmost' to stop the tens of thousands of Boers swiftly moving around on horseback from blowing things up or attacking Imperial troops. What steps could they take? How could they even know where the commandos intended to strike next? It was certainly not in the interests of the guerrillas to tell anyone what they had in mind. How could the residents convince the Imperial officers that they had tried 'their utmost', whatever that meant?

Roberts surely knew that local residents could do nothing to stop the attacks. Instead, he was simply bent on inflicting distress on defenceless civilians as an instrument of war. If the Boers attack us, we'll make someone pay, anyone, to discourage further attacks.

He was an old-fashioned general. In his view, wars were fought by two armies confronting and slaughtering each other until one had had enough and fled. In such a war, he was assured of victory because he had more young men available to be slaughtered than the other side. Guerrilla war was to him simply a reflection of cowardice. In his eyes it amounted to running away when confronted by a superior force and he called it by another name, banditry. He had no hope of defeating his elusive opponents in this unfamiliar struggle – his army was on foot, the Boers were all on horseback – so he turned to targets he could reach: the resident, stationary, civilian population.

The threat failed and the sabotage continued. So Roberts warned again on 16 June that *The houses in the vicinity of the place where the damage is done will be burnt and the principal civil residents will be made prisoners of war.*[36] Three days later he reinforced the message, proclaiming that if any further damage was done to public infrastructure in either of the two republics, the principal residents of the area where the damage occurred would be held responsible, farms in the district would be levied to pay for the damage, goods would be requisitioned from the residents of the district without payment, and yet again he declared that *The houses and farms in the vicinity of the place where the damage is done will be destroyed.*[37]

Thomas Pakenham, in his excellent history of the war, records that the Secretary for War, Lord Lansdowne, sent a message to Roberts supporting farm burning.[38]

And so began the emergence of homeless women and children. With the men mostly out on campaign, the brunt of the policy fell on their wives, children and, sometimes, their aged parents or disabled family members. When troops arrived at a farm to do the bidding of their commander-in-chief, the occupants were given ten or fifteen minutes to gather their things and get out. Then the house was torched.

Some generals, like Buller and Methuen, destroyed homes sparingly, interpreting Roberts's orders narrowly. They had both been in South Africa before the war; they knew the Boers, had fought alongside them in wars against the natives and had perhaps even enjoyed hospitality in Boer homes. Others, like General Archibald Hunter, exercised no such restraint. Some of his exploits are chronicled in the next chapter.

Chapter 6

Ventersburg

The establishment of camps for refugees began in September 1900, more than three months before Emily Hobhouse arrived in Cape Town. They were initially created for the rural residents of the two republics who had never taken up arms against Britain or who had surrendered and returned to civilian life. These people were vilified by those Boers who were still committed to the independence struggle and they came under moral pressure to join or re-join the fight against the invasion. Sometimes the pressure was accompanied by threats. Feeling isolated and at risk, many of these families packed their wagons with what possessions they could and sought safety in the proximity of British garrisons. Some drove their livestock with them and arrived with flocks of sheep and herds of cattle.

As their numbers grew, it became evident that some arrangements should be made to accommodate and support them. The Military Governor of Pretoria, Lieutenant-General JG Maxwell, was asked to take the matter in hand. Maxwell announced that two camps would be created, one in Johannesburg and one in Bloemfontein, to provide accommodation and support for these refugees. Later more camps were set up.

With their families intact – husbands and fathers in attendance – and having moved in their own time with their own transport and with the opportunity to think through the implications of a protracted absence from home, these people were much better equipped than those who were evicted minutes before their homes were destroyed. Some did not need support. The better-off had second homes in town where they usually stayed during *Nagmaal* – the monthly celebration of the Holy Communion. If there was a garrison in their town, one presumes that they simply moved into their own town house. Others found refuge with relatives or friends. The remainder gratefully accepted the offer of accommodation and food in the fledgling camps.

However, from the outset, these camps also harboured some of the people made homeless when the arid breath of the Empire torched their homes – the displaced, helpless, suddenly indigent people who had little choice but to find their way to the garrisons and place themselves at the mercy of the military authorities, the very people responsible for their misery. In these families, the men were almost all absent. They were on campaign, fighting for their independence.

As Emily would learn firsthand on her travels from camp to camp, the two categories of people lived uncomfortably together: the first supportive of, defensive of or resigned to the Imperial conquest; the second deeply embittered by their sudden loss and determinedly committed to their republican independence. All of them went voluntarily to the camps – though some, in reality, had little choice – and both categories might be termed refugees. This is the name used to describe the camps – 'refuge camps' in Maxwell's early communications, 'refugee camps' in later official documents. The more neutral term, burgher camps, was also used.

Soon a third category emerged: people brought forcibly to the camps and who, in most cases, were not permitted to leave. They became the overwhelming majority. Although they, too, were called 'refugees', they did not regard themselves as refugees and resented the term. 'Prisoners' seemed more accurate. The authorities recognised the differences among camp residents and gave preferential treatment to the loyalists.

Once Lord Roberts had marched his army through the Orange River Colony (the renamed Orange Free State) and into the southern Transvaal, he established the central command in the capital, Pretoria. In this location, the army was critically dependent on the two railway lines to the coast, one through Natal, the other through the ORC. These long, vulnerable arteries carried all their supplies and fresh troops and were the avenues by which they would all one day go home. Each track supported the garrisons in the towns along its route and was, in turn, protected by those garrisons. There was a third line to the coast, one that terminated in Lourenco Marques in Portuguese East Africa (now Maputo in Mozambique), but it could not be used because it ran through territory still under Boer control.

The ORC line passed about 15 kilometres to the west of Ventersburg, a town near the centre of the new colony (see map pages 10–11). In October 1900, it was sabotaged several times in this general vicinity. Military intelligence suggested that there were many burghers in the area.

General Archibald Hunter was dispatched to put an end to these attacks. The number of soldiers placed at his disposal for this endeavour is not clear, but they must have been in considerable strength as two more generals were appointed to share the command under him. The troops travelled by train, regrouped at the station nearest Ventersburg called Ventersburg Road (now the small town of Henneman) and at midnight on 29 October they began to advance towards the town.

At 4.30 am they were ambushed by Boers who had let the advance guard pass by undisturbed. The British suffered casualties of one officer and eleven men. The horses stampeded and a disaster was narrowly averted.

Hunter was not amused. The bungling was on the part of his advance guard, but he directed his attention to the nearby town. The locals would have to pay for the humiliation and loss he had suffered. Some of the medicine prescribed by Dr Roberts would have to be administered.

Some insight into what followed can be gained from the diary of one of the men who participated in the ensuing events, a young English officer with the remarkable name of Major John Edward Pine-Coffin. He was from a wealthy Devon family and had been educated at Eton and Cambridge. The relevant entries begin a day after the ambush:

31st October: Dispatched all the remaining inhabitants of Ventersburg Town to Bloemfontein … Gen Hunter left for Bloemfontein. Work very heavy, sending off the refugees, but the country is being cleared by degrees. Any amount of women and children came in late at night, they had to sleep in open Cattle trucks.

1st November: Ventersburg Town was burnt today. All refugees sent off. I collected several more families & sent them away, sending men in one direction & the women in another, so that after the war they will have some difficulty in getting together.

5th November: Boers still in the neighbourhood. Removing all the Dutch & burning their houses, have now got rid of a good many. … Shall soon take steps to deal with the Kaffirs. [This term was used at the time by both British and Boers for the indigenous people. It was and is derogatory but was probably used carelessly by Pine-Coffin.] *No other news of importance. Am furnishing my room very well.*

6th November: … More families being removed. Hope soon to see the last of them. Enemy on the hills about Ventersburg

& Gen Botha still in the Town. [Unlikely!] *Went out with the gun in the evening & shot a couple of duck.*[39]

The attitude is as remarkable as the events. This officer was apparently not troubled by spending his days evicting families, many with young children, and burning their houses. For recreation he went duck shooting in the evening, as the diary shows he often did. It was just all in a day's work. Orders were orders.

Pine-Coffin continued to remove residents from the surrounding area throughout November, helping himself to their furniture and possessions as he went. He presumably allowed his men to do the same after he had had his pick, then they torched what remained.

The official return of buildings burnt in June 1900 to January 1901[40] lists the fifty-three houses and farms that were destroyed in the town and district. A section of the report covering this destruction at Ventersburg in the beginning of November 1900 is reproduced on p 61. The names of those who lost their homes or farms include Widow Erasmus, Widow Fourie, Widow Vonburgen, another Widow Erasmus (perhaps the same widow, perhaps she had a farm and a town property) and a Dr Leith. Reasons are given for the destruction, none of which would justify the actions taken. Moreover, the destruction was without warning and none of the reasons offered could have been tested by any kind of due process. Was Widow Erasmus really 'on commando' as the list suggests?

One of Hunter's subordinates, Major-General Bruce Hamilton, was left in charge of the destruction and he posted the following notice on 1 November 1900 in the midst of the devastation:

The town of Ventersburg was cleared of supplies and partly burnt, and the farms in the vicinity destroyed, on account of the frequent attacks on the railway line in the neighbourhood. The Boer women and children who are left behind should

District.	Name of Village or Farm.	Name of Owner.	Date of Destruction.	Reasons for Destruction.
Ventersburg ..	Houses in Ventersburg Town	W. Kotzee ..	1/11/00	Owners on commando.
Do. ..	do. do.	L. Erasmus ..	1/11/00	do.
Do. ..	do. do.	J. C. Potgelter ..	1/11/00	do.
Do. ..	do. do.	M. B. Kruger ..	1/11/00	do.
Do. ..	do. do.	Widow Erasmus	1/11/00	do.
Do. ..	do. do.	J. Hoosthuzen ..	1/11/00	do.
Do. ..	do. do.	Kleinham ..	1/11/00	do.
Do. ..	do. do.	Cronje ..	1/11/00	do.
Do. ..	do. do.	Wessels ..	1/11/00	do.
Do. ..	Blaawbank, 20 miles N.E.	B. S. Venter ..	1/11/00	Harbouring Boers and on commando.
Do. ..	Vaalbank, 2 miles S.E. of Ventersburg	Fourie ..	1/11/00	do. do. do.
Do. ..	Steynsrust, 15 miles E.	Widow Fourie ..	1/11/00	do. do. do.
Do. ..	Christianral	W. Prinsloo ..	1/11/00	do. do. do.
Do. ..	Eved Hoep, 4 miles S...	L. J. Le Clus ..	1/11/00	do. do. do.
Do. ..	Wilderbeestefontein, 4 miles S.E.	J. F. Venter ..	1/11/00	do. do. do.
Do. ..	Kookspruit, 7 miles E.	—	1/11/00	do. do. do.
Do. ..	Kool Kraal, 20 miles E.	H. Steyn ..	1/11/00	do. do. do.
Do. ..	Ongegundevreiheid, 3 miles N.E.	M. C. Stander ..	1/11/00	do. do. do.
Do. ..	Moolpan, 8 miles N.E...	J. Cronje ..	1/11/00	do. do. do.
Do. ..	Kleinfontein	J. J. Odbergh ..	1/11/00	do. do. do.
Do. ..	Pieters Rust	Widow Vonburgen	1/11/00	do. do. do.
Do. ..	Likkerleven	Widow Eramus	1/11/00	do. do. do.
Do. ..	Fraamtzicht	Potgeiter ..	1/11/00	do. do. do.
Do. ..	Tanee	Dr. Leith ..	1/11/00	do. do. do.
Do. ..	Bloivbols Fontein, near Ventersburg	J. Claremont ..	2/11/00	Mounted Infantry fired on from surrounding district.
Do. ..	Armoed Spruit, 10 miles N. of Ventersburg	S. S. Fourie ..	2/11/00	do. do. do.
Do. ..	B. von Vesthuzen ..	B. von Vesthuzen	2/11/00	do. do. do.
Do. ..	J. Minty	J. Minty ..	2/11/00	do. do. do.
Do. ..	Braklaagter, 12 miles N. of Ventersburg	Botha ..	2/11/00	do. do. do.
Do. ..	Koornfontein	Hoofman ..	1/11/00	Harbouring enemy.
Do. ..	Bigensil	J. S. van Joorstelat	1/11/00	do.
Do. ..	Biskop	W. Breet ..	1/11/00	do.
Do. ..	Green Point	W. Venter ..	1/11/00	do.
Do. ..	Kraanvogelcht.. ..	S. van Renshaw	1/11/00	do.
Do. ..	Petersrust	R. P. Odendal ..	1/11/00	do.
Do. ..	Van der Beers Farm ..	Mrs. Ferrerias ..	3/11/00	Harbouring Boers.
Do. ..	do. do.	Mrs. De Plessis	3/11/00	do.
Do. ..	Volsack..	Mrs. Sapsford ..	3/11/00	do.
Do. ..	Reitfontein	Mr. du Prietz ..	3/11/00	do.
Do. ..	do.	Mrs. de Beers ..	3/11/00	do.
Do. ..	do.	Govans.. ..	3/11/00	do.

Extract from the official report of buildings burnt in June 1900 – January 1901

61

apply to the Boer commandants for food who will supply them unless they wish to see them starve. No supplies will be sent from the railway to the town.[41]

Not only was the town bereft of foodstuffs, so were the surrounding farms. With the area under British occupation, Hamilton knew that it was impossible for the Boers to provide food. Any burgher who came near the town would be shot or captured. For the remaining residents, starvation loomed.

The notice came to the attention of David Lloyd George, then a young, anti-war member of the British Parliament, later a prime minister. He read it to the House and said, *This man is a brute and a disgrace to the uniform he wears.*[42] But Lloyd George was in England and Hamilton was in the Orange River Colony following orders.

Major Pine-Coffin rounded up cattle, sheep and horses from the farms whose owners had now conveniently been removed. The diary informs us that he was developing his own farm near the railway line. It was amply stocked in no time.

Eventually, he showed signs of compassion. The entry for 28 November reads, in part: *Had a row with Col Lea AAG* [his superior officer] *about feeding refugees, said I should not feed them, suppose he wishes them to die of starvation. Asked him by wire if that is what he wanted.*[43]

What sort of farms were being destroyed by Pine-Coffin and other Imperial soldiers? At that time Australians were among the wealthiest people on the planet on account of their progressive and productive farms, and AB (Banjo) Paterson, the war correspondent for the *Sydney Morning Herald*, was well able to give an informed impression. He had strong ties with the agricultural regions of Australia and had a good eye for a farm. In March 1900, seven months before the attack on Ventersburg, he recorded his impressions near Bloemfontein, 160 kilometres to the south:

*This is the grandest bit of country we have seen in Africa ...
The grass is knee deep almost exactly like our kangaroo grass.
Below us is a flat of about 600 acres, covered with maize,
growing very well and about eight feet high. And all among
the maize there are thousands of melons – water-melons,
pie-melons, rock-melons, pumpkins – the fruit so thick on
the ground that a horse can hardly avoid smashing it as we
ride through the rows of corn. From the ridge at least six
farmhouses are in sight, each with its dam of water, its mass
of willows and poplars, and its fruit garden. ... The owners
of these farms and their farm hands are the 'Boers' of whose
uncivilised ignorance we have heard so much. They have the
latest aer-motor windmills, they use the springs of water to
their best advantage in irrigation, and in the towns we can get
everything that could be got in an Australian town of similar
size.*[44]

The countryside near Ventersburg is just as productive as that
described by Paterson, and maize is still grown in the region on a
large scale.

From east to west and north to south, homes were becoming ruins in most of the districts occupied by British troops. The
destruction was recorded and the results presented later – much
later – in a report to the parliament.[45] This is the report from
which a section was extracted and shown on page 61. As the reader
can see, it is detailed, farm by farm, house by house. It shows that
in June 1900, 2 houses were burnt, in July, 3, in August, 12, in
September, 99, in October, 189. By November 1900 when Lord
Roberts relinquished command, 621 homes no longer existed.

Some officers were more thoughtful than Major Pine-Coffin
about these actions and their likely consequences. Two months
before the events at Ventersburg and 50 kilometres to the north,
Captain L March Phillipps was confined to bed with the flu. He
wrote this from the hospital in Kroonstad:

The army seems to be adopting very severe measures to try and end the campaign out of hand, and the papers at home are loudly calling for such measures, I see, and justify them … The various columns that are now marching about the country are carrying out the work of destruction pretty indiscriminately, and we have burnt and destroyed by now many scores of farms. Ruin, with great hardship and want, which may ultimately border on starvation, must be the result to many families. These measures are not likely, I am afraid, to conduce much to the united South Africa we talk so much of and thought we were fighting for.

I had to go myself the other day, at the General's bidding, to burn a farm near the line of march. We got to the place, and I gave the inmates, three women and some children, ten minutes to clear their clothes and things out of the house, and my men then fetched bundles of straw and we proceeded to burn it down. The old grandmother was very angry. She told me that, though I was making a fine blaze now, it was nothing compared to the flames that I would be consumed in hereafter. Most of them, however, were too miserable to curse. The women cried and the children stood holding on to them and looking with large frightened eyes at the burning house. They won't forget that sight, I'll bet a sovereign, not even when they grow up. We rode away and left them, a forlorn little group standing among their household goods – beds, furniture, and gimcracks strewn about the veldt; the crackling fire in their ears, and smoke and flames streaming overhead. The worst moment is when you first come to the house. The people thought we had called for refreshments, and one of the women went to get milk. Then we had to tell them we had come to burn the place down. I simply did not know which way to look. One of the women's husbands had been killed at Magersfontein. There were others, men and boys, away fighting; whether dead or alive they did not know.

*I give you this as an example of what is going on pretty
generally. Our troops are everywhere at work burning and
laying waste, and enormous reserves of famine and misery are
being laid up for these countries in the future.*

*How far do you mean to go in this ... We can't
exterminate the Dutch or seriously reduce their numbers.
We can do enough to make hatred of England and thirst
for revenge the first duty of every Dutchman, and we can't
effectively reduce the numbers of the men who will carry that
duty out. Of course it is not a question of war only. It is a
question of governing the country afterwards.*[46]

The fate of the displaced people varied. Some – like the residents
of Ventersburg – were railed to the larger towns and cities. But
during much of Lord Roberts's tenure as commander-in-chief,
many people were simply abandoned beside their burning homes
as March Phillipps describes. As the British Army was short of
transport and of horses in particular, all horses, oxen, mules and
vehicles were usually confiscated. The newly destitute people were
left on their farms, often very large farms, without any means
of transport. Their only option was to walk many kilometres to
find sustenance and shelter – women, children, the elderly and
disabled, all. Pregnant women, women with babes in arms and
women with little children clutching at their skirts – all had to
cope somehow.

Some were able to send for assistance from neighbours who
had been spared the destruction. Others could neither move nor
obtain help and simply remained where they were to be discovered later, half starved, foraging for whatever they could find to
eat and living under a nearby tree, in a shanty made from materials salvaged from their derelict house or even in its burnt remains.

Gradually, forlorn people began to accumulate in the towns
where their destitute state and their tales of what had had happened to them caused embarrassment and practical difficulties

for the authorities. A solution was needed. Lord Roberts had two goes at this. His first plan was to hand them over to the Boers in the parts of the Transvaal still under republican control. For good measure, he decided also to expel the relatives of the Boers on campaign who had always lived in the towns and cities. Even the elderly wife of the former President Paul Kruger and Mrs Botha, wife of the SAR's commander-in-chief, both residents of Pretoria, would have to go.

There was a hidden agenda in this stratagem. Encumbered with wives and children, the burghers would be less mobile and more easily cornered. Their food supplies would be depleted faster, too.

The Boers, however, were equal to this challenge. After several hundred women and children had been railed out of Johannesburg and Pretoria to the eastern Transvaal, Commandant-General Botha wrote to Lord Roberts asking that he be given early notice if more women and children were to be sent. He wished to appeal to Europe to accept these people as refugees. Reports of the way the war was being conducted were already appearing in Dutch and French newspapers. Boer refugees appearing in Europe would have confirmed all that they were saying, that Roberts was using punitive actions against the civilian population as an instrument of war. It would have been a diplomatic disaster. The plan evaporated.

Instead Roberts sent the destitute to the camps that had already been established, as described earlier. The camps grew in size and number.

All this happened before Emily Hobhouse arrived in Cape Town and she knew little of it.

Chapter 7

The camp at Bloemfontein

The camp was about three kilometres from Bloemfontein town on the slope of a bare hill. When Emily arrived, it contained about 2,000 residents of whom about 900 were children. She does not offer a concise description of the camp. Instead she told Lady Hobhouse about her first visit in a letter dated 26 January 1901:

> *It was about four o'clock of a scorching afternoon when I set foot in the camp and I can't tell you what I felt like so I won't try.*
>
> *I began by finding a woman whose sister I had met in Cape Town. ... Imagine the heat inside the tents and the suffocation! We sat on their khaki blankets rolled up inside Mrs Botha's tent and the sun blazed through the single canvas and the flies lay thick and black on everything – no chair, no table, nor any room for such, only a deal box*[A7] *standing on its end served as a wee pantry. In this tent lived Mrs Botha, five children (three quite grown up) and a little Kaffir servant girl. Many tents have more occupants.*

*Mrs Pienaar came in and Mrs Raal, Mrs Roux and others
and they told me their stories and we cried together and even
laughed together and chatted bad Dutch and bad English all
the afternoon. Wet nights, the water streams down through
the canvas and comes flowing in (as it knows how to in this
country) under the flap of the tent and wets their blankets as
they lie on the ground.*

*The women are wonderful: they cry very little and never
complain. The very magnitude of their sufferings, indignities,
loss and anxiety seems to lift them beyond tears, and these
people who have had comfortable, even luxurious homes, just
set themselves to quiet endurance and to make the best of their
bare and terrible lot. Only when it cuts fresh at them through
their children do their feelings flash out. Mrs Meintjes, for
instance, she has six children in camp all ill. Two in the
hospital with typhoid and four sick in the tent. She ... expects
her confinement soon. Her husband is in Ceylon [captured
Boers were sent to prisoner-of-war camps in Ceylon, India,
St Helena Island, Bermuda and elsewhere]. She has means
and would gladly provide for herself either in town or in the
Colony where she has relatives or by going back to her farm. It
was not burnt, only the furniture was destroyed. Yet there she
has to stay, watching her children droop and sicken. For their
sakes she did plead with tears that she might go and fend for
herself.*[48]

One of the women she met that first afternoon, Mrs Pienaar, was
in an advanced state of pregnancy and after hearing how difficult
she found it to sleep on the hard ground, Emily bought a mattress
for her the next day.

However, Emily decided not to rush into the distribution of
the goods she had brought until she understood the circumstances
better. She had made a crucial, instinctive decision: she wanted to
see the situation through the eyes and experiences of the inmates.

They were her concern. The official view, the opinions of the administrators, could wait. She visited the camp repeatedly and did meet with members of the camp administration. General Pretyman gave her a permanent pass and introduced her to a Captain Nelson who had been in charge of the camp until shortly before her arrival. She met several times with Major Cray, the man responsible for the management of all the camps in the Orange River Colony and who, at the same time, was also the superintendent of the Bloemfontein camp. Gradually her understanding of the situation deepened.

One of the central issues was food. The women in the camp did not complain. 'We know it is wartime and we cannot expect much' was their attitude.[49] As a result, Emily did not at first realise how meagre and monotonous the rations were, and we must turn elsewhere for information.

About six weeks after her arrival, in a report dated 8 March 1901, Captain AG Trollope, the chief superintendent of refugee camps in the Orange River Colony (Cray's successor) listed the daily rations per person as follows:[50]

½ lb of fresh or tinned meat,
¾ lb of meal or rice or samp or potatoes,
1 oz. coffee,
1 oz. salt
2 oz. sugar,
$^1/_{12}$ part of a tin of condensed milk.

(In metric terms, approximately 225g of meat, 340g of meal or rice or samp or potatoes, 30 grams each of coffee and salt and 60 grams of sugar. The size of a tin of condensed milk is unclear but archaeological evidence observed by the author at another camp site suggests the tins were about the same size as the 395 gram tins currently sold in Australia. If so, one-twelfth is 33 grams or about one-thirtieth of a litre. Meal in this context meant maize-meal. Samp is coarse-ground or cracked dry maize kernels. The cracking loosens the husk, which is removed, and makes the kernels easier to cook.)

That was breakfast, lunch and dinner, the same every day. According to the report, everyone received the same rations, adult or child, no matter what age. Later, when she realised the implications of such a diet, Emily tabulated the rations herself in a letter to her brother[51] and also in her post-war book.[52] Her account does not differ materially from Trollope's official report.[53]

The food was all raw and could not be eaten without cooking. Tinned meat – mostly corned beef – was an exception, but it was expensive and supplied only infrequently when fresh meat was unavailable. There was no camp kitchen, no central or communal cooking facilities. With not a table, a chair or even a bed to sit on, the women had somehow to cook to feed their large families. For this they received some cooking utensils and a weekly ration of fuel – wood or coal – but Emily relates how the women scavenged for more fuel in the scrub on the treeless hill beyond the camp to supplement the inadequate quantity they were given.

The food could keep adults alive but, if sustained, it would have adverse health consequences – it was and did. For children, the implications were more significant. The very young – babies just weaned and those in their first years of life – experienced the greatest difficulty with a diet that was wholly inappropriate for them. There were many of them in the camp.

Inadequate as the diet was, Emily discovered that it was sometimes reduced. The capacity of the railway serving Bloemfontein was inadequate for the demands that the war placed on it. Rolling stock was insufficient and the single track was often congested. Troop movements had priority so that trains carrying the supplies from the coast had to wait when a major military redeployment was underway. At other times, trains were attacked by the guerrillas or bridges were blown up. The upshot was that food did not always arrive when due. When stocks ran low, the camp super-

Bloemfontein Concentration Camp

intendent had little choice but to cut rations and scramble for supplies in the town or at nearby garrisons.[54]

Another serious difficulty for the women was maintaining hygiene. Water was limited to two buckets per tent per day – for drinking, cooking, washing up, washing clothes and keeping everybody clean. Factor in the absence of soap and it is not surprising that hygiene standards often fell far short of what was desired. The water was from the river – untreated – in a town where typhoid was common.

If everyone was healthy and remained well despite the conditions, if the mother was robust and some of the children old enough to help her, she and her children could get by. If the children were little or became ill, the difficulties mounted. And already, as Emily found, many were ill. If the mother took ill, the family was wholly dependent on the support of neighbours, who were often stressed themselves. The situation could get out of hand quickly.

Emily was not alone in her attempts to assist the women and children. A small number of local townspeople, supported by churches or charities, were also active in the camp. They and Emily began to work together and they assisted her in distributing the aid she had brought.

However, they all realised that their collective efforts fell far short of what was required. *Whatever you do, wrote Emily, whatever the Military Authorities may do – and Major Cray, I believe, is doing his very best with very limited means – it is all only a miserable patch upon a very great wrong; whatever you do is only temporary alleviation and can only touch a very few. The whole system is a mistake and has placed thousands physically unfit in conditions of life which they have not strength to endure.*[55]

After just days in Bloemfontein and deeply concerned, Emily's thoughts turned to addressing the issue politically. Her first suggestion was unrealistic. *Dear Aunt Mary,* she wrote, *couldn't you write such a letter about it to The Times as should make people listen and believe and understand – which would touch their conscience? Is England afraid of losing her prestige? Well, that's gone already in this country, but maybe some of it might yet be won back by an act of mercy, however late. To keep these camps going is murder to the children.*[56]

This was strong language. Her aunt, presumably in discussion with her husband, the judge, wrote no such letter. Much more information was needed before Emily's supporters in England would take her pleas into the public domain.

Chapter 8

Solutions?

The camps were based on the accommodation provided for soldiers. This was the quickest and cheapest option available. The tents were to hand, the rations already in store or on order, meat supplies already arranged. It did not occur to General Kitchener, the chief architect of the policy and a childless bachelor, that what was acceptable for soldiers was not suitable for women with children of all ages.

If there were deficiencies in the military accommodation, the soldiers could look after themselves in ways that women with large families could not. If they did not like the position of their tent, they could move it or dig a trench to keep stormwater from running through it. Soldiers could supplement their rations out of their pay; the camp inmates had no pay. The men could buy their own cleaning materials and fetch more water to wash and do their laundry if they cared to do so. The women had no soap, no shop, were not allowed to leave camp and their water was tightly rationed and unsafe. Managing the hygiene of babies and small children was extremely difficult. Soldiers were fed in a mess or shared fires if cooking for themselves; the women had to struggle with inadequate equipment and inadequate fuel to make the raw food edible for themselves and their families.

It was news to General Pretyman, too, that the Bloemfontein camp was inadequate. He had not meant to make life easy for these people who, after all, were the enemy. He was discharging his responsibilities, he thought, by providing shelter and food. Considering the friends that Emily was making in the town, he thought it hardly surprising that she should be critical. Nevertheless, he was prepared to give her a hearing and Cray was also prepared to listen. Cray, at least, was well aware that there were difficulties and not just at Bloemfontein.

Emily wrote to her aunt: *The Authorities are at their wits' end and have no more idea how to cope with the one difficulty of providing clothes for these people than the man in the moon. Crass male ignorance, stupidity, helplessness and muddling. I rub as much salt into the sore places of their minds as I possibly can, because it is so good for them; but I can't help melting a little when they are very humble and confess that the whole thing is a grievous and gigantic blunder and presents an almost insoluble problem, and they don't know how to face it.*[57]

But what should be done? While she was withering in her assessments, Emily was out of her depth, too, and grasping for answers herself. The suggestions she put in her letter to her aunt reveal her line of thinking:

First and foremost, I mean to ask for a matron speaking both Dutch and English for every camp – besides the officer in charge. She would keep an eye on the morals of the camp – most necessary here with the soldiery all around – and the women could come to her with all their wants.

Next, a mortuary tent. It is horrible that the corpses should lie in the hot tents with eight or ten living beings.

Then, more water. For seven or eight persons two buckets for washing, cooking and drinking are not enough.

Next soap. Think of the heat, the dust-storms, etc. and no soap in the rations; evidently because the military supply was short.

Then some sort of school for the children – and so on.
But do what you will, you can't undo the thing itself,
which is odious.[58]

As Emily realised, these suggestions would not be enough, even if
fully implemented.

She wrote to Cape Town to obtain more nurses. If none were
available, she hoped the Distress Fund's committee could find
some in England and send them out.[59] The authorities, she said,
would provide tents, rations and pay once they reached the camps.

We have much typhoid and are dreading a great outbreak, so I
am directing my energies to getting the water of the Modder River
boiled. As well swallow typhoid germs whole as drink that water. Yet
they cannot boil it at all; for first, fuel is very scarce. That which is
supplied could not cook a meal a day and they have to search the bare
koppies [hills] for a supply. There is hardly a bit to be had. Secondly,
they have no utensil to hold the water when boiled. I propose therefore
to give each tent another pail or crock and issue a proclamation that
all drinking water must be boiled.[60] The next day she suggested that
a big railway boiler be installed to boil all the water before it was
dispensed to the occupants.

Realising how difficult it would be to make the camps suitable for women and children with the limited resources available,
Emily suggested to Pretyman that the occupants be allowed to
leave the camps by degrees, if they wished. Pretyman agreed that
this was wisest, but was powerless to implement such a policy.
The camp residents were captives and it was not within Pretyman's authority to release them. He promised to see what could
be done about her other suggestions.

Emily thought that the aid she was able to provide should be
allocated in a systematic way. She wanted to satisfy the committee
of the Distress Fund that she had made the most of the resources
they had placed at her disposal. With the assistance of people in
the camp, she conducted a simple survey to establish what the

greatest needs were and among whom.[61]

Just as she seemed to be making headway with the authorities, the structure changed around her. First Major Cray fell ill and a Captain Hume was appointed in his place as acting superintendent of the Bloemfontein camp. He was less sympathetic to the residents and to Emily, and even more out of his depth. Next Pretyman left and was succeeded as governor by Major John Hamilton Goold-Adams, a man close to Sir Alfred Milner. Milner had suggested his appointment to Kitchener. He was more competent than Pretyman, but he too was less sympathetic. He had no family connections with Emily, as did Pretyman, and he felt less inclined to take heed of what she was saying. To her face he was charming, and at first she was taken in by this, but he was not inclined to give sympathetic consideration to people he regarded as the enemy.

Then came a bigger change: the camps were transferred from military to civilian control. Lord Kitchener did not think he should be in the business of harbouring women and children, especially when things were becoming much more complicated than he had expected. He offloaded the responsibility to Milner.

However, the military officers in charge of the camps remained unchanged. They, for their part, were less than impressed that they were now under civilian control. In one's army career, being in charge of a camp largely full of women and children did nothing for one's promotional prospects, not when one's peers were out there leading men into combat. To be under civilian control was worse. Captain Hume and his counterparts in other camps were doing work they had no interest in doing.

Emily understood the buck-passing perfectly clearly. She wrote to Lady Hobhouse that the official line is to speak of 'refugee' camps, to make out that the people are glad of the protection. *It is absolutely false. They are compelled to come and are wholly prisoners. In fact, I consider we are all more or less prisoners in Bloemfontein. We cannot move without passes. Everything is censored – spies abound – barbed wire and piquets surround the town – newspapers nearly all prohibited we have no news and know nothing but vaguest rumours.*[62]

Emily was invited to see Bishop Webb, the elderly head of the Anglican Church in the Orange River Colony. He had known her deceased father and knew of one of her uncles, also a bishop. She learnt that he had been sent to Bloemfontein to conciliate. If it were not for a few agitators, he told Emily, everything would settle down. As for the camp in Bloemfontein, *He said one of his Sisters of Mercy had visited the camp some time ago and reported that all that was needed was a little cotton and a little soap. They were happy and well off otherwise.*[63]

We cannot know if this is a fair summary of what the bishop really did say for we have only Emily's account, but whatever it was, it produced a startling reaction:

Then I went straight to my camp and just in one little corner this is what I found. Nurse Kennedy, underfed and overworked, just sinking onto her bed, hardly able to hold herself up after coping with some thirty typhoid and other patients with only the untrained help of two Boer girls – cooking as well as nursing to do herself. Next I called to see a woman panting in the heat just sickening for her confinement. Fortunately I had a nightdress in my bundle to give her and two tiny baby gowns. Next tent, a little six months' baby gasping its life out on its mother's knee. The doctor had given it powder in the morning but it had taken nothing since. Two or three others drooping and sick in that tent. Next, a child recovering from measles sent back from hospital before it could walk, stretched on the ground, white and wan, three or four others lying about. Next, a girl of 24 lay dying on a stretcher. Her father, a big gentle Boer, kneeling beside her while in the next tent his wife was watching a child of six also dying and one of about five also drooping. Already this couple had lost three children in the hospital and so would not let those go, though I begged hard to take them out of the hot tent. 'We must watch these ourselves', they said. Captain Hume had mounted guard over me – he thinks I am too sympathetic – but I sent him flying to get some brandy and get some down the girl's throat. But for the most part you must stand and look on helpless to do anything because there is nothing to do anything with. Then a man came up and said 'Sister,' (they call me Sister) 'come and see my child, sick for nearly three months'. It was a dear little chap of four and nothing left of him except his great brown eyes and white teeth from which the lips were drawn back too thin to close. His body was emaciated.

'Captain Hume,' I said, 'you shall look.' And I made him come in and shewed him the complete child-skeleton. Then at last he did say it was awful to see the children suffering so.[64]

The attempt by the bishop to persuade her that the situation was acceptable had transformed Emily. Gone was the tentative Englishwoman who had left Cape Town not knowing what to expect and wondering how she would cope. She was a different person now. Concern and sympathy had turned to dismay and then to anger.

The next day she wrote: *It is almost impossible to describe the moral atmosphere of this town. It affects me so that I am beginning to feel paralysed and intimidated. I do not know how to put the feeling into words – like being in continual disgrace or banishment or imprisonment. Some days I think I must cut and run – escape on foot if a pass is refused, but escape somehow. The feeling is intolerable. To watch all these Englishmen taking this horrible line and doing these awful things, and if you are thought to be taking a different view, to be watched all the afternoon by a man like Captain Hume – it's insufferable. Oh how I wanted to box his ears! I never realized it would be so hard. I only thought of physical hardships but they are nothing to this terror.*[65]

To avoid military censors, Emily arranged for her letters to be conveyed to Cape Town by travellers she thought she could trust. In Cape Town, Caroline Murray, with Emily's permission, read her letters and shared her comments with the small group of sympathisers, then arranged for their safe transportation to London. But couriers were not easy to find and when General Pretyman relinquished his governorship and returned to Cape Town, she entrusted one of her letters to Mrs Pretyman. She did not know that Mrs Pretyman was even less tolerant of her 'agitation' among the Boer women than her husband was. These were not safe hands in which to place angry words.

By the end of January 1901, it was time for Emily to leave Bloemfontein. The town had become unbearable. And there were more camps to visit.

Chapter 9

Governor to High Commissioner

After a visit from Emily, General Pretyman wrote, by hand, a letter to Sir Alfred Milner.[66] It was one of the last things he did before relinquishing his post.

Government Offices
Bloemfontein
31st January 1901

Private

Dear Sir Alfred,

In accordance with your letter of the 19th instant, I have done all I can to facilitate Miss Hobhouse's mission to the Boer refugee camps.

She volunteered the statement that her mission was non-political. I hope so, but I hear that since her arrival the refugees in this camp have suddenly found out that they are very badly treated and ought to be supplied with many more comforts than at present afforded them. At the same time she told me today she was generally satisfied with what had been done for the refugees, with some small exceptions. I asked her to let me have these in detail and that I would try and comply with her demands.

She has now asked to be allowed to visit the camps South of this, and of course permission has been granted.

I can see she is very much in sympathy with our Enemies, and incidentally let fall that she rather thought De Wet was within his rights in shooting the unfortunate peace-emissaries who fell into his hands – Morgendaal & Wessels – on the score that they were 'traitors to their country'.[67]

I fear this class of fanatic will not do the cause much good – from our point of view. At the same time I could not help in my heart agreeing with her that this policy of bringing in the women & children to these camps, is a mistaken one.

She told me that the one wish of the refugee women is to get back to their homes, whatever the condition of them may happen to be.

Against this are undoubtedly a certain number of them who came in here with their families to seek protection from the Boer Commandos. That class should of course be accommodated to the best of our ability. She is a pleasant, well-educated woman to talk to, and I have forwarded her mission so far as I am able, but she cannot conceal her political sympathies and her misguided love of the Boer in general.

I also know some of her relations at home; and I found she knew some of mine.

[The letter concluded with brief comments about his own future and on the recovery of an invalid Captain Hitchcock.]

Yours sincerely,

G J Pretyman.

Chapter 10

Norvals Pont and Aliwal North

Emily left Bloemfontein on or about 2 February 1901 to visit the camps at Norvals Pont and Aliwal North to the south of Bloemfontein. Both were on the south bank of the Orange River in the Cape Colony. There was no village or town near the Norvals Pont camp. It was on the railway line where it crossed the great river about 200 kilometres from Bloemfontein. The town of Aliwal North is about 100 kilometres upstream, but there was no direct line and reaching it entailed considerable detours. (See map on page 83).

It became a remarkable journey, much more so than Emily had anticipated. About a week after setting out, a very tired Emily wrote to her Aunt Mary, Lady Hobhouse.[68]

> *Begun at Naauwpoort Station*
> *10 February 1901*
> *The Land of Nod*

> *… I wrote a few lines yesterday from Stormberg Station,*
> *and now should like to begin a more detailed account of*

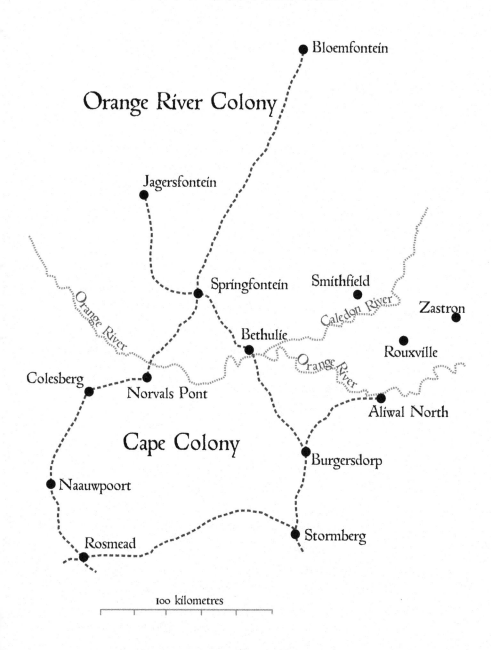

Places visited by Emily Hobhouse in early Feburary 1901

Norvals Pont and Aliwal North Camps. It has been an exciting week because I had picked on the same days as De Wet had done for careering up and down this line. At the best of times travelling is bad enough in this hot, dry, thirsty land, but add to that military control of everything, absence or partial disappearance of ordinary officials, permits and passes of endless kinds, the danger of travelling at night – the line occasionally torn up or a train burnt and the route blocked by countless strings of troop-trains and supply-trains all having to pass each other at sidings as the line is single – and you have some idea of the patience required.

One very hot day our eyes were refreshed by continual mirages presenting delicious views of cool stretches of water and imaginary cliffs. Sometimes I have slept in the train at sidings, sometimes at ghastly so-called hotels. A German Lutheran missionary has shown me much hospitality, and guards have been most kind in admitting me to their vans. Everything being in military hands it is all dirty and uncared-for.

I had great fears as to what I might find in the camp at Norvals Pont knowing there was no town to draw upon for supplies or help of any kind. But I am glad to be able to report that it is far superior to the camp at Bloemfontein. It was first organised by a Lieutenant Wynne and now Captain Du Plat Taylor is Commandant. The spot chosen is a slope surrounded by hills and about a mile from the station. From the Captain's tent there is a pretty stretch of the Orange River visible and far off the blue square-topped hill which marks Bethulie. The general character of the hills is similar to this – Table Mountains constantly recurring all through the land.

The population of this camp is about 1,500 and it is well laid out in rows and streets – with numbers so that you can find your way about. ...

The people I call prisoners-of-war occupy the centre and great bulk of the camp and beyond a broad space on the other side are pitched the tents of the single men – people who have surrendered or taken oaths or suchlike. Between the hours of 6 p.m. and 8 a.m. this part of the camp is prohibited from passing to the other side, and the soldiery have no tents, either, in the precincts of the camp. I must get this plan adopted in Bloemfontein.

Instead of drinking the waters of the Orange they use the river only for bathing and Captain Taylor had pipes laid on to a farm where a spring gives 14,000 galls. per hour, and this pure water is brought into the camp.

Much to my delight I found there was much less overcrowding in Norvals Pont and that each tent was supplied with a low wooden bed, one or more mattresses, a bench, [and] table utensils. Consequently the whole aspect of the people was different. The rations also were slightly better.

There was no violent outbreak of sickness though I understand that all the cases nursed in the hospital had died. This I attribute, and so did the people, to bad nursing. They have no trained nurse. I hope one may soon be procured.

The heat was very great. Captain Taylor told me himself that his large cool breezy marquee was usually 104° Fahr. [40°C] and he believes the bell-tents with single canvas rise to 110° Fahr [43°C]. The doctor said he could not use his clinical thermometer in them as it would not go down at all. I get greatly exhausted after sitting in these tents talking to people a whole day, especially as there are six or seven in the tent, and others from outside come and throng round the narrow opening excluding any possible breath of air.

Captain Taylor had employed the men in the camp to make a tennis court and this was just completed – sports of some kind are needed for exercise and to give something to do: the idle life is so demoralizing.

Sir Alfred Milner ... is sending round the Education Commissioner to arrange about schools ... In Norvals

*Pont two large marquees are set apart and mistresses duly
certificated are available from the camp population. Now the
need of clothing for the children is very great.*

*Captain Taylor had been so unhappy about the
clothelessness that he had ordered £150 worth and had given
it out, but had received a reprimand for his extravagance. So
I undertook to forward some and chose some women in the
camp to store and distribute it where most needed. ...*

*As we sat having tea at the door of the officers' tent, we
could see horsemen sweeping across the plain about three miles
off in a cloud of dust, and so near are the Boers that Major
Legh thought it was a Commando.*

*The death rate is not nearly so high in this camp – less
overcrowding and better water. I felt a great deal relieved.*

Emily found the commandant at the station a vague sort of person
and inveigled a pass out of him to go on to Aliwal North. She was
obliged to follow a zigzag route: north-east back into the Orange
River Colony to the rail junction at Springfontein, then south-
east into the Cape Colony to Burghersdorp and finally north-east
again to her destination.

It was a difficult journey. Food was often unobtainable. The
stations were under military control and the ladies facilities were
mostly locked up or being used as offices. One sleepless night
was spent sitting bolt upright in the guard's van as the train was
shunted all night. For another night she sought accommodation
at a station, but all the meagre offerings were taken. Then a gal-
lant commercial traveller offered her his hotel room if he could
leave some of his things in it:

*It was an appalling room; you had to stand in it with your
skirts drawn round you – and to add to the misery a sand
storm came on and the heat was the most excessive I have felt
out here. My tongue felt as if it were tied into a knot. After*

much worry I got two black ladies to come and wash the place
out, and then made a ring with insect powder and lay down
in the centre of it. It was a very ghastly night and though not
amusing at the time, I feel very much amused now in thinking
of my absurd hunger, thirst, fatigue, dirt, loneliness and
general misery.

I stayed as short a time as I could at this lovely lodge and
then made off for Aliwal North. After endless difficulties
I succeeded in getting there, and a dear little town it is.
Unfortunately, as I had come unexpectedly, I had left my
introduction to people there behind and could hardly tell
where to begin. So after reporting myself I went to the Post
Office and finding a fascinating young clerk got him to write
me down a list of the chief inhabitants. So I managed to pick
out the right ones to call upon, beginning with the Mayor
and working down to the Medical Officer. They had formed
a town committee to deal with the camp and have done their
work really well.

Poor little Aliwal with only 800 inhabitants had in
four weeks to receive and provide for a population of over
two thousand – nearly three times its own number. And it
does them credit for it is far away beyond the other camps –
but then, they have a most helpful Commandant in Major
Apthorpe who could not speak highly enough of the people,
their patience, good conduct and uncomplainingness under
their privations and losses ...

His camp can barely be called a prison, he has no soldiers
or sentries and everyone is free to walk into the town or to
receive visits from the people in the town without passes.
The [inhabitants of the] towns of Smithfield, Rouxville and
Zastron are all there and so far only two deaths have taken
place. Everything is beautifully arranged and provided for.
He gives two tents to large families and offers sailcloth to any
who care to put up wooden framework to make extra rooms.

He encourages them to come and state their needs. The rations here are better – compressed vegetables are given and 1 lb. of potatoes twice a week. And potatoes are 6d. a pound or eight times as dear as in London. …

Clothing for children is much needed, especially now the schools are opening, and I chose some women to receive and distribute the goods. The great lack has been soap. In neither camp has any been supplied, and those without money have been unable to wash clothes or persons properly. This seems to have been due to a careless order from Headquarters with regard to the rations, and men don't think of these things unless it is suggested to them, they simply say: 'How dirty these people are!'

The fact is, I believe, the military supply is very short. I bought soap in the town and sent [it] into the camp for immediate needs, also material for the women to make up for themselves. Many have brought their sewing-machines when they saved nothing else.[69]

The Aliwal North camp was different for reasons Emily did not mention. The explanation may be found in correspondence between General Pretyman and Sir Alfred Milner. The sudden influx of people was caused when Lord Kitchener withdrew the protection that until that time had been afforded the towns mentioned in Emily's letter – Smithfield, Rouxville, Zastron – and other small towns in the southern Orange River Colony. Kitchener decided he could not spare the troops necessary to secure these localities and ordered the garrisons to evacuate the inhabitants and report for duty elsewhere. The evacuations were not enforced and residents were allowed to stay at their own risk if they wished to do so. Most Boer supporters chose to remain, but the loyalists decided they could not take the chance of being raided by the burgher commandos and made their way, with assistance, to the camp at Aliwal North.

General Pretyman disapproved of this policy and in the month before Emily's visit wrote several times to Milner to complain.[70] Milner did nothing; he made a practice of not involving himself in military matters.

The evacuations were thus the opposite of what had happened further north where loyalists remained in the towns under protection and republican sympathisers were forcibly removed. The people in the Aliwal North camp had mostly chosen to go there for their own safety, had travelled in friendly hands and had arrived with their most precious possessions intact. They were not the enemy, as in other camps, but Imperial sympathisers. Their homes were not destroyed (although rogue Imperial troops looted Rouxville as they left). Major Apthorpe, the man in charge of the Aliwal camp, had been the district commissioner at Smithfield. He knew or recognised some of the people now again his responsibility and he was well disposed to them. Small wonder then that their experience of camp life was better than the experience of the occupants of the Bloemfontein camp and even the Norvals Pont camp – so far.

Emily resolved to return to Bloemfontein to see if she could persuade the authorities to run the camp there in the manner of these southern camps:

> *I am more satisfied with affairs at Aliwal North (as they concern my work) than I could have anticipated and so also, in less degree, at Norvals Pont. Now therefore I am hurrying back to Bloemfontein as quick as may be, having much to do there, and I live in hopes of going further north where I am much needed. The distances are so huge.*[71]

Emily was required to take a longer route back, going south via the junctions at Stormberg, Rosmead and Naauwpoort (see map on page 83). The landscape through which she travelled was far different from her native Cornwall. There were no green fields, no hedgerows and laneways and few trees. Though not as barren as the Karoo and never quite featureless, the plains rolled on, shimmering in the summer heat. The farms were huge, the population largely unseen and the homesteads far apart, mostly out of sight of each other.

South of the Orange River, the monotony was occasionally broken when the train penetrated a ridge through a gap or crossed over a saddle. Now and then a nearby hill rose to greater heights, like the striking Coles Kop, visible over a great distance. North of the river, the scenery was becoming familiar and offered nothing much to attract the gaze of a weary eye until Bloemfontein drew near. Emily took what consolation she could from the meagre visual offerings.

The prospect of this journey had filled Emily with trepidation, mostly for the discomfort, hunger, heat and physical hardship that it might entail. It had exceeded her fears on all those counts and on top of that she had found danger. Inadvertently, she had arrived in what was the most active region of the war at that particular time. And yet she remained resolute and determined to carry on. Her work 'simply had to be done'. Aborting her mission or staying in one place for a while until things cooled down never seems to have entered her mind.

Chapter 11

De Wet

It is remarkable that Emily was able to visit the southern camps at all. The De Wet mentioned at the start of her letter (see the previous chapter) was Commandant-General Christiaan Rudolf de Wet, the commander-in-chief of the former Orange Free State. He and the Boer leadership had resolved to carry the war into the Cape Colony and Emily had inadvertently entered the border region just when he was doing the same, intent on making his break across the Orange River.

An old map suggests there were only four road bridges from the Orange River Colony to the Cape Colony at that time, including those at Norvals Pont and Aliwal North.[72] He might well have chosen one of these two for his offensive. Then again it was recognised that he might choose to ford the river instead.

Both Milner and Kitchener were anxious that De Wet should be stopped. They were aware that the Dutch-speaking population of the Cape Colony was mostly in sympathy with the Boers. If the colonial citizens were to support De Wet in large numbers, in short, if De Wet's incursion should trigger a general uprising, the war would become immensely more difficult. The Colony was considerably larger in area and its Dutch-speaking population was greater than that of the Transvaal and Orange River Colonies combined.[73] Containing an insurrection there would be a nightmare. Moreover, the Colony straddled key supply routes to the interior, routes that might come under attack, and maintaining the military operations in the former republics would become much more difficult.

The Boers, for their part, hoped to achieve just such an uprising but expected, at worst, that they would succeed in recruiting young men to join their guerrilla movement. Lesser Boer commandos were already operating deep in the Colony and they were indeed succeeding in raising recruits as they went.

The Boers had another reason for fighting in the Colony: on colonial territory the British could hardly take punitive action against the civilian population as they did near any places of military action in the former republics. The colonials were British subjects and the destruction of their homes would be illegal. Moreover, if homes were destroyed it would greatly increase the risk of a general uprising, so home and farm destruction was simply not on. By taking the struggle onto colonial territory, the guerrillas would thus reduce the impact of the war on women and children.

Kitchener did everything he could to prevent De Wet from crossing the river. Lesser campaigns were abandoned and thousands of troops were transported to the border region causing the chaos on the rail lines that so inconvenienced Emily. Garrisons at the bridges were reinforced and detachments were deployed along the river.

De Wet was, however, the master tactician of the war. He sent spies ahead who let it be known among the local population that he intended to cross the Orange River somewhere upstream of its confluence with the Caledon River, its major tributary, somewhere not far from Aliwal North if not at Aliwal North itself. Perhaps they indicated that they had come to scout for a suitable ford. He moved some of his burghers in that direction with instructions to pass near enough to Imperial contingents to be seen. As the British commanders rushed troops to the area to cut him off, he forded the river with about 3,000 men at Zanddrift, well below the confluence of the two rivers and downstream of Norvals Pont.

The date was 10 February 1901[74], the date on which Emily began the letter to her aunt from Naauwpoort (now Noupoort), the letter of the previous chapter. Emily was thus south of the river in the Cape Colony as De Wet entered the territory. To get back to Bloemfontein, she threaded her way through the border region going against the flow of troops streaming down to pursue De Wet.

On their way to the river crossing, some of the guerrillas under Froneman, one of De Wet's generals, had captured a supply train on a branch line to Jagersfontein by the simple expedient of blowing up the track in front of and behind it. When they had helped themselves to much-needed supplies, including a large quantity of ammunition, they torched the train.[75] Emily had passed nearby just days earlier and passed through the area again after the attack.

Once De Wet was in the Cape Colony, Kitchener deployed yet more resources to contain and, if possible, capture or kill him; 14,000 soldiers in seventeen columns were thrown into this effort.[76] Against such odds, De Wet did not get far, but he managed to escape back over the Orange River – much to Kitchener's frustration – after eighteen vulnerable days on colonial soil. Back on his home ground, he dispersed his guerrillas and melted into the countryside once again.

Kitchener had the consolation that De Wet had suffered considerable attrition. Uncharacteristically, it rained heavily during the incursion and the guerrillas' supply wagons and heavy guns became bogged. All had to be abandoned. The grazing on the veld was poor – it had not had time to respond to the rain – and they lost many horses. Many burghers had to walk carrying their saddles, supplies, rifles and ammunition. Pressured by the pursuing British and driven by the relentless De Wet, hundreds deserted to make their way back to the ORC on their own. Many were picked up and became prisoners of war.

In his ensuing dispatch to the War Office, Kitchener reported on De Wet's invasion and concluded: *His losses in killed and wounded during the various engagements must have been very considerable, and seeing that over 200 prisoners, all his guns, ammunition, and wagons fell into our hands, he undoubtedly quitted Cape Colony with great loss of prestige.*[77]

Chapter 12

Kitchener's strategy

Emily's hopes that conditions would improve for the residents of the camp at Bloemfontein were destined to be short lived. Far to the north where she was not permitted to go, greater forces were at work.

The developments had been some time in the making. In 28 November 1900, one month before her arrival in Cape Town, Lord Roberts had relinquished overall command to Lord Kitchener with the assertion that the war was all but over and only mopping up remained to be done.

But the circumstances were not as Roberts had asserted they were. He had left Kitchener with a difficult situation. There were still tens of thousands of Boers under arms in the countryside, led by capable commanders like De Wet in the Orange River Colony, General Louis Botha in the eastern Transvaal and General Koos de la Rey in the western Transvaal. The Boers were resourceful, courageous, mobile, possessed local knowledge, had the support of most of the rural white population and gathered military intelligence expertly. Above all, they were determined not to yield.

Kitchener was left to work out how to contain and conquer them in a vast and sparsely populated land, and the supposed proximity of the end of the conflict made life more difficult for him. The troops were thinking of going home. Hadn't Roberts said it was all but over? Some of those who could, actually departed – the Canadians, the volunteer Yeomanry. Kitchener needed more men, not fewer. He needed a focus on the tasks that lay ahead, not thoughts of leaving. He wanted fresh troops to replace the war-weary ones he had. But Roberts's comments made it difficult to persuade London to supply what he asked for. Indeed 'London' for the most part meant the War Office, soon under the thrall of Roberts himself.

A large proportion of the men on hand had to be used for guarding the thousands of kilometres of railway lines without which Kitchener could not function. Away from the railways, Imperial forces could not move safely across the land except in large, heavily guarded convoys. Leaving a small detachment any-where was to risk its annihilation and present the guerrillas with a potential supply of munitions. Kitchener was compelled to con-centrate his resources. Only centres that warranted a substantial garrison could be occupied. The result was that he controlled the urban centres, the immediate countryside around them and, cru-cially, the connecting railway lines. Away from the railways, cities and large towns, the Boers still moved at will and Kitchener had not nearly enough men to bring them to heel.

The guerrillas were supplied from the surviving farms. Able wives, experienced if elderly parents and black farm hands managed to continue production satisfactorily, especially when advised during occasional secret visits by the man of the house. Besides food, the farms offered the Boers clothing, fresh horses, saddles, all manner of necessities, rest and recuperation and places to stash ammunition. They also provided intelligence on British troop movements. A farm would usually assist any guerrilla who called there.

As for supplies of ammunition, the Boers obtained what they needed by raiding and sometimes routing British convoys or garrisons. On 3 December 1900, for example, just days after

Kitchener had assumed command, the Boers captured a convoy of 120 wagons laden with supplies and munitions on its way to Rustenburg in the western Transvaal. Ten days later they defeated General Richard Clements who had camped with 1,500 men at Nooitgedacht in the same region. Clements lost 638 men – killed, injured or captured – and again the Boers acquired significant quantities of military supplies. With losses of this magnitude and defeats on this scale, the war was clearly not over.

When St John Brodrick, the Secretary for War, asked how long it would go on, Kitchener replied: *I cannot say how long it will go on. Not counting voluntary surrenders we reduce their forces at the rate of about a 1000 a month. … It is a most difficult problem, an enemy that always escapes, a country so vast that there is always room to escape, supplies such as they want abundant almost everywhere.*[78] This was not the kind of answer Brodrick expected or wanted.

Kitchener needed a new strategy and he struggled to find one. Then, in early 1901, even as Emily was visiting Bloemfontein, he settled on a carrot and stick approach – one part carrot, three parts stick. The carrot would be a new attempt to end the war by negotiation and he initiated efforts to engage the Boer command in discussions. If they were prepared to concede defeat and accept British rule, he would be generous in the terms of settlement. He had difficulty in getting them to talk and when he eventually did, agreement could not be reached. By May 1901, this part of his strategy had come to nought.

The first stick was a resolution that whenever a concentration of Boers was discovered, he would attack it with overwhelming force, using his greatly superior numbers and the mobility afforded by control of the railways. He would provide mounts for as many infantry as he could to match the mobility of the burghers in the field. Acquiring a large and steady supply of horses became a major task for his supply chain. This stick was applied during De Wet's incursion into the Cape Colony, for example.

Kitchener had started his military career as an officer in the Royal Engineers and the second stick was a large construction project. He developed a plan to build a series of fortified lines to crisscross the land and thus segment it, large as it was, into a patchwork of regions that he could clear out one by one. The fortified lines would prevent the Boers from returning to an area once cleared and would generally limit their mobility.

Each line would consist of barbed-wire fencing, sometimes with an adjacent trench, stretching between fortified positions. The fortifications, called blockhouses, were to be within rifle range of each other to ensure that no one could pass between them without coming under fire. They would be manned twenty-four hours a day by soldiers operating in shifts, seven or eight at a time. Each blockhouse would be stout enough to protect the occupants against the weather and rifle fire. The guerrillas no longer possessed heavy guns and there was no need to take artillery attacks into account.

The scale of the project was huge and the strategy expensive to execute. It required labour and materials to build the blockhouse lines, soldiers to protect the builders and a further large allocation of troops to man all the fortified posts as they were completed. London was persuaded to supply the money and the men, and construction continued until the end of the war. By then, the lines extended for 6,000 kilometres and contained more than 8,000 blockhouses occupied by more than 50,000 soldiers.[79]

The third stick is relevant to the story of Emily Hobhouse.

The resounding welcome Roberts had received on his return home implied a message that Kitchener evidently understood. Roberts had authorised the destruction of homes and farms in a very visible way by public proclamation. In the wake of this destruction, women and children had been confined to the hopelessly inadequate camps. The message was that these things would be overlooked, even encouraged, if they hastened the end of the war.

Kitchener decided that it was time to clear the land of

anything that could support and sustain the guerrillas. All farms and rural communities had to be removed. This, too, was a plan executed on a grand scale.

The first sweep was under the command of Major-General John French, Kitchener's most effective field commander and a future British field marshal. Rayne Kruger, in one of the leading histories of the war, takes up the story:

> The operation was destined to be the prototype of what was called a 'drive'. French's target was not only the enemy commandos. Strict instructions were issued that every farm was to be visited and all women, children and their Native employees were to be sent to the nearest railway depot for subsequent internment. All crops, stocks and wagons were to be seized or burnt and all bakeries and mills destroyed. In short, the army was to fall like a plague of locusts upon a territory of over 10,000 square miles and leave it not only uninhabited but uninhabitable.
>
> The advance started in sweltering heat on 28th January. Soon hundreds of old men, women and children, piling what possessions they could on to wagons and driving great herds of cattle and sheep, fled before the columns whom Boer rear guards tried sporadically to hold off. Across the undulating grassland of the high veld the troops moved with a slowness imposed on them by their gigantic task of devastation.[80]

The drive began a few days before Emily set off for her visit to Norvals Pont and Aliwal North. French lined up his troops along the Johannesburg–Pretoria rail line and moved east. The area they covered is about three times the size of Wales and happens to be excellent farming country with ample rainfall. By April, this prosperous region had been comprehensively laid to waste.

One of French's columns was commanded by Lieutenant-Colonel Edmund Allenby, also a future British field marshal.

More intelligent than most of the participants in this campaign, he wrote home of the extraordinary nature of their work. He recognised that the uprooting of thousands of families, with women and children given a few minutes to clear their homes and then driven off in wagons, was the making of a new Great Trek, a new mythology of bitterness and suffering, and he found it 'beastly work'.[81]

Many other accounts of French's drive may be found in British and Boer sources[82], including personal testimonies of officers and soldiers engaged in or observing these activities.[83] Kitchener's official report simply said that French *cleared the country through which he passed*.[84]

In military terms, the results of the drive were small. The 21,000 Imperial soldiers engaged in the operation succeeded in killing, wounding or capturing 473 Boers in four months. An additional 555 men surrendered voluntarily – mostly those too old, too infirm or too young to evade the advance.[85] Commandant-General Louis Botha was in the area and a prime target of the operation, but he and most of his commando of 2,500 burghers broke through the line with relatively few casualties and moved north. With such meagre results, this was not a tactic that would quickly end the war. But if it produced few military results, it generated a huge new flow of people into the camps. Kitchener called them concentration camps.

Roberts had given solemn undertakings that Boers who laid down their arms or who had never taken them up against Britain in the first place, and who pledged loyalty to the Crown, would be allowed to live their normal lives undisturbed. But under Kitchener, their properties were devastated just as completely as the rest. For the strategy to be fully effective, no producing farm could be left intact, no flock of sheep or herd of cattle could be overlooked, no crop left to be harvested. When it became clear that this would be done, many of these men did not wait for the drive to reach their property. They prepared their families as best they could, dug up their buried rifles, mounted their horses and joined or rejoined the Boer commandos in a deeply angry mood. Kitchener's tactic led to the most successful recruitment the Boers had had for months, offsetting the meagre casualties the drive had inflicted.

Emily, on her return journey to Bloemfontein, was unaware of these events.

Chapter 13

Return to Bloemfontein

After her difficult journey to Norvals Pont and Aliwal North, Emily needed a rest to recover her strength and plan. Kya Lami, the large and gracious home of the widow Fichardt, was just the place for this, and Mrs Fichardt welcomed her back.

The task before her now seemed clear: it was not so much to distribute the modest resources she had at her disposal but to influence the authorities to do what was necessary. Only the government had resources capable of dealing with the scale of the problem.

She started at the top and went to see the most senior person in the civil administration in Bloemfontein, General Pretyman's successor, Major John Hamilton Goold-Adams. Emily was apprehensive about the meeting but received a cordial reception. She wrote to her aunt:

Just come from a long interview with Goold-Adams who is agreeable, energetic, and very desirous of making the camps what they should be. He felt with me that this one is not what it should be. He is open and kind-hearted but evidently not a

*man of any particular mental power. He is trying to carry on
a Government with no money and seems a little perplexed, but
the faith of all of them in Alfred the Great and his policy is
implicit and they don't look beyond.*[86]

In response to their meeting, Goold-Adams inspected the camp in
person several days later and they had a further discussion on the
site. He gave the camp superintendent, Captain Hume, a dressing
down for failing to co-operate with Emily, and it had the desired
effect. *Captain Hume is reduced to a state of abject deference,* she
wrote afterwards, *continually asking what my wishes are and how
they can best be carried out.*[87]

There was progress of sorts. The brickwork necessary for
installing the boilers was complete and a few days later the boilers themselves arrived. Soon boiling could begin and germ-free
water would be available. Soap was promised. A hundred families were accommodated in rows of one-roomed corrugated iron
huts instead of tents – a consequence of Emily's persuasive efforts
with the departed General Pretyman. The hospital tents were likewise replaced with corrugated iron structures and were given hard
rather than dirt floors, but they remained hopelessly too small
and grossly unsuitable for their purpose.

Letters from England reported that many people were engaged
in supporting Emily's work. Kate Courtney wrote that a further
£500 had been raised and transferred to Emily's Cape Town bank
account.[88] Dorothy Bradby reported that thirty-three sewing cir-
cles were making clothes. Seven consignments had already been
sent and they were sending boots and shoes, too. She added, *more
work parties are starting … people are working with a real will – it
is very nice.*[89]

Emily continued to receive assistance from her team in Cape
Town, too. Caroline Murray, Mr Schultz, Dr Andrew Murray,
Mrs Elizabeth Roos and others remained keenly interested in
her efforts and ensured that consignments from England were

sent north as Emily directed whenever space on the railways was granted. Caroline wrote how interesting and informative they found the letters to Lady Hobhouse.[90]

In Bloemfontein, local people were also involved, despite the discouraging attitude of officialdom. Emily mentions Mrs Hannie Blignaut, wife of a prominent member of the Boer administration before the war and sister of the deposed president; Miss Maynie Fleck, a young and equally dauntless woman, and Mrs Marie Krause, also from a prominent family. According to Emily, Mrs Blignaut and Miss Fleck toiled *like slaves and take the bulk of the clothing work off my hands, so that I can devote the whole of my attention to 'squeezing the authorities'.*[91] Hannie Blignaut was not permitted in the camp herself because she was said to have 'talked politics' to the residents, while Maynie Fleck was followed by a trooper wherever she went.[92] Neither diminished their efforts on behalf of the women and children in consequence of this harassment.

But despite all these efforts, the situation was deteriorating. The people in the camp had arrived with very few possessions and their meagre clothing was wearing out just as the earliest signs of the southern autumn were bringing cooler weather. More victims were arriving constantly and the overcrowding was getting worse. Inadequate sanitary arrangements from the outset meant that one part of the camp was becoming uninhabitable from the stench.

Most telling of all, the three small hospital buildings were full of typhoid patients and many were ill in their tents. The single doctor, a military doctor assigned to the camp, was incompetent, overworked and unfamiliar with the medical needs of women and children. Boer war histories indicate that both Roberts and Kitchener were unimpressed with the medical support that accompanied their troops. It is unlikely that the army released the best of their unsatisfactory doctors to serve the camps.

Deaths were a daily occurrence and there were sometimes several funerals a day. The full extent of what was happening dawned on Emily when she realised that the people in the camp were about the same in number as there had been in her father's parish in Cornwall. There funerals had been rare, something of an event when they happened, and the deceased were usually old. Here the young were dying and the occurrence was frequent.

The military leadership, including Kitchener himself, thought that if the women were having a difficult time, if children were ill and dying, perhaps the women would see the wisdom of ending the war. Perhaps they could be persuaded to encourage their husbands and sons to lay down their arms and surrender.

A number of prominent Boers had also reached this view and had already surrendered. Commandant Piet de Wet, brother of the commandant-general, had himself come to the conclusion that the war was hopeless, that the suffering of the families and the continued war casualties no longer made sense in a war they could never win. The British recruited him to spread this message among his own people. If he could make the women see sense, they would perhaps get the message out to their menfolk.

Emily tells the story of his visit to the Bloemfontein camp. *This week they sent out Piet de Wet, brother of the General, to address the women and ask them to induce their husbands to surrender. A large concourse assembled. When he had finished he looked markedly at a prominent woman – a Mrs Botha – a nice good creature, asking her support. Mrs Botha returned the look, solemnly shook her head and moved off to her own tent followed in a string by all the women, till the wretched orator found himself on the platform alone.*[93]

The camp residents must all have wished fervently for the end of hostilities, but Emily reports that the predominant attitude was hardening in defiance. The women were beginning to think of themselves as having a role in the struggle for their nation's independence. While the men were risking their lives against the British army, they would play their part by enduring the conditions in the camps. On 13 February, Emily wrote to Lady Hobhouse: *From all accounts the mass of Boer prisoners are determined never to live under British rule and now this camp system with all that led up to it has consolidated the feelings of the women into one strong desire to retain at all costs the independence of their country.*[94] Later she expressed it more graphically to her brother, Leonard: *But those who are suffering most keenly, and who have lost most, either of their children by death, or their possessions by fire and sword, such as the reconcentrated women in the camps, have the most conspicuous patience, and never express a wish that their men should be the ones to give way. It must be fought out now, they think, to the bitter end.*[95]

The importance of clothing was escalating. Emily wrote: ... *the autumn nights have come and it is cold after the heat of the day. Soon it will be very cold ...*[96] The diurnal temperature range on the African Highveld is great, as it is in high country everywhere; nights are often 20°C colder than the daytime. But it was not within Emily's power to do what was necessary, despite the welcome stream of clothes from England. *The demand for clothing is so huge that it is hopeless to think that the private charity of England and Colonial working-parties combined can effectively cope with more than a very small portion of it. The Government recognize that they must provide necessary clothes and I think we all agree that having brought these people into this position it is their duty to do so. Yesterday, Captain Trollope, now Chief Superintendent of camps throughout the Colony, asked me right out if I would pay for all the clothes they provide and I refused most decidedly. You see they (the Government) are very hard up.*[97]

Emily recognised that the value of her presence was declining. The tasks of managing and distributing aid had been effectively delegated and had become a joint effort of women in the town and women in the camp. She had spoken all she could to the authorities. Slow progress was being made and, for the moment, there was not much more that she could do. Her thoughts again turned elsewhere.

She had permission to visit other camps and resolved to go to them all, including those she had already seen. She would then return to Bloemfontein, hoping that by then Lord Kitchener would have granted her repeated requests to be allowed to go north. If not, she would travel to Cape Town, confer with her supporters there and return home. It was time for the committee in England to begin making arrangements for someone to succeed her in southern Africa, perhaps even two people.

Other noteworthy events occurred between 12 February 1901 when Emily returned from the southern camps and before she left Bloemfontein at the end of that month. The first of these were events in England: When Emily arrived back, the letters waiting for her at Kya Lami were full of news about the death of Queen Victoria. She learnt that Uncle Arthur had assisted in the swearing in of the new king.

Although she continued to work for the camp residents, or perhaps because she did, she was slow to shake off the exhaustion of the journey. On 13 February, the day after her return, she wrote to Aunt Mary: *In this land of nod I fall asleep between sentences as I write them and waking up can't remember what I wrote on the last page. This terrible affliction of which I am much ashamed is the cause of the disjointed character of my letters. Now and then I have to give in, lie down and sleep soundly, then start again.*[98] On the 18th she wrote to Leonard: *I suppose I must in duty bound write to someone though I have become such a dormouse I would a great deal rather go to sleep.*[99] Three days later, she surrendered: *I have not much to add today because I was laid up yesterday and took a day off in bed – nothing really amiss, but I needed a rest.*[100]

Perhaps as a consequence of her tiredness during this time, there were lapses in her judgement. She decided to pay for some of the 'better class' of school-age girls in the camp to go to a boarding school in the town. The Distress Fund's committee was unimpressed and she desisted, but not before she had committed the funds needed to support four girls. She kept the commitment; the four went to the boarding school and became her lifelong admirers.

A more serious lapse was the carelessness with which she wrote, forgetting that letters might be opened in transit and read. Besides the letter carried by Mrs Pretyman, she sent a letter with an Inspector of Education. Both of them, to protect themselves, might well have submitted these letters to the censors before delivering them.

In these letters, Emily expressed herself most freely to her brother writing, for example:

> *Understand that since his [Goold-Adams's] arrival civil government is supposed to have begun and the camps, in particular, are supposed to be run on civil lines. … It is such a curious position, hollow and rotten to the heart's core; to have made all over the State large, uncomfortable communities of people whom you call Refugees, and say you are protecting, but who call themselves prisoners-of-war, compulsorily detained, and detesting your protection.*
>
> *The whole object, of course, is to enable Chamberlain to say in Parliament that the country is settled and civil administration begun. It's a farce.*[101]

And later: *It was very amusing to hear this man* [a Mr Webb] *give his views on the British army and above all on all the officers; their laziness, incompetence, and love of amusement. … This army, it is thought, will never catch de Wet; there is too much riding, and shooting, and picnicking, and polo, and golf playing, for war to have much place. Possibly a small fresh army with some fight in it, and before they fall into the habits here, might ride after him and catch him. But all those Tommies asleep upon the line and all the badly kept offices! Oh! dear it's dreadful. … So you see we are not in love with the Imperial Army.*[102] This was not exactly the diplomatic language of an apolitical humanitarian. We have no independent account of the verbal interchanges between Emily and the people in authority, but her opinions of them did not improve; nor their's of her. Censors wrote reports on what they found.

There was another concentration camp at Bloemfontein. On the outskirts of the town in another direction, there was a camp for indigenous, black people. As farms across the countryside were destroyed, the black people on them were also left homeless, equally indigent and just as devoid of the means to subsist as the white people who were turned off these properties. They were also concentrated into camps, separate camps, one of which was at Bloemfontein.

Emily never went there and one can only speculate why this is so. But it troubled her. She suspected that conditions there were even worse than in the white camp which she frequented. She hoped others would investigate and take up the cause of those people.

Her concern led to an unfortunate development. She was invited to address a meeting of 'loyalist' women in the town. The gathering included long-time residents as well as some who had arrived with the British occupation; wives of officers and civil servants, for example. She freely and forthrightly described the situation in the white camp, then took the opportunity to suggest that members of the audience, with the compassion of womanhood, might visit the black camp. Perhaps she thought that while they resiled from assisting Boer women and children – enemy people – they would not have similar reticence in helping the blacks who were, after all, supposed to be neutral in this conflict.

The suggestion was another error of judgement. There was no possibility that anyone would take up her suggestion and no one went. To these women, blacks were servants and they never interacted with them in any other context. They found the suggestion preposterous.

The audience did not much care for Emily's work among the Boer women and children either. A reporter from the *Bloemfontein Post*, a local paper, was present even though Emily had believed that the meeting would be a purely private one. The reporter wrote a highly critical report. In it she said it was presumptuous of Emily, a newcomer, to address ladies who had lived their whole lives in South Africa in the way that she had. The article ended *... we must certainly, by way of conclusion, express the earnest hope that Miss Hobhouse will not, as part of her mission, teach the refugees at the Refugee Camp, who have so much to be grateful for, to believe they have grievances – grievances quite unimagined hitherto.*[103] It is safe to assume that neither the reporter nor any other members of the audience had been to the camp.

War correspondents were present in the town. They picked up the story and it reached English newspapers, to Emily's deep dismay and the dismay of the Distress Fund's committee. It was her first experience of a hostile press.

Because of her position, Tibbie Steyn, wife of the former president, had freedom to move around the city, though always with a military escort. One evening, while travelling in her carriage and with a thunderstorm approaching, she encountered Emily walking home from the camp. She offered Emily a ride, thereby rescuing her from a possible drenching. It resulted in an invitation to spend the next afternoon in Mrs Steyn's company. Mrs Steyn's younger sister was an inmate of the Bloemfontein camp. Emily heard how she had been paraded through the streets on her way to incarceration.

To Tibbie Steyn, Emily's must have been one of the few voices of compassion in a war whose logic she rejected. She was constantly anxious for her husband who was roaming the country with the guerrillas, usually with Commandant-General De Wet. She was afraid for them, afraid they would be captured or shot. But it was more than that. They had to remain constantly on the move and she knew this was taking a severe toll on her husband.

Brandfort concentration camp

Most of the men in De Wet's commando were the toughest and best of the Free State resistance and most of them were young. Her husband, on the other hand, was a middle-aged city man inclined to be overweight and unsuited to spending all day in the saddle. She also knew that despite the hardship there was not the remotest possibility he would surrender. If he did so, the resistance might collapse. Instead he remained one of the staunchest, most determined patriots and the most inspirational of all.

Emily's fraternising with the ex-president's wife was noted with disapproval and reported to Milner and Kitchener. The establishment's disaffection with this Hobhouse woman was growing.

Now Emily faced a new journey over greater distances than the one she had so recently completed. She was not looking forward to it, but she felt compelled to see more camps and with good reason. For one, she did have tangible assistance to provide and the occupants of other camps were entitled to some of what the Distress Fund could offer. She knew it was much appreciated by the recipients. At every camp she had visited, she had been able to organise for the future distribution of assistance that might be sent directly to the camp from Cape Town, especially clothing. She could make similar arrangements by visiting more camps.

Her visit to a camp had other beneficial effects. Superintendents did react to her urging, and even if the resulting changes were small, they were changes nevertheless. The nursing staff were encouraged and the victims were comforted by the mere fact that she was there and taking an interest in their situation.

But the most important reason was perhaps this: the change of government policy, the fundamental change of direction that was required, could never be achieved in southern Africa. That much was becoming clear to her. She would have to argue the case when she returned home to Britain, and she needed more information, more evidence. Reporting on just the handful of camps she had seen so far would not be sufficient.

Chapter 14

A new journey

The heat of mid-summer had abated when Emily Hobhouse set off to visit the southern camps again and make her way to Kimberley and the west. (See map p 114.) On 4 March 1901, she wrote to her Aunt Mary from Springfontein, a place that was little more than a railway station and her first stop on this new journey:

> *It is a comparatively small and recent camp, but the people are poorer and more utterly destitute than any I have yet seen. This was largely because there was no adjacent town from which supplies could filter in.*
>
> *The Commandant, Major Gostling, is really a kind man willing to help both the people and me as far as possible, but his limitations (and mine) through lack of material are woeful. Fortunately I brought three cases of clothing with me but it is a drop in the ocean of their needs.*[104]

As she fitted one family after another with clothes, they told their stories – monotonously repetitive – and she noted the various ways in which the women responded to the events they had endured. *Some are scared, some paralysed and unable to realize their loss; some are dissolved in tears; some, mute and dry-eyed, seem only*

Bechuanaland

Molopo River

Cape Colony

Mafeking

Transvaal

Vryburg

Vaal River

100 kilometres

Warrenton

Orange
River
Colony

Kimberley

Magersfontein
Modder River

Bloemfontein

Enslin
Belmont

Organe River
Station

Orange River

Jagersfontein

Cape
Colony

Springfontein

De Aar

Colesberg

Norvals
Pont

Naauwpoort

To
Cape
Town

Rosmead

Stormberg

Places visited by Emily Hobhouse in March and April 1901

to be able to think of the blank, penniless future; some are glowing with pride at being prisoners for their country's sake.[105]

That first day she assisted sixty people with clothing. A visit to the village shop the next day yielded nothing but a packet of needles.

I had been giving some materials for women to make their own boy's clothing, but we are stopped by the utter famine of cotton or thread. Scissors are handed round from tent to tent, thimbles are very few.

Everything here is so scarce that the sight of my rough deal packing-cases created quite a sensation – not for what was inside but for the actual wood. They are destined to make low bedsteads, tables, etc and a few bits for firing. ...

The crying need in this camp is fuel – wood there is none – a little coal is served out, but so little that many days the people cannot cook at all, and their rations are raw meat and meal and coffee, so each of these needs fire. If you could peep at Springfontein you would at once realize the hopelessness of getting any fuel – a bare veld, covered with sparse short grass, ringed by the barest kopjes – stony and without even grass. ... there is nothing to burn.[106]

Ultimately, the most enduring legacy of her work would be the intangible:

Many women to whom I have given nothing nor even offered to, and who neither ask nor wish for charity, express deepest gratitude for the bare tidings that any English people feel for them. They are very sore at heart and are really helped by the knowledge that we understand at all the aspect of affairs as it appears to them. They are so tired of being told by officers that they are Refugees under the 'kind and beneficent protection of the British'.[107]

Springfontein concentration camp

Norvals Pont camp, her next stop, was only 60 kilometres down the line, but such was the congestion on the railway and so cautiously did the trains proceed that it involved an overnight journey. She was greeted on arrival by a friend from her first visit, a Miss Boshoff, who warned her of a new peril. The nurse and teacher had conspired to set a trap for her by pretending to be pro-Boer and so to draw her out. Any political comments she would make would be reported to the superintendent. Forewarned, Emily avoided sensitive topics. One morning in the camp, she was awakened by the roar of cannon and would have liked to ask what was happening. The camp officials presumably had some information. But she kept her curiosity to herself and learnt later that there had been a fight nearby.[108] She made nothing of the risks implicit in war raging within earshot.

Otherwise she was less circumspect. She wrote to Leonard: *I was rather upset by a nasty encounter with the doctor today. He was very insulting but he is an insufferable cad and I pretty plainly told him so. Also that I brooked no criticism, interference or impertinent questions from subordinate officers like himself. It was a real scene. I had to mount a very high horse and believe I had the best of it. This man has lived six years in Jagersfontein and is of the kind who cannot open their mouths without using invective against the Boers – going out of their way to do so. ... It is almost impossible to stand it, and it makes the work a great strain.*[109]

So there was, after all, a story against Emily to relate to Captain Taylor, the camp's superintendent. *Emily knew her tongue made her enemies yet was unable to govern herself,* wrote John Hall in his biography. He cited this incident as an example.[110]

Despite the conspiracy to entrap her and her confrontation with the doctor, Emily had positive things to say about the camp. The security guards at the gate had been withdrawn and the occupants were free to roam the countryside in the afternoons. They could go down to the river to do their laundry or collect firewood in the gullies to supplement the fuel in their rations.

Her next destination was Kimberley and to get there Emily had to make a circuitous, multi-day trip via Naauwpoort and De Aar. This leg of her journey began badly. She waited for a train in the Railway Staff Officer's office at the Norvals Pont station, but no train came. Eventually, it was too late to return to the camp. There was no adjacent town, no accommodation for the night.

It is now 9:30 pm and no train. I can't imagine where to go or what to do for the night – and yet be on the spot for the train at dawn. The floor of this office is all that presents itself to my mind but if leave is refused I don't know where to go![111]

The next day, well on her way, she completed the story:

*I was in luck's way last night at Norvals Pont station. About
10 o'clock they told me finally no train would come in. So I
asked if they were going to close the R.S.O.'s office, and learnt
it would be open all night. There was no resource [sic] but to
ask to sit there too, and was told I could.*

*Afterwards I went out for a turn in the air and to my
surprise was followed by the R.S.O. himself, who very shyly,
awkwardly, and gruffly asked if I would care to have his bed
for the night. He said he had a van. So he took me away to
a siding where an old guard's van stood by the soldiers' camp
and lo! he had made of it a bed and dressing-room. Then he
marched off with his pyjamas and left me in possession. I was
so undone by this unusual and unlooked-for bit of kindness
that when he was gone I collapsed into a fit of hysterical
weeping. ... Then I examined my van and found a bath ready
set with water – and a mattress and khaki blankets – no
sheets. But it was a lovely night.*[112]

The RSO's name was Bates and she canonised him in her mind,
St Bates of the Cheshires.

The weather was changing: *Today it has been so cold I have to
stand in the sun to warm myself,* she wrote.[113] The journey took her
deep into the Karoo again – arid, bleak, vast, thinly populated –
but she knew what to expect and her letters bear no complaint.

For the last 100 kilometres into Kimberley, the seemingly
endless plains give way to more varied country with hills and
ridges. At the beginning of the war, Lord Methuen's advance had
followed this section of the rail line – he was dependent on it for
his supplies, even to augment the inadequate water available on
the route. Emily noted the names of the isolated stations – Belmont, Enslin, Modder River – all familiar from the battles that
had raged at each of these places, all locations where the Boers had
taken advantage of favourable terrain to try to stop the invasion.

At Magersfontein (see map on page 114), Emily saw fresh

graves and Boer trenches from the train's windows. This is where, fifteen months earlier, Methuen had been defeated and his progress to Kimberley halted. Britain lost 902 soldiers in the battle (killed and wounded) and the Boers 236 men. When Lord Roberts arrived in southern Africa, he had moved his 50,000 soldiers up this rail line to a base on the Modder River, then marched them around the Boer positions at Magersfontein and, following the river, on to Bloemfontein.

When Emily arrived in Kimberley, she found accommodation in the comparative luxury of the Queen's Hotel, just twenty minutes on foot from the concentration camp. Diamonds had made the town prosperous; it was larger than Bloemfontein. The grey, kimberlite dumps were not as pretty, she thought, as the mine dumps of her native Cornwall.

With the size and prosperity that Kimberley possessed, one might have hoped that its camp would be better. Instead it was deplorable:

> *First I called on Major Wright, the [Camp] Commandant. He is an old resident – a Colonial Volunteer and a coarse, lazy, indifferent old man. He often does not go near the camp for days together and no wonder I found it in such a neglected condition. ...*
>
> *The camp is the smallest in area that I have seen – the tents too close together and the whole enclosed in an eight-foot-high barbed-wire fencing which is supposed to be impregnable and cost £500! Sentries at the gate and walking inside. No nurse; an empty unfurnished marquee (which might be a hospital); overcrowded tents, measles and whooping cough rife; camp dirty and smelling; an army doctor who seems to know nothing of children's ailments; fuel almost none; general laxity in the management.[114]*

Emily found that several women from well-off families were

confined in the camp. One of them, Mrs Snyman, soon became her guide and interpreter. Her father had owned a farm where diamonds had been found. He had been a director of a bank and she had travelled in Europe. This woman was more bitter and antagonistic to Britain than any she had met, perhaps because the scale of the family's loss was greater or perhaps because her worldly perspective gave her a sharper understanding of their predicament. Or perhaps it was just the state of the camp.

Three babies died in as many days following Emily's arrival. She was particularly disturbed by the death of one of them, the child of a Mrs Louw:

Lord Methuen came to her house with his column to sweep her away. The Louws have a large farm, a good house and are well-to-do people. Mrs Louw is a delicate-looking gentle woman with a white skin and beautiful scarlet lips so seldom seen out of books. Her baby was only 17 days old when Methuen came, and she was very weak. She could not nurse the child and so it, like all her children, was being brought up on donkey's milk. This she explained to Lord Methuen who gave special commands that wherever Mrs Louw went that donkey was to go ... Well, by degrees, she arrived in Kimberley and the donkey came also to the town. But once she was in the camp that donkey disappeared. They either couldn't or wouldn't produce it. The baby failed and pined. They tried everything – cow's milk, condensed milk, foods – all no good. It was a splendid child and it dwindled to skin and bone. In vain they begged Major Wright to send the donkey.[115]

Then a new superintendent arrived and the women appealed to him and showed him the dying child. *At once he produced that donkey. But it was too late; the baby had got past recovery. ... It was still alive this morning when I called. In the afternoon they beckoned me in to show me the tiny thing laid out.[116]*

Mrs Louw's husband was a commandant in the Boer forces.

On the positive side, she discovered a local committee doing good work for the camp and resolved to co-operate with them. She thought of leaving them a grant of money, but her correspondence does not say if she did so.

General Pretyman was now the civilian administrator of Kimberley, a demotion from his position as governor of the Orange River Colony. Emily went to see him to obtain travel passes and found that his attitude had changed considerably. She was, of course, unaware of his letter to Milner. They had a row over the dying children. Pretyman held the mothers responsible; Emily replied that their children did not die on their farms.[117] He refused to give her a pass to continue further or even to return to Bloemfontein, saying he had no authority to do so, and offered her one to Cape Town instead. She had no choice but to take it. In fact, it was a relief to bow to the inevitable. She longed for a break from the difficulties of working in the war zone and the tragedies of the camps.

Emily spent ten days in Cape Town and made the most of it. She addressed a meeting of sympathisers at the home of Mrs Koopmans De Wet, a *grande dame* in Cape society. Later that house, still containing the elegant furniture of her time, became a museum. She met the British commander in the Cape Town area, Lieutenant-General Sir FW Forestier-Walker, and the newly appointed governor of the Cape Colony, Sir Walter Hely-Hutchinson. (Milner had moved to Johannesburg and was still the high commissioner. Hely-Hutchinson reported to him.)

Both meetings proceeded cordially and Emily had no difficulty in securing the passes she needed to continue her camp visits and return to Bloemfontein. To her surprise, Hely-Hutchinson was unaware that there were concentration camps in the Cape Colony. (By this time there were five; six including the refugee camp at Port Elizabeth.) He listened attentively to her description of the conditions in them and her proposals for improvements.

Sir Joshua Rowntree and his wife, the philanthropists who had been on board the vessel that brought Emily to southern Africa, were about to return to England. Emily sought them out and told them of her experiences and of what she had seen. Later, when she was back in England, they became important allies.

Military censorship had been tightened, she thought, and she wrote to her correspondents to be cautious. *Be careful how you write to me*, she advised Lady Hobhouse in a letter from Cape Town that probably travelled safely with the Rowntrees, *and expect nothing of interest from me*.[118] Instead of committing her views to letters, Emily began a diary, the source from which we learn of some of her subsequent experiences.

The ladies beavering away in England and Cape Town had achieved much and Emily was able to take two rail wagons of clothing with her when she went north again. She was back in Kimberley by early April. The diversion to Cape Town and back had been 1,900 kilometres with all the slowness and difficulties of rail travel in southern Africa at this time. Emily did not say much about the travelling. She now knew what she had to endure.

En route, the train stopped for the night at Orange River Station on the south bank of the river. Here on the edge of the arid Karoo, Emily discovered a fledgling camp with just five or six women and twenty-four children. Later this small camp was moved a kilometre or two further from the river, expanded to take the overflow from Kimberley and became a substantial camp in its own right. The place is noteworthy for reasons that will emerge later.

Chapter 15
To Mafeking

A large part of Botswana's southern border with the modern-day South Africa is demarcated by the Molopo River. Yet, over most of its length, this river carries water only rarely. It is so reliably dry that a well-made, gravelled road runs for hundreds of kilometres in the riverbed. In part, the road has been tarred. When it rains sufficiently and water flows in the river - once a decade or so - travel is suspended until the water subsides. Why is the road in the riverbed? Because the orange-red dunes of the Kalahari Desert occupy the land on both banks and stretch away into the distance. A road through the dunes would be much more expensive to build and difficult to keep clear of the shifting, wind-blown sands.

At the headwaters – if that is the right word – of this 1,000 kilometre-long river lies the town of Mafikeng, 'the place of stones'. At the time of the Boer War it was called Mafeking and that is the name we'll use. There are no dunes here and the river flows more often before its waters disappear into the Kalahari sand, yet life is not easy.

Despite its remoteness, Mafeking was significant before the war. Its location at the northern boundary of the Cape Colony meant that it was the springboard for journeys into central Africa.

For a time it became the capital of British Bechuanaland (now Botswana) even though it is not situated within that territory. A railway line was built to this town and a garrison was stationed there permanently.

Commandos from the South African Republic laid siege to Mafeking at the beginning of the Boer War. It held out for 217 days under the resourceful Colonel Robert Baden-Powell. When the siege was lifted on 17 May 1900, the event triggered exaggerated celebrations in an England hungry for good news. Baden-Powell – as much a self-publicist as a soldier – later capitalised on his newfound fame to establish the Boy Scout movement.

En route from Cape Town, Emily spent a few days in Kimberley and then took the train to Mafeking, 360 tedious kilometres to the north. She did not have to ask the antagonistic Pretyman for a pass.

By now, she knew perfectly well what to expect. The camps on this long extension of her journey would be much the same as those she had already seen. It was plain that the way the war was being conducted and the paucity of resources was the same everywhere.

The journey nevertheless had some surprises for her. A quarter of the way to Mafeking, the line runs through a place called Warrenton where 300 displaced people were accommodated in the church and school because there were no tents to form a camp. Emily planned to visit them on her return journey. But when the train stopped there on her outbound trip, she had an unexpected encounter. A young army captain got into her compartment and Emily described what she learnt from him:

He only got into Warrenton that morning with a great convoy and he was dead tired. He had swept in the stock and the women and children, burnt all food and clothes behind him and allowed the Natives to loot the Boer houses as money is too short to pay them in a better way. He was very sick of it all and agreed it was a war of extermination. Every animal that lagged or did not keep up with the convoy had its throat cut and was left behind.

And there, in a great mass by the railway line, I saw all his sweepings, thousands of animals of many kinds, carts and wagons, soldiers and horses, crowds of human beings both black and white. And I happen to know there is not a tent in Warrenton to put them into![119]

She arrived in Mafeking on 9 April 1901, nearly eleven months after the famous siege had ended, and learnt that the local camp was far out of town. *I had to take a Cape-cart and drive out for it is a full six miles – a lonely, lonely spot. Mafeking itself feels like the end of the world and the camp seems like driving six miles into space.*[120]

She spent two days there, buying clothing and supplies for the camp in the town. The most important thing, she thought, was just to be there. It meant a great deal to the camp occupants that there were people in England who knew of their existence and cared about their circumstances. The nurse was especially grateful and took new heart.

The camp was the oldest of those Emily visited and the first and only one under the administration of the Transvaal authorities that she saw. The rations and fuel supply were better and the superintendent was sympathetic, but otherwise it was the usual story exaggerated by the camp's remoteness – no soap, a great want of clothes, few blankets, overcrowding in the tents …

The camp's subsequent history is especially unfortunate. It was moved closer to town and expanded from 765 occupants when Emily visited to 5,245 inmates in the ensuing five months. The superintendent was replaced and the camp went on to record the worst fatality rate of the war.[121]

As planned, Emily stopped at Warrenton on her return journey.

At the station were two train-loads full of [people being sent on to Kimberley], *quite half in open coal-trucks – all piled up and wedged in with such goods as they had been able to bring. They were tired and hot.*[122]

More than twenty years later she wrote in her memoir:

> *... the appalling tragedy of it all came home to me in the sight I witnessed at and near Warrenton both going and returning. Those truck-loads of women and children unsheltered and unfed, bereft of home, bearing the vivid recollection of their possessions in the flames; and that mass of the 'sweepings' of a wide military 'drive' – flocks and herds of frightened animals bellowing and baaing for food and drink, tangled up with wagons and vehicles of all sorts and a dense crowd of human beings – combined to give a picture of war in all its destructiveness, cruelty, stupidity and nakedness such as not even the misery of the camps (with their external appearance of order) could do.*[123]

The trains bearing the human 'sweepings' followed Emily's to Kimberley where the 240 people on board were accommodated in the concentration camp in just twenty-five bell tents, the only shelter available.

There was mail waiting for Emily at Kimberley with awkward news. The circumstances, it appears, were as follows:[124] In late January, Joseph Rowntree wrote to his brother-in-law and sponsor, John Ellis MP, from Cape Town criticising the British administration in southern Africa. Ellis, a leading critic of the war, used the information in parliament to attack the government. He then gave Rowntree's letters to the *Daily News*, a London newspaper supporting the opposition, which published extracts in early March. The difficulty was that some of Rowntree's information had been sourced from Emily. While she was not named, those who understood the situation could deduce that this was the case.

Milner, Kitchener and the government in London were now alerted to her ability to cause political embarrassment. On reading of the unwanted exposure, she realised she could expect more difficulties in her work. She became more aware of being watched, was more careful with her language when in the camps or when talking to officials, and she was more circumspect in the letters she wrote. She worried that no one would be allowed to succeed her.

Knowing that she would not visit Kimberley again before returning to England, Emily made arrangements for the delivery of assistance to the camp to continue, said her farewells and left for Bloemfontein on 18 April 1901. By the time she arrived back, this journey, with its forced detour via Cape Town, had lasted six weeks and she had covered 4,800 kilometres. It was a feat of great fortitude and endurance for a lone woman travelling under the difficulties of war.

Yet there were blessings, too. Herds of the supremely beautiful springbuck grazed, still graze, these arid lands. There were ostriches, usually in pairs, and the Kori bustard, the world's heaviest flighted bird, could be seen, though it is hard to spot. While the bustard is well camouflaged, a third large bird is conspicuous: the striking secretary bird struts through the veld searching for and expertly dispatching snakes, its favourite food. Near Mafeking, Emily might have encountered herds of the eye-catching oryx, an antelope so well adapted to arid conditions that it is quite capable of surviving among the dunes of the Kalahari Desert. The solitary, black-backed jackal trots through the veld, searching for small prey. On the koppies and in the thornbush thickets by the mostly dry water courses, baboons bark warnings to each other when someone approaches. In the same thickets there are sometimes vervet monkeys, too, conducting their own chattering conversations and scurrying to the treetops at the suspicion of danger. In Emily's day, leopards might still have lurked in those thickets, cheetahs still hunted on the plains and packs of the unusual and now much endangered Cape hunting dogs still roamed the countryside.

However, Emily's focus remained firmly on animals of the human kind. She was not on a sightseeing trip. She was returning to Bloemfontein with one principal, resolute purpose in mind: to get permission to visit the camps north of Bloemfontein and, if permission were to be granted, to make those visits.

Chapter 16

Departure

During Emily's absence, the situation in the Orange River Colony's camps changed rapidly. She had heard of this even before she left Kimberley.

Lord Kitchener's great drives were scorching the country to the north. As described in Chapter 12, these were no longer the punitive actions of Lord Roberts, targeted at those who overtly supported the Boers or failed to report or prevent their actions. Kitchener's objective was different. His aim was to remove from the country-side anything that could be of use to the guerrillas. That meant everyone and everything had to go, all food had to be removed, all shelter, all livestock, especially any arms and ammunition.

By the middle of April 1901, General French's drive was nearing the end of its mission in the eastern Transvaal Highveld, having swept across 150 kilometres in a swathe half as wide. While he was busy in the east, Kitchener sent Lieutenant-General Cunningham to the south-western Transvaal to scorch the area between the western rail line and the Vaal River.[125] Other columns, if not engaged specifically in drives, nevertheless destroyed farms and small communities wherever they went. General Clements, for example, laid to waste the fertile Magalies Valley west of Pretoria to the north of Cunningham's designated zone.

The Transvaal camps were bulging. On or about 22 March there were 20,671 people[126] in that colony's white camps; by the end of June the number had reached 45,659.[127] The camp at Middelburg – in the heart of French's operations – increased from 977 in mid-March[128] to 6,637 by the end of May.[129] Corresponding information for black camps was not reported until later, but they, too, would have increased significantly in occupation during these autumn months.[130]

To ease the burden on the Transvaal camps, people were railed south into the ORC. On her return journey, Emily's train stopped at Springfontein Station. She later wrote to Lady Hobhouse: *At Springfontein I left a manageable little camp of 500, now it has swelled to 3,000 and as we passed yesterday morning there was a trainload in the station of 600.*[131] Many were in open trucks and it was bitterly cold. There had been a downpour during the night and the people were trying to dry themselves and their goods. They had been given no food for two days and children were crying with hunger. Emily gave them all the food she had brought for herself and left money for more to be purchased at the station. Her pass did not authorise a stopover.

By 22 April she was back in Bloemfontein where the camp population had approximately doubled during her absence and the conditions had deteriorated considerably. She learnt that sixty-two people had died and found that the camp doctor himself was down with enteric (typhoid). Four young Boer women were being trained as nurses when she left and she noted that their work in the hospital was greatly appreciated. On her return to the camp she found that two of them had died. She was particularly dismayed about Poppy Naudé, a universal favourite. *The doctor, the nurse and all had said: 'We can't spare Poppy.' ... And I come back to find her dead!*[132]

Emily lunched with Goold-Adams who informed her that many more people would be coming. He and the camp superintendents were struggling to cope, but he was powerless to stop the flow. They were on the doorstep of winter, the nights were already very cold and for the families under canvas, the situation was serious. Emily's worst fears were materialising:

> *If only the camps had remained the size they were even six weeks ago, I saw some chance of getting them well in hand, organizing and dealing with the distress. But this sudden influx of hundreds and thousands has upset everything and reduced us all to a state bordering on despair. I feel paralyzed in face of it. I feel money is of little avail, and there are moments when I feel it would be wisest to stop trying and hasten home to state plain facts and beg that a stop may be put to it all.[133]*

She had made the return journey to Bloemfontein in the hope that a last appeal to Kitchener would result in permission to visit the camps to the north. But with the rapidly deteriorating situation and Kitchener's awareness that her visit could lead to adverse publicity in Britain, indeed had already done so, there was no possibility that her wish would be granted.

Emily had come to realise that the only person in southern Africa who had the authority to make the necessary urgent improvements in the camps was Lord Kitchener himself. It was with him that she should speak. She should go north, not just to visit more camps but to see the commander-in-chief himself. He was in Pretoria, hundreds of kilometres beyond her reach, and it had dawned on her for some time that he was not going to permit her anywhere near him. Her only option was to go to London where higher authority resided.

Exhausted, demoralised and losing her voice, she said her farewells and left Bloemfontein on 1 May 1901 bound for home.

As they parted, the former president's wife gave Emily a letter in which she expressed the wish that Emily would thank the committee of the Distress Fund and others in England who had provided aid for the poor women and children in the camps. Her letter concluded:

> *Above all I thank them for having sent you. I was deeply touched that from England such a warm friend was sent to us. Once more 'Goodbye' dear Miss Hobhouse. God bless and reward you. Ever think of me as a loving and grateful friend.*
>
> *R. Isabel Steyn.*[134]

But Emily had not quite done with the Orange River Colony, nor it with her. *I broke my journey at Springfontein*, she wrote in her memoir. *There, to my horror still massed on the railway siding, I found the same unfortunate people whom I had seen when passing north 10 days previously – their condition beggars description; the picture photographed on my mind can never fade.*[135]

One scene, in particular, touched her deeply. She was called to a makeshift shelter where a mother sat on a trunk with a fast-fading child on her lap. She tried unsuccessfully to get a little brandy from the camp, a kilometre or so away, in a last-ditch effort to save the little one. The camp refused; its meagre supplies were being husbanded for the camp itself.

> *There was nothing to be done and we watched the child draw its last breath in reverent silence.*
>
> *The mother neither moved nor wept. It was her only child. Dry-eyed but deathly white, she sat there motionless looking not at the child but far, far away into depths of grief beyond all tears. A friend stood behind her who called upon Heaven to witness this tragedy and others crouching on the ground around her wept freely.*[136]

Emily arrived in Cape Town early on the morning of 5 May in a dishevelled state, hair and clothes permeated with red dust.

The Louvain camp near Winburg, a camp beyond Emily Hobhouse's reach.

Washing, even of face and hands, had been impossible for days.

On arrival, she learnt that a single berth, a first-class berth, remained on the *Saxon* sailing for Southampton three days later. She had thought of spending a little more time in Cape Town and had never intended to travel home first class. But she took the berth and departed from southern Africa four eventful months after arriving. She was now a profoundly different woman. South Africa would never leave her.

PART 2

The work of others

Chapter 17

Brodrick's request

What were Kitchener and Milner being told about conditions in the camps during the period that Emily Hobhouse was in southern Africa? What information did the War Office and the Secretary for War, the Colonial Office and the Secretary for the Colonies receive? Was the British Cabinet informed?

The first formal report to mention the camps to London was probably Lord Kitchener's routine dispatch on the progress of the war dated 8 March 1901.[137] In this lengthy report, the reference to the camps was just two sentences long. He wrote:

> I some time ago took measures for the establishment of properly organized camps at certain selected sites on the lines of railways, at which surrendered burghers are permitted to live with their families, under our effective protection. The families of all burghers still under arms are, as far as possible, brought in from the adjacent districts, and similarly lodged in these camps, the administration of which has recently been wholly taken over by the civil authorities.

Kitchener was taking credit for something he presented as a good deed and good strategy while at the same time absolving himself of all further responsibility. The government ignored his cop-out. Ten days later, the Secretary for War, St John Brodrick, asked Kitchener by telegram for more information: *Please send by next mail a despatch giving full report on refugee camps in Cape Colony as well as Orange River Colony and Transvaal.*[138]

This request was a direct consequence of Emily's work. Lady Hobhouse had given copies of Emily's early letters to the supportive and sympathetic Sir William and Lady Harcourt. He was an opposition member of parliament, but the Harcourts were friends with members of the government and Lady Harcourt showed the letters to Arthur Balfour, the Deputy Prime Minister. He and Brodrick felt this called for more information, hence the telegram.[139]

No systematic reporting was in existence, so Major George A Goodwin, the chief superintendent of refugee camps in the Transvaal, hastily assembled information on the camps in that colony. The response was limited to burgher camps, white camps, although Brodrick's request makes no such distinction.

Major Goodwin was in a civilian role following the transfer of the camps from military to civilian control. He had arrived in Pretoria to take up his position just six weeks earlier but had already visited several camps and had reported on them to General Maxwell, Military Governor of Pretoria. He was thus able to give a reasonably informed if not comprehensive response to Brodrick's request. His report is dated 22 March 1901 and it provides the first substantial, official view of the camps.[140] It also introduces us to camps in the Transvaal, camps that Emily was not allowed to visit.

In Goodwin's report, we read of the contempt of the Boer families brought in under duress for those who had surrendered and entered the camps of their own volition (the loyalists); the men, especially, were scorned. We discover that local charitable and religious organisations and concerned individuals were providing assistance to camp residents, for example in Pretoria, Johannesburg and Heidelberg, just as Emily discovered they were in Bloemfontein and Kimberley. There is a broad hint that all is not well when we learn that he and Governor Maxwell had themselves launched appeals on behalf of the camp occupants to supply what the government could not or would not provide.[141]

But it is from the numerous appendixes to Goodwin's report that the more revealing insights emerge. It is here that we learn that by 22 March 1901, the number of refugees in the eleven burgher camps under Transvaal administration already exceeded 20,000. The camps at Johannesburg and Potchefstroom already had more than 5,000 each at a time when there were 2,000 in the Bloemfontein camp. Children outnumbered adults in many cases, sometimes by a considerable margin.[142] (See the table below.)

Census returns of number of refugees in the different Burgher Refugee Camps in the Transvaal Colony, including the camp at Mafeking. Note that all over the age of twelve appear under the column, 'Adults'.[143]

Camp	Adults	Children	Total
Baberton	346	357	703
Heidelberg	615	692	1,307
Irene	866	631	1,497
Johannesburg	1,452	4,035	5,487
Klerksdorp	213	243	456
Middelburg	499	478	977
Potchefstroom	2,221	3,152	5,373
Standerton	384	958	1,342
Vereeniging	336	325	661
Volksrust	1,045	1,023	2,068
Mafeking			800
Total			20,671

In addition there were 434 self-supporting refugees resident in the camps.

According to Goodwin, the weekly rations for adults were initially just the following:[144]

Meal or flour	7 lb (3.2 kg)
Salt	4 oz (113 g)
Coffee	6 oz (170 g)
Sugar	8 oz (230 g)

Loyalists were allowed 12 ounces (340 grams) of sugar instead of 8 and given one pound (450 grams) of meat twice per week. From 27 February 1901, after civilian administration had commenced, the meat ration was extended to all. The meal, flour and meat were, of course, raw.

Children, no matter how small, were given half the adult rations, even half the coffee, except that they were allowed the full adult ration of sugar.[145] There is no mention of the inadequacy or unsuitability of this diet for children or of the lack of equipment and facilities for preparing the food and the consequent difficulties the women faced in making the raw food edible. However, Goodwin was able to report confidently that the cost of running the camps was likely to be less than one shilling per person per day, including the cost of the superintendents, doctors, nurses, food, medicines and all the rest.

Goodwin's visits to the camps were brief, typically a day or two, and he was careful to emphasise the positive, seeing that he himself was responsible for them. Nevertheless, his comments on individual camps make interesting reading.[146]

He reported first on Heidelberg, one of the earliest camps, where everyone seemed 'normal'. In this camp, the local management had put the camp occupants to work building sod houses roofed with galvanised iron sheeting, an innovation that took advantage of the suitable turf in the proximity. These abodes provided much better protection against the elements than tents.

In other camps, things were not so good. Of Irene, the camp

nearest the capital, Pretoria, he wrote: *Many of the children here have suffered from measles, and in spite of the isolation of all known cases, the disease appears to be spreading. Diarrhoea is also prevalent among the women and children.*[147] At Johannesburg he found *many of the women looking hopeless, helpless, sick and vermin-ridden. Among the children measles and sore eyes prevailed and diarrhoea.*[148] He thought the camp doctor unsuitable and dismissed him, appointing Dr H Crook in his stead. Considering the size of the camp, the condition of the occupants and the preponderance of children, the camp needed several doctors, not just one. At Vereeniging, *the refugees seem of a superior class ... and appeared in good health, happy and contented. ... Notwithstanding this, a large amount of enteric exists.*[149]

At Potchefstroom, sufficient tents were not available and many of the refugees were accommodated in the town in private homes, some commandeered for the purpose. However, the building of reed houses had commenced and soon, it was hoped, all those drawing rations would be accommodated in the camp. Goodwin saved his longest comments for the camp at Standerton.[150] These are extracts:

> *The condition of the refugees here was pitiable in the extreme. There had been 4 days of heavy rain, the soil, which, throughout the district, is a black pot clay, had in camp been worked up to a deep thick glutinous mud, making the condition of tents and passages deplorable. ... There was no list showing the numbers in camp. Refugee families were being brought in continually and at the same time families were being deported to Natal, or to camps nearer the district they had been brought in from. This caused much confusion and hardship, and might, in my opinion, have been deferred until drier weather set in.*
>
> *Dr Leslie, who ... left Pretoria on 17th instant to act as Medical Officer for the camp, on arrival at Standerton*

definitely refused to take over the duties. I consider he had no valid excuse for adopting this course, and his doing so caused us considerable inconvenience.

Standerton is in the south-eastern Transvaal and Major Goodwin's visit was on 22 and 23 February 1901. It is through this region at this time that General French was conducting Lord Kitchener's first great 'drive', scorching the earth and harvesting people.

Goodwin had only one general recommendation to make after his tour of inspection. Believing that the camp inmates either had or could obtain money, he thought it urgent that camp shops be established at which the residents could purchase what they needed. Writing to the Chairman of the Central Relief Committee, Cape Town, to ask for storekeepers, he said, ... *the matter must not be delayed, as these people are barefooted and in rags. The goods required to be stocked are – flannel, calico, linen, cotton, women and children's boots, socks, &c, corned meat, sardines, milk, jam, coffee, sugar, rice, &c.*[151]

After he had been appointed to the Johannesburg camp, Dr H Crook wrote to Dr George A Turner, Principal Medical Officer for the Transvaal, expressing concerns of his own: ... *unless we provide sufficient warm covering for the large number of small children and babies (who are insufficiently clad) I am of opinion they will be exposed to great danger.*[152]

Dr Turner went to see some camps for himself. His reports, addressed to General Maxwell, were also appended to the report Goodwin assembled for Brodrick. He wrote at much greater length and in more detail about the three camps he saw, focusing on matters affecting the health of the occupants.

He went first to the Irene camp, the nearest, and declared himself 'very well pleased with it'. However, regarding the water supply,

I noticed one or two little matters that require attention.
    1 There is a bridge across the water furrow, above the intake [of the camp's water supply] which is frequently crossed by cattle and sheep. The animals are liable to pollute the water; this happened while I was looking on this morning. ...
    2 Sheep, calves, goats, &c., are kept in the camp itself. This should not be allowed; they foul the soil, and if they do not pollute the water used in the camp, they foul that used further down the water course.[153]

Dr Turner's report continued at length about other, presumably 'little', matters that also required attention in this camp that pleased him so much. Regarding the health of the camp residents, he quoted statistics for the week of his visit and wrote: *The number of sick is apparently great. If all the other 52 weeks are equally sickly, it would mean that every man, woman and child would come under the doctor's hands six times per annum.* He was especially troubled by the prevalence of and prognosis for measles patients: *Taking the period from 6th February to 3rd March as a lunar month, then the death rate would be 15 percent per 1000 living* [sic]. *It is unnecessary to dilate upon this mortality, which is enormous.*[154] All but two of the deceased were children.

Dr Turner likewise had much to say about the camp at Johannesburg, where, in his view, much needed doing. It was on the site of a pre-war racecourse and people were housed under grandstands, in totalisator booths (betting facilities), stables and large, purpose-built corrugated iron sheds with walls that did not reach down to the ground. Privacy was non-existent. The accommodation was so poor that Turner thought tents would be better.

At Vereeniging he was particularly concerned about the cases of typhoid that Goodwin had mentioned. He noted that all the cases had been contracted in the camp itself, not brought in by already diseased individuals, and concluded that the cause lay in the unsafe water supply.

These official reports, all on the situation in the Transvaal, were all by civil servants anxious to cast matters in a positive light and writing about a situation for which they themselves bore some responsibility. They, like Emily Hobhouse, told of a camp system grossly unfit for purpose and out of control.

The Orange River Colony also supplied a report on their camps a week after the Transvaal.[155] It bears the name of Captain AG Trollope, the chief superintendent of refugee camps in the ORC and Goodwin's counterpart. In contrast to Goodwin's comprehensive document, it is just one and a half pages long with a single appendix on food rations. Trollope's report would have us believe that the situation in ORC camps was satisfactory, even good. A few extracts illustrate the tenor of the document.

The ration scale, he declares, *has given every satisfaction and is found to be ample …*

> *All persons who arrive in camp, and who are not provided with bedding, blankets, plates, knives, forks, cups, &c., have these articles supplied to them at the expense of Government.*
>
> *Ample accommodation is provided in all camps for the refugees, some are in wood and iron buildings, each family having a separate room, some in marquees, while others have bell tents; overcrowding in all cases being strictly forbidden.*
>
> *Shops are established in the largest camps, so that refugees can buy any luxuries, &c., they require, over and above what is supplied by Government.*
>
> *Clothing is supplied by Government to all destitute refugees who are unable through poverty to pay for same.*
>
> *Hospitals are established in all the camps and one Medical Officer allowed for each 1,000 refugees. Trained nurses in proportion of one per 1,000 refugees in addition to which paid female refugee nurses and hospital orderlies are allowed*

at about three per 1,000, the hospital establishment being increased in case of any grave sickness or outbreak of fever. ... all linen, clothing and hospital luxuries of every description are supplied without stint.

The report contains no mention of hospital occupation nor of the incidence of disease and it makes no reference to fatalities. There are no medical reports. No data on individual camps appear.[156] There is no reference to fuel supplies and the report fails to mention the lack of cooking facilities. The food is said to be satisfactory even when the appended ration scale is patently inappropriate for children and hardly more than emergency food for adults.

Trollope's superior, Major Hamilton Goold-Adams, knew perfectly well that this was a misrepresentation of the situation and it is remarkable that he allowed Trollope to file such a travesty of a report. But we should recall that Goold-Adams was close to Sir Alfred Milner who now carried responsibility for the camps. No point in embarrassing your sponsor and mentor, is there?

There is, however, something that is noteworthy about Trollope's report: he included blacks. During the week ending 16 March 1901, the camps contained 11,563 whites and 8,811 natives, total 20,374. We are led to believe that the rosy picture painted in the report applied not only to the white camps but also to the native camps as there is no indication to the contrary. The only difference between whites and blacks, according to the report, is in the food. The cost of feeding a white person was nine pence per day – adults and children got the same food in the ORC – whereas the cost of feeding an adult black was less than half, four and a quarter pence, and a black child even less. Whites, by this time, received fresh meat daily; blacks tinned meat only once per week. Whites were given one-twelfth of a tin of condensed milk, whereas blacks and, in particular, black children, received no milk at all.

After these reports were delivered, Kitchener accelerated the clearing of the land and the rounding up of people. The camp population rose rapidly, as already noted in the previous chapter.

There was a curious interchange between Sir Joseph Chamberlain, the Colonial Secretary, and Sir Alfred Milner in the following month. Chamberlain telegraphed Milner on 15 April 1901:

> *Reports by Dr Mackenzie, 19th December, and Dr Johnston, 9th January, condemning food supplied to Boer Refugee Camps, Johannesburg, as unfit for human consumption have been published here. It is stated that death rate among women and children is extraordinary high, and also that food and money are not allowed to be sent to them, on the grounds that they have all they want. Report by telegraph about this as soon as possible.*[157]

Chamberlain was the smartest of politicians and his telegram was carefully crafted. He had not seen Goodwin's or Trollope's reports, which were sent to the Secretary for War and the War Office. Rather, he had become aware of Emily's letters, but, knowing her to be controversial, he chose to use other reasons for asking. As Milner's superior, he had ministerial responsibility for the camps and yet was in the dark about them. He could expect questions in the parliament and he needed answers. Milner replied:

> *Whatever the defects in the first instance the food now is, and has been for some time, wholesome and sufficient; it is not fact that the death rate was extraordinary high, or that no food or money was allowed to be sent though certain individuals were not allowed to go to the camp.*[158]

Chamberlain was presumably reassured – for the moment at any rate. By the time of this response, Milner must have been well aware of the comments made by Major Goodwin and Dr Turner in the Transvaal report issued nearly a month earlier and he wrote this response in the face of evidence to the contrary. Since Chamberlain had asked only about the Johannesburg camp, he presumably thought he could defend his answer. He, after all, was responsible, nominally anyway, and if the state of the camps was unsatisfactory, he was accountable.

The reality was that responsibility for the camps was hopelessly unclear. Kitchener had transferred responsibility to the civilian authorities under Milner, but most of the superintendents were military officers seconded to the camps. The army supplied everything: tents, food, clothing, even the doctors and many of the nurses. The military administration controlled the railways and therefore the transport of camp supplies. Because the camps arose out of military strategy, it was accepted that their cost should be met by the army. Milner had responsibility, but little information, few levers to pull and at best weak control while Kitchener could argue that he had no responsibility at all.

Brodrick's request for information on the camps had wrong-footed Kitchener. He would not allow that to happen again and from that time onwards, information about the camps was systematically recorded and monthly reports followed. The fact that these reports were prepared under the imprimatur of the commander-in-chief and supplied by him to the War Office and the Secretary for War, rather than by Milner to the Colonial Office, again illustrates the divided responsibility.

Since the reports contained ever bleaker news, they were slow in reaching London. Only the first one had arrived by the time Emily was home. Nevertheless, the triggering of regular reports was a crucial achievement. It would eventually have significant consequences.

At first, regular reporting applied only to the white camps. Systematic reports on the camps where black people found refuge, willingly or unwillingly, were not prepared until months later.

No Emily wrote their stories; no whites cared enough to speak for them. The few champions they had of their own who were sufficiently articulate to express their suffering in white man's language were ignored and dismissed even more easily than the well-connected Emily Hobhouse.

Chapter 18

Other Voices

Emily Hobhouse was not alone in her concern for the people in the concentration camps. There were others outside the system who expressed views much like hers.

Afrikaners in the towns where the camps were located knew very well what was happening and worked to alleviate the hardships, sometimes alongside Emily. She mentioned, as we have seen, Mrs Blignaut, Mrs Krause and Miss Fleck in Bloemfontein and 'an active and kind-hearted committee' in Kimberley.[159] Goodwin drew attention to the voluntary assistance provided by the communities in Johannesburg, Pretoria and Heidelberg. These volunteers were regarded as partisan, of course. No one asked their views and, when offered, their opinions counted for little.

But other views could not be dismissed so lightly. Mrs Maxwell's, for example. She was close enough to the system to appreciate what was going on. Her husband, General Maxwell, Military Governor of Pretoria, had, as noted in the previous chapter, lent his support and authority to a campaign to solicit donations for the camp occupants.[160] He knew from personal visits that all was not well and he supported the appeal in the face of opposition from Kitchener. Kitchener thought it was an inappropriate public statement that implied the government was not doing all that was needed.[161]

Louise Maxwell was sufficiently concerned to take the matter further. She was American and launched an appeal for funds in the United States. Her letter was printed in the *New York Herald* on 16 or 17 April 1901 when Emily was in Kimberley.[162] She wrote, in part: *It is in the name of the children who are living in open tents without fires, and possessing only the scantiest of clothes, that I ask for help.*[163] She knew the winter was coming and would be cruel.

The United States maintained an official stance of support for Britain in the war. It had invaded Cuba in 1898, the year before the Boer War had started, and could not very well defend its own invasion of a small country while condemning Britain's invasion of two. But Mrs Maxwell knew that many Americans sympathised with the Boers. Americans had fought the British for their independence just as the Boers were doing and she hoped that many people would contribute to her appeal.

In the autumn of 1901, six young Boer women of Pretoria worked in the camp at Irene as volunteer nurses. Each was allocated a section of the camp and they lived in their allotted section under canvass. One of them was Johanna 'Hansie' van Warmelo, a feisty young woman who, as Johanna Brandt, later wrote a popular book on the spying activities of Afrikaner women in Pretoria during the war, activities in which she took part.[164]

But the spying came later. Her mother, the widow of a church pastor, was prominent among the women of Pretoria, and she visited Hansie in the camp on 21 May 1901.[165] Maria van Warmelo was so disturbed by what she saw and heard from her daughter that day that she endured a sleepless night. At 3 am she sat down and wrote an appeal for assistance to the diplomatic corps in the city. She wanted their governments to intervene. Later that morning she went to see the Consul-General for the Netherlands, Mr Domela Nieuwenhuis. Nieuwenhuis advised her to contact Mr D Cinatti, the Portuguese Chargé d'Affaires, who at that time was the doyen of the diplomats in the city.

Portugal was unusual among Continental European countries in not criticising Britain over the war. However, Cinatti was undeterred by his government's position and indicated that he was willing to lay Mrs van Warmelo's appeal before the diplomats in Pretoria if she would obtain more signatures in support of her petition. They agreed that absolute secrecy was necessary, and that this should be impressed on any additional signatories. Mrs van Warmelo soon obtained the support of other leading women. Cinatti then called a meeting and representatives of ten nations attended. The upshot was that Mrs van Warmelo's petition was translated into French, the diplomatic language of the day, and sent to their governments and to Kitchener.

Cinatti was invited to meet General Maxwell, who demanded to know who the petitioners were. Cinatti refused to say and their identities were never discovered until the petitioners themselves disclosed their names many years after the war.

A month later, when Kitchener had not replied and the situation in the camp had deteriorated, the women under Mrs van Warmelo's leadership petitioned the diplomats again. Cinatti called a new meeting and this time the diplomats decided to investigate for themselves. They deputised three of their number to prepare a report: Cinatti, Baron Pitner (Austria) and Baron Ostmann (Germany). Those present at the meeting and party to the decision included Mr Nieuwenhuis (Netherlands), M Aubert (France) and Mr William D Gordon (USA).

The committee obtained permission from General Maxwell to visit the camp at Irene and called for official reports and statistics on all the camps. They were only partly successful in obtaining what they wanted, but they received enough information to produce a seven-page document, *Rapport au Corps Consulaire De Pretoria*.[166] It was written in measured, diplomatic language, cited the official reports, contained detailed information on individual camps and said, in part:

Although the returns are not complete through absence of returns for whole weeks in the official publications, we may arrive at the following conclusions:

1 *That the death-percentage in the Camps surpasses all hitherto-known proportions.*
2 *That the death rate amounts to 14 times that of Pretoria, which has, according to Dr Stroud, an average of 25 per thousand per year.*
3 *That the death rate of the children confined to the Camps has increased to an alarming extent.*

The committee spelled out the principal causes as they saw them: the misery and privations of the families after being driven off their farms (their journey sometimes lasting twenty days), the insufficiency and poor quality of the food which was unsuitable for children 'in every respect', the low temperatures especially at night, the ineffectiveness of the protection against the elements provided by the tents, the lack of clothes and blankets, the insufficiency of medical facilities and medicines and the insufficiency of medical personnel. The report was sent to Kitchener and Maxwell and to the governments of the participating diplomats.

William Gordon wrote two confidential letters to accompany the copy of the report he sent to the State Department in Washington. They are now in the national Archives of the United States. He wrote a covering letter for the report and a further explanatory letter, and he did not mince his words. The formal letter said, in part[167]:

The Consuls recognise that by no international law have they a right to interfere in a matter purely between Briton and Boer, at the same time they cannot in the name of humanity see practically the annihilation of a nation, without doing what may lie in their power to stop the ill-usage, or at any rate

*to assist in some way, the helpless women and children, who
probably are being made to suffer in this war as women and
children have never suffered before.*

*We believe this state of affairs to be absolutely unnecessary
which makes one think we are back in primeval times, instead
of what we are pleased to call the enlightened present.*

*It may be through ignorance – but more likely through
peculation of subordinates – that the supplies are short; that
improper and insufficient clothing is given these poor creatures;
at any rate, the results are appalling, and we think the nations
present by official representation, will be implicated if they do
not stop this crime against humanity.*

*We believe that the Governments of all civilized nations
have the right and duty to interfere in favor of women and
children,...*

In his explanatory letter he wrote[168]:

*The enclosed confidential letter may be considered to be
written in strong (possibly too strong) language, but I feel very
strongly on the subject and am willing to go to any sacrifice,
personally, to help these poor people.*

He briefly described the background and the failure of Kitchener
to respond to the first petition. Then he continued:

*All the Consuls are a unit in this matter, and by this and last
week's mail, the following governments were sent a copy of this
report: Austria, Belgium, Denmark, France, Germany, Greece,
Holland, Italy, Portugal, Russia, Switzerland, Turkey. With
two exceptions, representatives of the above Governments have
been here throughout the war.*

*You will, of course, understand that the reports reaching
the American press always pass the British Censor, and we*

have experienced, frequently, that misleading information is
published, and at other times the truth is suppressed.

Gordon's dispatch to Washington is dated 26 July 1901. The British Government must have been informed of the contents of the diplomatic report at about that date or earlier. By then, it was mid-winter on the South African Highveld.

Emily Hobhouse was unaware of Maria van Warmelo, of the work of the diplomats and of the secret report sent to the thirteen governments. It would have been a great comfort to her to know of a document that so fully vindicated her position, a document bearing the authority of the representatives of so many nations.

After the war, in July 1903, Emily visited Pretoria and spent an afternoon at Harmony, Maria van Warmelo's home[169], but her hostess did not disclose that she, too, had attempted to bring about a change in the concentration camp policy. The secret was still intact.

Back in Irene camp, Hansie van Warmelo also did not know of the events she had precipitated. On many mornings, when she did her rounds, she would find children who had died in the night. One day, counting five little corpses in her ward alone, she could bear it no longer. She left the camp, took the train to Pretoria and went straight to General Maxwell's office. Maxwell listened.

At about this time – the sequence of events is not clear – Maxwell invited the diplomats in the city to accompany him and his *aide-de-camp* in a surprise visit to the camp.[170] Some improvements followed immediately – Hansie's ward got more blankets – but the benefits were at best local and the fundamental issues remained.

In his report for the month of May, the medical officer at the Irene camp, Dr Percy Green, had commented on the work of

Hansie and her colleagues. He described the nursing that they did and said: *These ladies do their work well and it would be difficult and impossible for the present medical staff to do their work without them.*[171] Nevertheless, as the winter set in, as illness and death increased, all the volunteer nurses were expelled from the camp.[172]

Chapter 19

Meanwhile in England ...

M ajor Goodwin's first report on the concentration camps of
the Transvaal was much too long to telegraph and it probably reached London by mail around the middle of April 1901. As
the Secretary for War, St John Brodrick, leafed through that document, he must have known that Emily had grounds for her concerns and that he had a problem on his hands. It would be best
if this material did not reach the public. The document was not
passed on to the Colonial Office or the cabinet, and it seems that
Joseph Chamberlain, Secretary for the Colonies, remained, for a
time, ignorant of its contents, even though he, through Milner,
had nominal responsibility for the camps.

Nevertheless, the issue was beginning to emerge into public
view. The unfortunate report in the *Bloemfontein Post* had already
been reproduced in the London papers and the Rowntree letters had appeared in the *Daily News*. Then the committee of the
South African Women and Children Distress Fund released a
fundraising leaflet that disclosed some of the information they
had received from Emily. It was cautiously worded and said:

There are, undoubtedly, many persons who have not yet
realised that under the special circumstances under which the
war has been carried on, a very large portion of the Women
and Children of the two colonies ... have, perforce, been swept
out of their homes and collected into large camps where they
have entirely to depend for maintenance upon the military
authorities, whose hands and resources are already fully
occupied with the necessary provision of the troops. Of these
circumstances it has been an inevitable consequence that their
hardships have become terrible.[173]

The leaflet quoted from Emily's first long letter from Bloemfontein (see Chapter 7) and described the work she was doing 'with
the full sanction of Sir Alfred Milner and Lord Kitchener'. The
leaflet had limited circulation and from the government's point
of view, it did not say enough to scare the horses – it was the sort
of thing people would say if they were raising money. Yet the use
of that word 'terrible' by such responsible people in a carefully
considered document must have seemed a bit strong.

Lord Hobhouse was next. He was sufficiently troubled by the
news arriving from his niece that he wrote a long letter which was
published in *The Speaker*, a current affairs journal, on 15 April
1901.[174] He, too, used sober language and his letter said, in part:

Whatever may have been the cause of the disputes, whatever
the rights and wrongs alleged on either side, it has been
abundantly clear for more than a twelve-month that we are
engaged in the subjugation of two communities: small ones, it
is true ... and that they are fighting with all their strength to
preserve [their] liberty. That species of war, war with a nation,
leads to dreadful misery. It has led us on to lay waste large
portions of the country, and to drive a portion of their male
inhabitants and large numbers of women and children, who
either would not or could not escape, into camps where they

are kept in confinement. This is done in order that they may not afford sustenance to the males who are in arms. But thus they are deprived of the ability to sustain themselves, and are dependent on the arrangements made by their captors.

The difficulty of such arrangements is very great. The results, of which we have received accounts at first hand, are such as to rend the heart and shock the conscience. Numbers crowded into small tents; some sick, some dying, occasionally a dead one among them, scanty rations dealt out raw; lack of fuel to cook them; lack of water for drinking, for personal cleanliness; lack of bedding or of beds to keep the body off the bare earth; lack of clothing for warmth and in many cases even for decency; no needles or thread to mend tatters; shelter only in tents of single canvas, now scorched by a very hot sun, and now drenched by rain, and very slender appliances to meet the maladies consequent on such exposure. It is not that our people are cruel; we are not casting blame; certainly many are doing what they can with the resources at their disposal, and doing it with pity in their hearts. But the evil comes of the nature of the war in which we are engaged, and of the magnitude and novelty of our undertaking to uproot a population and to keep it at a distance from its own home …

… there is one sense … in which our enterprise can hardly fail to have a political result. Whatever differences of opinion there are as to the merits of the war and the course it has yet to run, all agree that, after it is over, English people and Dutch will have to live in the same political society. Anything that attracts the two component parts of that society to one another will diminish its friction and strengthen its union. And it may well be that the help – and perhaps still more the sympathy – brought by English people to the women and children of the Dutch in their direct need will soften the feelings of the weaker party and make it easier for them to unite in one community with the stronger.

John Ellis questioned Brodrick about the camps in the parliament on 22 April. A few days later Brodrick telegraphed Kitchener to inform him that stories about the camps were circulating in England. He said he thought he could keep the House of Commons at bay, but added, *All the same, Harcourt had some very harrowing stories.*[175] It reveals something of Brodrick's state of mind. This was an issue he would have to deal with and he saw it mostly in political terms. At the same time, he was unsure of where right lay.

He must have noted that the three public disclosures of the conditions in the camps – by the Distress Fund, Lord Hobhouse and John Ellis – had the same origin: that woman who had provided Lord Hobhouse with firsthand accounts, such as to rend the heart and shock the conscience.

On 3 May, Ellis and Rowntree went to see Brodrick to plead for humanitarian action in the camps. Their request was modest, far too modest to achieve the necessary degree of change. Their proposals were summed up in the telegram Brodrick sent to Kitchener the next day:

> *As regards the Refugee Camps, we have a demand from responsible people headed by some MP's to allow (1) Extra comforts to be sent in (2) Some access by responsible and accredited people who can assist in measures for improving the life in the camps (3) Some latitude as to visitors – friends of the refugees.*
>
> *'As regards (1) and (2) I propose if Lord Roberts and Mr Chamberlain concur to make proposals to you by telegraph. The object of these people is good, and they are ready to provide funds for those women who have lost household goods with some necessaries at the close of the war. They have also shown considerable discretion as they have had and shown to Govt. some harrowing accounts of conditions in the earlier camps / Jan and Febr/ and have not used them publicly.*[176]

Kitchener immediately sent the telegram to Milner, who was on the brink of departing for England. Milner replied:

I do not think it is reasonable to ask us to do anything which could cause transport difficulty at this time, as we require all the transport there is for the troops and for such of our own people as are returning to their homes, from which they have been exiled for nearly 2 years. Surely they have first claim. Besides, though it is said this proposal is humanitarian and not political, experience shows that persons who from sympathy with the enemy visit camps on these so-called humane missions are, as a matter of fact, unable to control their political sympathies, and do mischief sometimes without intending.[177]

It is perfectly clear who Milner had in mind when he wrote this. Kitchener was more than happy to agree with Sir Alfred and he passed the response on, offering to arrange for the distribution of any funds that might be made available. This was unacceptable to Ellis and Rowntree and their initiative came to nought.

It is apparent that neither Rowntree, Ellis, Brodrick, Chamberlain, Kitchener nor Milner grasped the gravity of the situation. No tinkering at the edges, not all the extra comforts the Distress Fund and others charities could possibly supply, no provision of household goods and necessaries at the close of the war, no increase in the numbers of visitors would achieve what was urgently necessary.

Early May 1901 was a critical time. If lives were to be saved in the camps, now was the time to move quickly. It was late autumn in southern Africa and the coldest months lay just ahead. The lives of the camp occupants were very much at risk.

It was also the time when the men who mattered most – Milner, Kitchener and Brodrick – were crystallising their attitudes to the revelations that one way and another had originated with Emily Hobhouse. All three, for their various reasons, were making up their minds to do nothing.

PART 3

Taking the
message home

Chapter 20

Voyage

The RMS *Saxon*, at 12,385 tons, was the largest liner in the Union Castle Line's fleet in 1901. It could sustain a speed of seventeen and a half knots – impressive for its time. This meant that the voyage from Cape Town to Southampton lasted about fifteen days after allowing for a few hours to refuel and replenish supplies at Madeira. When it sailed from Cape Town, just before 1 am on 9 May 1901, its passengers included not only Emily Hobhouse, but also Sir Alfred Milner and some of his staff.[178] Milner was making his first visit home to Britain since the beginning of the war.

Emily had arrived in southern Africa with an upper-class accent, the support of a committee that included Lady Ripon and Sir Thomas Acland and introductions from Lord and Lady Hobhouse. She had a bishop for an uncle and cousins in the House of Commons. With connections like these, Sir Alfred and the senior military men she met in Cape Town and Bloemfontein, all of similar social backgrounds, could reasonably regard her as one of them, someone who might do good deeds but could be trusted not to do or say anything that would embarrass those of her own kind.

This was the implicit bargain that Emily knew existed and

the reason she sought no publicity for herself or for what she had discovered. Her supporters in England likewise believed that publicity would damage her work. In returning to England, she intended to bring about change by speaking privately with people of influence and to maintain confidentiality.

But it was too late. Her behaviour was the first to give her away. In Cape Town she had fraternised with people known to be against the war. In Bloemfontein, Pretyman was shocked when she stayed with Caroline Fichardt and developed a friendship with Tibbie Steyn, the former president's wife.

Then came the newspaper reports in the *Bloemfontein Post* and the London *Daily News*. Correspondence intercepted by the military censors confirmed that her attitude was not sympathetic to Britain's conduct in the war. They knew, on the contrary, that she strongly condemned it. Her actions had breached their unspoken understanding: she could not be trusted to remain discreet. If she chose to speak out, this lady could create great embarrassment and political difficulties. Her connectedness made her all the more dangerous. It was time to neutralise the threat, cast her out before she could inflict too much damage.

On board the *Saxon*, the attitude of other passengers was distinctly cool. Milner's staff had been talking.

Emily was not entirely ostracised. Just before her departure, Caroline Murray had introduced her to the Potgieters who were also on board. They were a large family with eleven children and maids to assist in the child minding. They befriended her and she sat at their table at dinner.

But this was another indiscretion for the Potgieters were prominent Boers. Mr PT Potgieter had been the mayor of Pretoria when Lord Roberts marched into the city and he had spurned Roberts's invitation to remain in that position under British control. By coincidence, one of Mrs Potgieter's sisters was Maria van Warmelo[179], although no one on the ship knew of the significance of this connection, except perhaps Mrs Potgieter herself.

Emily told other passengers she was using the opportunity to improve her Afrikaans, the Dutch-based patois of the Boers, so that she could speak it better on her next visit to the new colonies. Ossie Walrond, Milner's secretary, scoffed: she would never be allowed to return. Emily was shocked; it was the first she had heard of this.

Her main objective during the voyage was to discuss the situation in the camps with Sir Alfred. They were confined on board for two weeks; no better opportunity would arise. But Milner kept to himself, sheltered by his staff. He let it be known that he was not a good sailor; on board he felt 'mentally torpid'.[180] However, during the stop at Madeira he received good news; his mental torpidity disappeared and he became more sociable, and he agreed to a meeting with Emily.

Emily reports that they had a full discussion. She was astounded to learn that he had received sixty-four reports on her.[181] She would have been equally dismayed had she seen the telegram that Milner had sent to Kitchener and Brodrick just before their departure. She asked if she would be allowed to return to southern Africa but did not receive a clear answer. She misjudged him and was perhaps deliberately deceived by him. To her, he was a 'charming, sympathetic, gracious and cultivated man' whose private, liberal leanings, she believed, were at odds with the task he was honour-bound to fulfil. She saw nothing of the Milner who had largely, almost single-handedly, engineered the war, whose ambition was to go down in history as the man who had unified South Africa under the British flag and to reap for himself the accolades that would follow. She did not know that he wished to make the country politically and culturally English, irretrievably English, and that for him all things Dutch were obstacles to be pushed aside or extinguished.

At the meeting, Sir Alfred undertook to write to Emily after he had talked with the government. In this letter he would respond to her suggestions for ameliorating the suffering in the camps and indicate whether she would be allowed to return to southern Africa.

The telegram Milner had received at Madeira was from Joseph Chamberlain, the Colonial Secretary. It informed him that they had arranged a rather special homecoming for him. With the recognition he would soon receive, Emily Hobhouse and anything she might say would count for very much less than his words.

There was another passenger on board who kept to himself throughout the journey, one Adriaan Hofmeyr. Since he will reappear, a brief introduction to this man is warranted.

Hofmeyr was once a minister of the Dutch Reformed Church in the Cape Town suburb of Wynberg, but he had been suspended from his religious duties for alleged immoral conduct with a music teacher. He resigned from the ministry, left the Cape and became an agent for Cecil John Rhodes in far-off Bechuanaland. After the war began and while serving his British master, Hofmeyr was captured by the Boers and imprisoned in Pretoria. They released him, perhaps on account of his evident Boer nationality and former position – the Boers held their pastors in high regard – but expelled him into Portuguese East Africa (now Mozambique). From there he made his way to England and undertook a successful lecture tour during the mid-war British election. His message was popular, pro-war, pro-Britain, pro-Unionist, anti-Boer.

With the re-election of the Unionists, he returned to southern Africa and visited the concentration camps, most likely at the behest of the administration.[182] One day, he and Emily were in the Bloemfontein camp at the same time. His mission, like that of General Piet de Wet, was to influence the attitude of the Boer women. Unfortunately for him, his reputation had preceded him. Among these devout women, his indiscretion with the music teacher while a minister of the church was as unforgivable as his traitorous relationship with the enemy.

Emily was puzzled by his presence on the *Saxon*. Hofmeyr had let it be known that he was travelling in Milner's party and that he had been summoned to England by Joseph Chamberlain. Walrond, Milner's secretary, denied any such connections.[183]

As the ship was approaching Southampton, the captain was asked to slow down so that their arrival would synchronise with the preparations being made to greet Sir Alfred. When they docked, Milner took the train to London.

The most senior ministers in the government were at Waterloo Station to greet him: Lord Salisbury, the Prime Minister; Arthur Balfour, the Deputy Prime Minister and Joseph Chamberlain, the Colonial Secretary, among others. He left with Salisbury and Chamberlain in an open carriage through cheering crowds and they went directly to Marlborough House where the King conferred a peerage on him. By the end of the day he was Baron Milner of St James and Cape Town.[184]

Historian Thomas Pakenham's comment on this event is interesting in the context of our story:

How Milner was later to regret his own fatal blunder at this moment of triumph. He still dismissed Emily Hobhouse as a 'pro-Boer' and a 'screamer'. In fact, the story she told was only too true. Over sixty thousand men, women and children were now stuffed in those 'refugee' camps set up by Kitchener. Their population was rising like the waters in a dam. But where were the doctors, the matrons, the orderlies; the clothes and blankets; the medicines and comforts? It was the twin spirit of neglect and red tape ... that had haunted the white tents at Bloemfontein a year earlier [when soldiers had died in large numbers from typhoid]. *And this year the rows of tents were not intended for soldiers used to the ways of the barrack room. They were for women and children, used to the free life of the veld, and (for the richer farmers) ubiquitous African servants. Now they were ... herded in, exhausted, destitute, starving, to*

Kitchener's camps of 'refuge'.[185]

Milner was a senior civil servant returning home on holiday. By staging a triumphal welcome for him, the government had found a way of creating a much-needed good news story out of no special event. The press sang his praises, he was the man of the moment and his homecoming had exceeded his most extravagant hopes. The social invitations piled up.

Meanwhile, Emily Hobhouse was greeted at the dock by a few friends and well-wishers, unknown and unnoticed by everyone else. Where was she to begin? The last thing Britain wanted at that moment was bad news from southern Africa. How could she persuade the nation that a major change in the conduct of the war was needed? It was unavoidable, if she were to succeed, that she would implicate the object of their current adulation in the unfolding humanitarian disaster at the southern end of Africa.

If there is a tide in the affairs of man, it was flowing strongly, and Emily faced the daunting prospect of swimming against it.

Chapter 21

Back on British soil

Many people were ready to assist Emily, and first among these were her brother, Leonard, and her Aunt Mary and Uncle Arthur, Lady and Lord Hobhouse. Leonard and Mary had been her main correspondents while she was in southern Africa while Arthur had remained in close touch and understood the situation, including the politics in London, as well as anyone. Upon her return, Emily went to stay with Mary and Arthur at their country home in Oxfordshire. Leonard, a journalist at the *Manchester Guardian* (and later a distinguished sociologist) came down at her request so that they could all discuss what to do next.

Equally supportive was the South African Women and Children Distress Fund, her sponsor and the body she herself had founded.[186] Emily was soon in touch with the committee members to seek their advice and assistance; Kate Courtney was especially involved. Emily also met others sympathetic to her work. A meeting with John Morley MP, a staunch critic of the war, stood out in her memories of this time.

Besides Morley, she had the backing of other parliamentarians. They included Leonard Courtney, the founder of the South African Conciliation Committee (Kate's husband), John Ellis, Sir William Harcourt, Lord Ripon and, most outspoken of all, the young Welsh MP and future prime minister, David Lloyd George. All were able and distinguished people. Emily's letters had been circulated among them and they knew what she could tell the British people in person.

However, going public was a step not to be taken lightly. The message she carried would embarrass the government. Her family and supporters had kept her letters from the public eye lest their disclosure made things more difficult for her in Africa and politically harder for the government to give sympathetic consideration to her message. Discretion ruled and this was still their line of thinking.

They wished the work in the camps to continue. Two women sponsored by the Distress Fund, Miss Monkhouse and Miss Mellor, sailed for Cape Town the day after Emily arrived in Britain, a move that seemed hasty to her. She would have preferred to spend time with them and give them the benefit of her experience, but the committee feared that one of the consequences of Emily's return would be a refusal by the authorities to allow more representatives to go and the women were packed off before this could happen.

Emily's inner circle advised her to seek a meeting with the Secretary for War, St John Brodrick, as soon as possible. She felt she ought to wait for Milner's promised letter. She believed that he had heard her sympathetically, would intercede with the government on behalf of the people in the camps and would accede to her requests, including her wish to be allowed to return to continue her work in the camps. But no letter arrived from Milner.

Days passed. The urgency of the situation in the camps demanded action and she wrote to Brodrick requesting the meeting. He agreed to see her on 4 June.

Meanwhile, the pressures upon her were increasing. Her letter to Caroline Murray on 29 May 1901 said, *Mr Molteno* [Caroline's brother] *came to see me last night and several others to discuss my best line of action. I am quite overcome by the responsi-*

*bility resting upon me and by the importance attached to every word
I speak. My letters, too, are regarded as strong documents and are to
be printed in some form as soon as I can break from the Authorities.
But first I am to appeal to them and give them their chance. Editors
are after me and interviewers and people clamouring for meetings
and I am vainly trying to keep my head cool and my facts clear and
distinct.*[187]

Emily's brother helped to prepare her for the encounter with
Brodrick. Fearing she would go into too much detail, he agreed
with her the points she should raise.

Just before the meeting, Emily became aware of a report prepared by Dr Henry Becker, who had recently taken up duties
at the Bloemfontein camp.[188] It had much in common with the
reports of Drs Turner and Crook in the Transvaal, offered a long
list of causes for the disease and death prevalent in the camp and
suggested much that should be done to address the situation.
Becker said he expected the death rate to increase in the coming
week due to the excessively cold weather. Pneumonia would be
the most common diagnosis. The report comprehensively con-
troverted the rosy picture Trollope had presented on the OFS
camps (p 144). It was the first Emily knew of such reports and
she resolved to urge Brodrick that it be heeded.

The meeting was not as difficult as she had anticipated. She
wrote to Leonard:

*I have just seen Brodrick and come away with a strong
impression of his gentlemanly incompetence – slippery but
pleasant, mediocre and agreeable; ready to listen, ready also to
drift. Standpoint: How good we are, how right we have been.*

*Did not feel I got my claws into him anywhere. Brought
in almost all our points and brought him quite up to date
by letters fresh from the camps last night. ... He asked me to
write fully my suggestions for ameliorating matters and will
discuss with Colonial Office and Milner. ... Poor Brodrick!*

When I ended by telling him I should be obliged to make public his refusal to let me go again, he turned white as a sheet![189]

It was Emily's misfortune to have in this critical position a minister too weak to stand up to the stronger men in the fray, Roberts and Kitchener, Chamberlain and Milner, especially Milner. Here was a crisis whose proper solution involved a major change of direction but the change was beyond Brodrick's power to deliver. He had evidently hoped he could placate Emily by listening and with reassurances and courtesies, and his alarm about her parting statement was the realisation that she was in no way mollified and was prepared to take her campaign into the public domain.

Emily put her proposals in writing and delivered them the same day. She urged[190]:

- that all who could leave the camps be allowed to go
- free passes into towns for all wishing to find work there
- equality of treatment for all
- a resident minister of religion for every camp
- that no further women and children be brought in
- the appointment of a matron conversant with both languages for every camp
- that any new camps be in the Cape Colony nearer supplies and sources of charitable aid
- free access to the camps for at least six accredited representatives of philanthropic societies
- that the doctor's report on Bloemfontein camp be acted upon
- that three individual women, whom she nominated, be at once allowed to leave Bloemfontein camp on account of their poor state of health and that of their children.

Decades later, when writing her autobiography, Emily acknowledged that these requests were inadequate. She had been impetuous and her response had been too hasty. She had made no mention of the urgent need to modify the food, provide warm clothing and blankets, improve water and fuel supplies, provide more tents and better shelter, improve the hospital accommodation and appoint more doctors and nurses. Fortunately the official medical reports from southern Africa were stressing the need for all of these and more.

Brodrick put the recommendations to Milner, as he had said he would; Milner had heard most of it before. As John Hall wrote, Milner's response would have astonished and outraged Emily.[191] He rejected most of her proposals or dismissed them as purely military matters to be referred to Kitchener. In his reply to Brodrick, he wrote:

> *It is possible to be too stingy about the camps. We don't want to make them too comfortable, but neither ought anything necessary for the health of the inmates be neglected. But this can and ought to be done by persons, preferably S. Africans, appointed by the Government, not by philanthropic or other private agencies outside. It is admitting neglect on our part that such persons should be necessary.[192]*
>
> Emily should not be allowed to return, nor should any other outsiders be allowed to meddle with the camps. On the other hand, said Milner, if the government *thought it necessary to allow such meddling, then Miss Hobhouse had better be one of the meddlers. As long as she is working in the camps, she will not be able to carry on a crusade in England, though, of course, she can write mischievously.[193]*

Since this man had just come from southern Africa, had direct responsibility for the camps, had a better understanding of the situation than he and had been freshly lauded for the excellence of his work, why would Brodrick disagree?

Chapter 22

Out of obscurity

June 1901 was a difficult, demanding and sometimes frustrating time for Emily. While she waited for the government to respond to her pleas, the committee of the Distress Fund met to discuss what could be done. It was becoming increasingly obvious that their preferred approach – direct discussion with the government out of the public gaze – was failing. While they waited, human beings were suffering and dying in the camps. The situation demanded urgency. If the government would not act when asked quietly, their only choice was to bring the weight of public pressure to bear. The government would probably react defensively and going public could be counter-productive. But doing nothing was not an option. So a strategy was formulated to escalate the political pressure and inform the British people of conditions in the concentration camps of southern Africa.

It was agreed that Emily would produce a report, which would be printed and given to all members of parliament. When the press picked up the story, as they surely would, she would address a large public meeting in central London. This would be followed by meetings in Manchester, Birmingham, Bristol, York, Leeds and wherever a significant audience could be mustered. In the August holiday season, she would tour the coastal resort towns.

To begin the process, Emily spoke at a large gathering, mostly of ladies, hosted by Lady Hobhouse at their London house on 10 June. Emily was nervous, but she received an encouraging response.

A few days later she met the leader of the opposition, Sir Henry Campbell-Bannerman. He listened for two hours and as Emily recounted how homes were burnt and women and children swept into the ill-prepared camps, he muttered 'methods of barbarism, methods of barbarism'.

Campbell-Bannerman was in an awkward political situation. His party, the Liberal Party, had split into anti-war and imperialist factions. Public support for the war had cost him victory at the last election. He strove to hold the party together by occupying the middle ground, muting his own anti-war position and being content with holding the government to account on points that could garner consensus in the Liberal ranks. But, moved by what he had heard, he decided that he could not sit on the fence on this issue.

That evening he and Sir William Harcourt were guests at a dinner given in their honour by the National Reform Union at the Holborn Restaurant in London. In his speech, Campbell-Bannerman wasted no time in using the insights he had newly obtained. *A phrase often used*, he said, *is that 'war is war'. But when one comes to ask about it, one is told that no war is going on – that it is not war. When is a war not a war? When it is carried on by methods of barbarism in South Africa.*[194] It was the language he had used while listening to Emily. The press was present and his words flashed around the world, even to southern Africa.

Campbell-Bannerman understood, as politicians in the government refused to acknowledge, that it was the entire policy of destroying properties and confining families to camps that was at fault, and he roundly condemned the government for it.

On 17 June, Brodrick was asked in the House of Commons about the number of people now in the camps and the mortality among them. He replied that in the Transvaal there were 37,739 occupants, in Natal 2,524, in the Orange River Colony 20,374 and in the Cape Colony 2,490 – 63,127 in total.[195] The real number in the white camps was at least 5,000 higher at the end of May and rising, and he made no mention of the number in black camps. Nevertheless, these figures were news to the members of the House. He gave the white fatality figures for May in the Transvaal: 39 men, 47 women and 250 children. No figures were offered for the other camps. The opposition realised that the fatalities were nearly one hundred more than in April.

Later that day, David Lloyd George moved that the House debate the situation in the camps as a matter of urgent public importance. He extrapolated the figures and said they amounted to a death rate of 12 per cent per year, a policy tantamount to one of extermination: *I say that this is the result of a deliberate and settled policy. It is not a thing which has been done in twenty-four hours, for it has taken months and months to do it. The military authorities knew perfectly well it was to be done and they had ample time to provide for it.*[196]

It was disgraceful, he said, that after six months children should be dying at the rate of hundreds per month, and he made a fateful prediction, one that would prove all too accurate: *We want to make loyal British subjects of these people. Is this the way to do it? Brave men will forget injuries to themselves much more readily than they will insults, indignities, and wrongs to their women and children. ... When children are being treated in this way and dying, we are simply ranging the deepest passions of the human heart against British rule in Africa ... It will always be remembered that this is the way British rule started there and this is the method by which it was brought about.*[197]

John Ellis, William Redmond, Herbert Lewis and Campbell-Bannerman supported Lloyd George, calling for action and urging that this was a humanitarian issue that should be treated apolitically.

Brodrick bore the brunt of it and refused to treat it apolitically.[198] It was largely the Boers fault: militant Orange River Colony farmers had returned to their farms on parole, then re-joined the commandos; many people would not be in the camps if the Boers recognised that it was their responsibility to take care of their own women and children; some had come in voluntarily; the government was having difficulty supplying not only the camps, but also their own soldiers; if the women and children were released, they would either starve to death or again support the enemy; the conditions in the camps had been steadily ameliorated; the many deaths in the Johannesburg camp were the result of an epidemic of measles that was the responsibility of the mothers who refused to follow the dietary guidelines of the authorities; the food provided was sound and the same as provided to the soldiers; what would benefit the refugees more than anything else would be the cessation of the war (meaning, of course, that the Boers should surrender).

Emily watched in despair from the public gallery. She wrote the following year: *Very clearly in my remembrance of that debate stands out Mr Herbert Lewis's attempt to fix the attention of the House on the humanitarian side of the question. The House was unsympathetic and neither knew nor cared to hear. Humanity was appealed to in vain, and Mr Lewis was literally howled down. ... In common with the Boer women, I had felt sure that English humanity would not fail to respond instantly if the facts were clearly understood. I was wrong; no barbarisms in South Africa could equal the cold cruelty of that indifferent House.*[199]

The Times newspaper saw it differently. Its editorial the next day said, *Mr Brodrick's reply to the attack upon the system of refugee camps in South Africa ... was clear, vigorous and convincing.*[200] It pointed out that the opposition was divided and that many of its members had supported the government. In a long defence of the government, it said:

*The British people and the British Army, whose methods of
warfare Sir Henry Campbell-Bannerman … brand[s] as
'barbarous', deeply grieve over the privations and the hardships
endured by the wives and children of their enemies. But, as Mr
Brodrick proved last night, they cannot take blame themselves
for what are necessary consequences of the war and of the
fashion in which the husbands and fathers of those now in the
refugee camps have chosen to conduct it. We have done all in
our power – more than has ever been done by any nation at
war – to mitigate those consequences. Throughout the long and
trying campaign the humanity of our troops and of our methods
towards all classes of our opponents has been without a parallel.*

The Times carried considerable weight in the market of public
opinion; it was the authoritative voice of its time. By supporting
the government in this way, it and other newspapers that took
a similar line were extending the responsibility for the concentration camps beyond the members of the government into the
wider British population.

It was clear that Brodrick was not going to respond with the
urgency the situation demanded and was unlikely to bring about
a change in policy. Lord Hobhouse had repeatedly expressed the
view that the government would act only out of fear of public
opinion. It was time to mobilise that opinion and Emily's fif-
teen-page report[201] was distributed, as planned, to all members of
parliament on or about 18 June[202], the day after the disappointing
debate in the House of Commons. As expected, it immediately
became public.

The report was largely an edited version of her letters from
southern Africa, and in it she listed again the things that should
be done. She summed up: *There is no doubt that the general discomfort could be vastly alleviated by attention to the points mentioned, but it should be clearly understood that they are suggested only
by way of amelioration. The main thing is to let them go. The ruin*

of most is now complete, but let all who have friends or means left go. Above all one would hope that the good sense, if not the mercy, of the English people will cry out against the further development of this cruel system which falls with such crushing effect upon the old, the weak and the children.[203]

Emily Hobhouse had high hopes for the release of this document. Her appeal was now before the English people, and she had confidence that they would understand and put an end to the suffering in the camps. It was for this that she had come home.

The defenders of the citadel were ready and waiting. The next day, *The Times* newspaper carried a report on her document, reproducing her recommendations in full. The accompanying, breezy editorial said:

Miss Hobhouse describes some painful sights she witnessed and repeats some painful tales she heard, and, it would seem, accepted without much investigation. Her statements, at the same time, by no means bear out the declamation of the pro-Boers. She admits that she received particular facilities for the work she had in hand from Lord Milner and Lord Kitchener, and it will be seen that most of the suggestions she makes which are at all practicable either have been carried out or are now under consideration. ... we are gratified to know, on the authority of Miss Hobhouse, that the steps taken or contemplated by Mr Brodrick will materially lighten the sufferings of the refugees.[204]

As for further assistance to the camps, Mr Brodrick explains that Lord Milner, Lord Kitchener and the Government are most anxious to avail themselves of the services of local committees. There is, on the other hand, another class of persons whom Miss Hobhouse and others would like to see in the camps, but whom the Government will on no account admit. They absolutely refuse to have the camps turned into centres of agitation by the action,

*intentional or unintentional, of real or sham philanthropists,
who write blood-curdling descriptions and disseminate false or
inaccurate stories. They are perfectly right.*[205]

First a screamer, then a meddler, now Emily had been promoted
to agitator.

During his previous visit to London, in 1899, Milner had met
the editors of the London papers one by one and had explained
his pro-war position to them. Had he been at it again? The words
in the editorial, not all of which are reproduced here, suggest that
he, Brodrick or their staff had briefed the press in advance of
Emily's report.

A public meeting had been arranged for that evening, 19 June,
to permit two members of the Legislative Assembly of the Cape
Colony, Mr John X Merriman and Mr JW Sauer, to express their
views on the situation in southern Africa. It may be recalled that
Emily had been a guest at the Merrimans' home when she first
arrived in Cape Town and that the Sauers had warmly welcomed
her involvement in southern Africa. Sauer represented Aliwal
North in the legislature and had local knowledge of the camp in
his constituency. Admission to the event was by ticket only but a
large crowd supporting the government gathered outside. Scuffles
broke out, the police had difficulty in controlling the situation
and minor damage was done to the hall (broken glass).

On the night, Merriman was indisposed, but Sauer spoke and
so did several of the prominent 'pro-Boers'. David Lloyd George,
brandishing Emily's report, devoted much of his anti-war address
to the plight of the children in the camps. A resolution urging the
government to stop the war and restore the independence of the
republics was adopted. Mr John Dillon then moved the following
resolution, which was carried: *That this meeting expresses its horror
and indignation at the action of the Government in employing the
British Army in South Africa in the barbarous work of farm-burn-
ing and in capturing women and children and confining them in*

pestilential camps, and demands the immediate abandonment of this policy of 'concentration', ... as being an outrage against humanity and as casting dishonour upon the troops who are compelled to carry out orders so repulsive to honourable men.[206]

Resolutions like this had no effect, of course, but they demonstrated, at least, that many people did not support the government's intransigence.

Emily was scheduled to address a public meeting five days later at the same venue, the Queens Hall at Langham Place near Oxford Circus in central London. The Bishop of Hereford had agreed to take the chair and the committee of the Distress Fund advertised the event and sold tickets. The audience would again be restricted to ticket holders to reduce the risk of disturbances during the meeting. But it never happened. The lessor of the hall, citing the rowdiness at the preceding meeting, terminated the contract. An alternative venue was offered by the deacons of Westminster Chapel, an independent church near Buckingham Palace, not to be confused with the Anglican abbey or the Catholic cathedral in the same part of London. However, after discussions with the police, they also withdrew. Emily saw interference by 'the Authorities' in both decisions.

After seeing Brodrick, Emily wrote to Milner asking if he would now send her the letter he had promised her on the *Saxon*. She especially wanted to know if she would be allowed to go back to the camps. His reply arrived on 27 June and was again evasive. As she had now taken the matter to the government, he said, it was better that they deal with it. He did not disclose that he was advising the government to stop her from returning.

Chapter 23

Reaction

The publication of her report on the camps changed Emily's life overnight, though not in the way she expected. She had made the evidence available to all; surely now everyone could see how urgently change was needed. But the reaction was different. In political terms, hers was a serious challenge and it elicited a concerted response.

Two days after her report was released, *The Times* carried its own report on camp conditions.[207] It was written, allegedly, by their 'special correspondent' in Bloemfontein and the camps discussed in it included those that Emily had visited.

It said there was nothing in Bloemfontein that did not point to progress: *In no department is this more marked than in the burgher refugee camps under the administration of the Orange River Colony. Five months ago ... this stupendous undertaking was in its infancy, and from its very magnitude was somewhat unsatisfactory; but in the middle of February it was taken over by Captain Trollope and in the ensuing months was brought to its present state of management, which, when the following statistics are read, will convince readers that everything possible under the unique conditions is being done for the people who suffer from the prolongation of hostilities.*

It reported that there were 24,800 white refugees in twelve

camps in the ORC and, as an afterthought, mentioned a further 15,500 natives in nine camps. The rest of the discussion dealt with the white camps only. It gave the statistics on the number of tents and marquees provided and, at Bloemfontein, also wood and iron shelters. Next to housing, medical care was the most important, it said. *The Executive have* carte blanche *in this respect,* they can spend as much as they want. There were doctors and nurses in the camps and more on the way from England. The hospitals were generally accommodated in marquees, but in Bloemfontein and Kimberley £1,500 had been spent on building hospitals. It went on:

> *Clothing and blankets are distributed to all the needy, but great difficulty is experienced in preventing the well-to-do people from appropriating Government property under pretence of poverty. Over £1,800 has already been expended on clothing and more than 15,000 blankets have been distributed. The daily ration consists of half a pound of meat and meal ... Vegetables were issued, but the Boers, not being inclined to such diet, showed no inclination but to waste it.*

Dairies were established at each camp to supply the hospitals and children with milk.

> *According to all reports from the camp superintendents, the burghers are very amenable to discipline and law-abiding. Passes are issued in rotation to visit towns and camps, amusements are encouraged and light work is found for able-bodied adults.*
>
> *But,* wrote the correspondent, *the most startling development of these camps is the educational progress. Schools have been established in all the camps, in which the education is conducted in English. Attendance is voluntary, but all the parents have shown alacrity in having their children thus*

taught. It purported to show that there was a preference for classes in English rather than Dutch.

This was all a rather positive picture. Trollope, to whom all this was attributed, could be relied on to produce a good report. A pity for him that his counterparts in the Transvaal, Goodwin and his successor, Tucker, insisted on taking the word of the doctors and painting a much more depressing scenario. But *The Times* was not going to inform its readers of what they were reporting, possibly because the government did not let it have access to their reports.

The editorial in the same paper emphasised Trollope's version.[208] *The account of the refugee camps in the Orange River Colony which our Special Correspondent sends us from Bloemfontein this morning will enable the public to form a juster view of these establishments than the sensational descriptions drawn by irresponsible investigators with a pro-Boer bias. He shows how immense was the labour cast upon us by the determination of the Boers to abandon the care of their dependants, how unwearying have been our efforts to perform it to the utmost of our ability and how high has been the measure of our success.*

One gulps when reading 'the determination of the Boers to abandon the care of their dependants'. Just who was it that burnt the farms and destroyed anything that could sustain human life? And were not many women and children brought into the camps under duress? The report was, of course, simply false. Milk was not on the official rations for children and was usually provided only in the hospitals. Vegetables never appeared on rations sheets, not according to Captain Trollope's own reports. Dr Becker of Bloemfontein pleaded for them. And 15,000 blankets? For 40,000 people living in tents in freezing conditions?

And as for education, the report also does not mention that only teachers who taught in English were paid. Milner was deliberately attempting to anglicise the captive next generation. The

Boers were not deceived. Some schooling for their children was better than none; they would take care of Dutch at home.

The fatalities contradicted all the rosy claims. In May, the average for all camps in the ORC was at an annualised death rate of 117 per thousand. For Bloemfontein, the annualised rate was 383 per thousand.[209] This meant that nearly 40 per cent of the camp occupants would be dead if this rate were sustained for a year! The rate was high, said the report, but it was getting better.

It was the Boers' own fault, of course, a refrain repeated again and again: *The Boers are accustomed*, said the editorial, paraphrasing from their report, *to living on isolated farms on the open veld, where the commonest sanitary precautions may be neglected with comparatively little danger. They neglect these same precautions in the camps, with the results that may be imagined. Another factor which has raised the rate of mortality in the camps has been the exhausted state in which many of the refugees arrived. Their constitutions had been ruined by the inevitable hardships of the war, and they died with the winter's cold.*[210]

'The hardships of the war' implied the refusal of the Boers to stop fighting – their fault again. Not the transportation in open trucks in all weathers without food or water for days.

So Emily presented one view, *The Times* and other pro-government newspapers another. There was a third rich source of information, the monthly and other official reports from the camps themselves, available to the government but not to the public. What did they have to say?

Take the 'sanitary precautions' that the Boer occupants were said to be neglecting. Major A Baird inspected the Bloemfontein camp at the request of the General Officer Commanding (Kitchener) on 17 April 1901. His report contains the following:

Latrines: The accommodation did not appear to me to be sufficient, but the commandant informed me that more were being added. ...

At 11am the latrine buckets had not been emptied for the previous day and night and remained outside the latrines in the hot sun. A fearful stench was emitted by these, I had to keep my handkerchief to my face, and finish the inspection as quickly as possible. The commandant said this was the fault of the Town Council in not removing the pails regularly.[211]

Neither Baird nor the Camp Commandant, Captain Arthur Hume, attributed any responsibility for this appalling situation to the Boers. Baird did mention that the dongas (ditches) in the vicinity were also used as latrines and even, rarely, the spaces between the tents. Who could blame the residents for declining to use the latrines? Many were children; many were small children.

Dr Henry Becker, the newly arrived medical officer at the Bloemfontein camp, filed his first report on 1 June 1901, two and a half weeks before the report on the camps in *The Times*. This is the report to which Emily drew attention when she met Brodrick on the 4th and also in her written recommendations. Faced with a camp of nearly 4,000 people in which large numbers were dying, Becker nevertheless made the time to write a lengthy report.[212] It has this to say about the health of the camp residents:

But now to come to the real causes of disease and death prevalent in this camp, the following must be enumerated:-

1   *The indiscriminate massing together of people of all sorts from different parts of this Colony in a large camp, whereby, no doubt, contagion is bound to assert itself.*
2   *Insufficient hospital accommodation for infectious cases.*
3   *Insufficient housing and covering, absence of warmth to people who have been suddenly removed from houses. Some of the tents are useless as a covering. In many cases the supply of blankets is insufficient.*

4 *Overcrowding in many tents.*

5 *Insufficient latrine accommodation [six weeks after Hume promised there would be more].*

6 *Slops thrown about the tents.*

7 *Insufficient supply of water as well for the washing of clothes as for the person.*

8 *Bad nursing on the part of the people themselves, cold, want of room and breathing space.*

9 *Insufficient food supply. I think half a pound of meat for an adult not sufficient. The Boer Afrikander is used to a great deal more. Fresh milk and vegetables (even though compressed or preserved in tins) should be supplied two or three times a week. Diarrhoea is very prevalent amongst adults as amongst children, and is in many cases due to the food, in other cases undoubtedly to the water. Water cannot be kept clean in tents into which wind and dust constantly are blown. The quality of the meat supplied to the camp might with safety be improved.*

The Times made a point of the building of a hospital at Bloemfontein camp. It did not mention that this was a timber and iron shack and one of Dr Becker's many concerns. He found the wards excessively cold and draughty and regretted that the improvements that had repeatedly been requested were not granted. The nurses were untrained and the two doctors, he and a colleague, were swamped and could not do justice to each case. Another dispensary was needed to serve a distant part of the camp. So much for *carte blanche* expenditure on matters medical.

The official reports on the camps for this period were released only in November 1901, many months later when the worst of the tragedy in the camps had already unfolded. Among those reports there is curiously no report from any camp under the jurisdiction of the Orange River Colony except Bloemfontein. But there *were* reports from each of the Transvaal camps. Not the breezily positive version of *The Times*, seeing nothing but progress, but troubled narratives of doctors like Becker, pleading for resources and earnestly suggesting changes and improvements:

- From Volksrust (4,810 inmates): ... *the cold is intense at night and when a breeze is blowing the days are also very keen. Aged persons and young children as well as those not in perfect health suffer considerably from this cause.*[213]
- From Middelburg (6,636 inmates), a new doctor pleaded for one Dutch-speaking matron per thousand inmates, for residents to be able to purchase condensed milk, butter and warm clothing, for better shelter for the hospital than tents.[214]
- From Krugersdorp (1,531 inmates): *The condition of the families lately brought in is deplorable as they are very short of clothing and have very little bedding.*[215]
- From Potchefstroom (6,149 inmates of which 4,447 or 72 per cent were children): ... *the health among the Boer refugee women and children has been anything but satisfactory and mortality among the children has been very great.*[216] In the following month, 235 inmates of this camp died, 206 of whom were children.[217]
- Standerton (2,983 inmates): *The cold latterly has been intense and the refugees, many of whom are scantily supplied with clothing, have suffered severely.*[218]

In England, the only person able and willing to tell of the real state of affairs was Emily Hobhouse; a story she knew only partly and imperfectly, but nevertheless, in another sense, wholly.

The public were unaware of the official reports. They had only their newspapers to inform them. *The Times* had distinguished itself in the Crimean War and it meant to capitalise on and maintain its reputation. It had more reporters and correspondents in southern Africa than any other newspaper. For the man in the street, its voice was the most authoritative. But it was not alone in its assaults on Emily and her credibility. *Punch*, the satirical magazine, parodied her. Their version of her list of necessities for the ladies in the camps included hairpins and spirit lamps for heating their curling tongs. British officers were castigated for their brutality in failing to appear for afternoon tea.[219] And: *Vying with The Times in the ferocity of its assaults was the Daily Mail, owned by the future Lord Northcliffe, Alfred Harmsworth. Emily was an interfering woman who was not impartial, had no balance in her judgements, and knew nothing of war, editorialised the Mail. According to a Fleet Street legend, one brave journalist who protested over the proprietor's pro-war, anti-Emily stance was silenced by Harmsworth reaching down the circulation ledger. 'Look,' said the press baron, 'here we began our campaign. See, up, up, up.'*[220]

Yet it was *The Times* that continued to lead the campaign against Emily. On 26 June it published a long letter by the Adriaan Hofmeyr who had sailed to England on the *Saxon* with Milner and Emily. He wrote:

> *I too have visited these camps and seen how they were conducted, and have come away with impressions vastly different to those of Miss Hobhouse and the party she belongs to. ... after my visit I can only say that I thanked God that England was acting so generously and kindly towards the women and children of my poor people. I went among them as their well-wisher, not hiding the fact, however, that I was a loyal British subject. I spoke their language, I met them alone, and got them to pour out their hearts to me. The universal opinion entertained by the men and the women was that they were treated by the officials with the greatest courtesy, and that under the circumstances nothing more could be done for them unless it was to send them home.*[221]

However, the wisest among them, he said, were afraid of trouble should they be found on their farms.

> *Miss Hobhouse's report errs more in what she fails to say than*
> *in what she says ... First, Miss Hobhouse does not know how*
> *the poor in the Transvaal and the Free State [the ORC] are*
> *accustomed to be housed. We out there know that thousands*
> *of the roving farmers and poorer classes live in tents year*
> *in and year out, care very little for the heat by day and the*
> *cold by night, and rejoice in a thorough washing out by a*
> *fertilizing thunderstorm. What is apparently a hardship to*
> *Miss Hobhouse and other gently-nurtured English people we*
> *out there make light of.*

He related how he visited the Bloemfontein camp the day after a visit by Emily and met with the men in the commandant's big tent. There he was surprised by the questions he received: Was it true the Liberals would be in power in Britain soon; that public opinion about the war was changing in England; that independence would be restored; that a foreign power would intervene on the side of the Boers soon? In his turn, he asked, *'Who told you all this rubbish?' Their answer was, 'The English lady who was here yesterday.' Imagine my surprise and sorrow. I do not say that Miss Hobhouse did make such communications to them. I only repeat what happened to me.* This was a particularly nasty insinuation. Not only was Emily spreading false stories about the camps, she was now also a traitor.

The letter purported to reveal that Hofmeyr had discovered who the real leaders of the republican Boers were and who was behind their determination to continue fighting for their independence. It was not the aged President Paul Kruger in exile in Holland, not President Steyn, not the two commanders-in-chief of their forces in the field, Louis Botha or Christiaan de Wet. No, they were none other than the two politicians from the Cape Colony, JW Sauer and John X Merriman, who were at that very time in London speaking out against the war – two British subjects, two traitors in their midst.

Strange that no one else had noticed their supposed authority over the republican forces then and no historian has discovered it since. But mud sticks. How were the readers to know?

The Times did not say who Hofmeyr was. There was no mention that he was a former minister in the Dutch Reformed Church who had been hounded out of his parish in suburban Cape Town in disgrace and who had worked for the British since that time.[222]

The British Government were now so morally compromised that no objective discovery of the facts could be allowed and no reasoned debate could occur. They were compromised at the outset by the invasion of the two small republics that wanted only to be left alone – by Britain in particular. They were subsequently compromised by the manner in which the war had been conducted with Lord Roberts's small-scale but pernicious actions against civilians and thereafter by Lord Kitchener's massive burning of homes and scorching of the earth. Now that a further consequence of their deplorable war was turning up – the widespread suffering of women and children with high fatalities – they could only put up all the defences they could think of. If it meant shouting down the opposition in the House of Commons or preventing Emily Hobhouse from presenting her version of the situation to the public or resorting to the tawdry, threadbare propaganda of blaming the Boers themselves, so be it. Any alternative opinion, any half-truth would do.

Emily thought she had discovered suffering, disease and death and was doing what she could to ameliorate them. Since her return, another alarming discovery was dawning on her, something perhaps even more disturbing: her own government's moral bankruptcy.

For the government, everything was at stake here. If they were to ask Kitchener to stop clearing the countryside and cease the herding of women and children into the camps, it would be more difficult for Kitchener to win the war. They would either have to give him more soldiers, more arms and more, hard-to-obtain horses – much more at great expense – or face the equally expensive option of a much longer war, a war of which the British people might tire. More than that, if the government admitted they had erred in the way the war was being waged, British public support for the war might evaporate quickly. Why, the public might ask, were they paying extra taxes for a war incompetently managed? Worse still, the public might begin to question the ethics of the conduct of the war. Down that road lay certain defeat at the next election. This was the danger posed by that Hobhouse woman. She had to be stopped from persuading the public at all costs. For them, it had nothing to do with the survival of Boer women and children in southern Africa; it had everything to do with the survival of the Unionist government in Britain.

Chapter 24

In search of the national conscience

Emily now began the speaking tour that had been planned to follow the release of her report. After the aborted Queens Hall meeting in London, her next destination was Oxford. Again the venue where she was to speak was withdrawn at the last minute. But the reaction was different. The university community did not fear differences of opinion and was less than impressed by an apparent attempt to silence Emily. Supporters rallied, alternative arrangements were rapidly made and she was able to address two alternative meetings, one at the Liberal Hall, the other at Balliol College.

The second happened when the wife of the Master of Balliol invited Emily to address an audience in the Master's Lodge. The Master, Edward Caird, a distinguished scholar and moral philosopher, presided over the meeting himself and concluded by expressing his support for Emily. The things she had described, he said, could not possibly go on.

Balliol was then already renowned for the academic achievements of its students, many of whom became prominent in public life.[223] Its alumni included Emily's deceased father who had maintained contact with the college during his lifetime and had been a friend of Caird's. Ironically, the alumni also included Alfred Milner and St John Brodrick, who knew each other from their undergraduate days there.

Caird's comments carried weight. The press was present and reported his remarks – positive publicity for Emily for a change[224] – and the meeting assumed a special significance for her. It provided encouragement at a critical moment when she might have feared that she would never get to put her case. At subsequent meetings, she referred to Caird's supportive words.

The Times reported the meeting objectively but carried the story on the same page as Hofmeyr's nasty attack[225] (see the previous chapter).

On 27 June 1901, Brodrick replied to Emily's request for government intervention to ameliorate the situation in the camps. His tone was conciliatory: the government had already taken the steps she recommended or would do so, as far as this was possible in the midst of war. These were weasel words, and Emily and her supporters realised that little would change. However, the letter did seem to contain one important concession: women who wished to leave the camps would be allowed to do so. It seemed a substantial step in the right direction and Kate Courtney congratulated Emily on this achievement.

It was, however, also a mirage. Camp departures required the permission of the military authorities and in the months that followed, that permission was granted to only a few, too few to have any material effect on the overcrowding and misery in the camps.

Emily continued her work, and in the weeks that followed she underwent a remarkable transformation. The concerned welfare worker became a resolute public campaigner. She travelled the country, addressing meetings wherever her supporters and friends could arrange an audience. That summer, she presented the case for urgent change in the camps at forty meetings.[226]

Just as she had travelled from camp to camp by herself in

southern Africa, so she made these travels mostly on her own, demonstrating again the great strength of character she possessed. This time she had assistance with the arrangements and was greeted and guided by sympathetic hands wherever she arrived.

There is no single record of her itinerary, but reports of individual events allow a reconstruction of her hectic and often tumultuous journey through England, as shown in the table below.

Some of the meetings addressed by Emily Hobhouse during June to August 1901

25 June	Oxford – two meetings[227]
28 June	Hull[228]
29 June	Scarborough[229]
30 June	York[230]
1 July	Leeds[231]
2 July	Manchester
3 July	Southport[232]
5 July	New Southgate (London)[233]
7 July	Liverpool[234]
8 July	Bristol[235]
9 July	Bristol[236]
11 July	Birmingham[237]
12 July	Scarborough[238]
14 July	Heywood[239]
17 July	Northampton[240]
18 July	Halifax[241]
19 July	Darlington[242]
20 July	Darlington – private meeting[243]
22 July	Huddersfield[244]
23 July	Bradford[245]
On or before 23 July	Gateshead[246]
On or before 24 July	Cheltenham[247]

14 August	Rochdale[248]
15 August	Oldham[249]
18 August	Sheffield[250]
25 August	Portsmouth[251]

As in London and Oxford, the advertised venues at Hull, Scarborough and York were withdrawn by the owners, the police or the local council just before the gatherings were due to take place on the grounds that they would cause a disturbance.[252] As at Oxford, meetings were hastily rearranged at alternative venues, all of which were provided by the Quakers. At York, Emily addressed an adult school at a meeting presided over by Joshua Rowntree, her strong Quaker supporter. He hailed from this region.

She was confronted with rowdy audiences almost everywhere she went. After her address at Southport, the police considered it prudent to escort her to safety. At Bristol, a reader wrote to the local paper of her second meeting as follows: *Mr Joseph Storrs Fry, the chairman, had a very trying time of it the whole of the time the meeting lasted, but he did his duty well. It was 20 minutes past 8 really before the meeting commenced and during the 20 minutes that was wasted Mr Fry rose from his seat 6 or 8 times trying to demand a hearing for Miss Hobhouse, and during this time chairs were uplifted, broken, and scattered in all directions. The scene was most exciting and tumultuous. I am of the strong opinion that there must have been arrangements made by the noisy mob amongst themselves prior to the meeting ...*[253]

At Darlington, County Durham, Emily had the toughest reception. *The Times*'s report on the event was brief: *Miss Emily Hobhouse attempted to hold a meeting at Darlington last evening on behalf of the South African war victims fund, but was unable to obtain a hearing. There were about 300 people present and Sir David and Lady Dale both unsuccessfully attempted to procure order. The audience sang the National Anthem and refused to listen.*[254]

Emily reminisced about this event later. *There was something extraordinarily impressive that night in the silent platform facing the silent massed hall – for one and a half hours. We sat out the time the speeches would have taken if delivered. In the midst of this order and silence, this serious purpose and repose, a tiny group of noisy roughs, empty and aimless. There was something symbolic about it, and in one way it was the most wonderful and impressive of all my meetings ...* [255]

She did succeed in addressing a small audience at the Dales' house the next day, so even this stop in her travels was not wholly fruitless.

In contrast, a large audience gave her a sympathetic hearing at Manchester and the meeting was followed by a supportive report in the *Manchester Guardian* the next day. The latter was a foregone conclusion; her brother, Leonard, was a journalist at this newspaper and sat by her side on the platform.

It was a difficult, lonely time. She was greeted by supporters and well-wishers wherever she went, but they were strangers and she had constantly to make the effort to socialise and deliver her message both privately and publicly. She wrote in her memoir:

Before me as I write lies a letter from the Chief Constable of York, suggesting that there would be a disturbance if I held my meeting there and that 'the results would be serious'. Pure nonsense! In Manchester the same effort was made to prevent the meeting, but the Chief Constable refused to give in and the meeting, the largest I held, was crowded and quiet and enthusiastic.

Such matters, contemptibly small in themselves, would not be worth mentioning were it not that it was continued throughout the country. For it shewed the determination on the part of the Government to prevent my appeal to national sentiment, and this opposition was accompanied by a whisper to the Chamberlain Press to vilify me – which it did, I believe, quite successfully do. I never read that Press but now and then

*picked up a paper in a railway carriage during my many
journeys and got a glimpse of the sort of thing that was said.
I also experienced much rudeness and ostracism in London
drawing-rooms. You see I have survived to tell the tale. Lived
also to sum up Governments as poor things more careful of
their own prestige than of justice and right. And always, when
the conduct of war is in question, devoid of conscience. ...*

*To me the great disappointment was that I was prevented
from adequately keeping my word to the Boer women, viz.
that I would tell the English People of their sufferings, and
I could not prove my assurances to them that our People, if
they knew, would set things right. Something, however, was
accomplished for considerable reforms were set going in the
camps ...*

*It would weary you to tell of all the meetings I spoke
at during those summer months. It was hard work, more
so than I could have imagined. I so well remember Lord
Ripon warning me it would be so. He had had experience of
stumping the country and he said: 'It's not the travelling or the
actual speaking that so fatigues, it's the social part ...'*

*I found he was right. Strength was drained by private
talk and the necessary civilities to a daily changing circle of
hospitable but quite unknown hosts. My Uncle was so good; he
gave me money to travel first class. Consequently I could write
and rest and think in the trains, and arrived fresh.*

*The meetings themselves were a joy. Though the larger halls
were made impossible by Government action, and the large
audiences whose sympathies were first deterred by being told
I was a rebel, traitor and such other libellous terms a foolish
Press delights in, halls there always were and crowded at that
and the relief was good of thus unburdening my message.*[256]

She steadily made converts. After one meeting she was approached
by an elderly man who drew a letter out of his pocket. ... *he said*

he had written [it] *denouncing me and all my works to The Birmingham Post. Then, hearing that I was to speak that night, he judged it prudent to refrain from posting it until he had heard what I was to say. 'And now,' he said, 'having heard you, it will not be posted.'* [257]

Towards the end of July, Emily was able to write to her brother Leonard, *Very good meetings everywhere, full and orderly.* [258] A few days later she described her meetings, again to Leonard, as *orderly, interested – moved – large everywhere except Cheltenham – it has been a feature that at most places large parts of the audience file past platform to shake hands. Have had to refuse many meetings through lack of time.* [259]

Brodrick agreed to see Emily again on 18 July and she again requested permission to return to southern Africa with a group of like-minded women. Attending to all the camps was more than one person could accomplish. The Secretary for War again declined. Later he put his decision in writing:

> *It would have been impossible for the Government to accept your services in this capacity while declining others, the more so as your reports and speeches have been made the subject of so much controversy; and I regret, therefore, we cannot alter the decision which I conveyed to you on 18th instant.* [260]

Despite ever-worsening news from the veld, the government was able to counter Emily's campaign effectively by trotting out a steady stream of letters from southern Africa to paint the opposite picture. *The Times* faithfully published them, then reinforced the comments in editorials. Hofmeyr's letter is a good example. The most egregious to follow was from Mrs KHR Stuart, who described herself as a Delegate of the Guild of Loyal Women of South Africa. She commented in a lengthy letter on Emily's report:

> *One realises the inherent goodness of her heart; but her report is apt to give wrong impressions to those who are*

*unacquainted with the habits of life and conditions of things
in South Africa, where intense heat, crowded tents, flies,
scarcity of milk, snakes, &c, are every-day occurrences. We
South Africans wonder to hear so much made of things which
we have always had to put up with.*

After more in similar vein, it ends: *I believe I am voicing the feeling
of women of South Africa, the British Isles, and the colonies when I say
that our soldiers have gained the heart of the Empire's womanhood by
their chivalrous treatment of the women and children of their bitter
and deadly foes. They have not only done splendidly against Boer shot
and shell, but have come off victors in the more deadly campaign of
calumny and slander that has been carried on against them.*[261] The
writer had read much into Emily's report that did not exist and
Emily said so in a full response, also published by *The Times*.[262]
But again doubt was effectively sown and the effort of dealing
with attacks like these took its toll.

Towards the end of July, a disheartened Emily decided to
withdraw for a few weeks and work on a substantial article to
further her objective. Despite her huge effort, the groundswell
of outrage against the government was not materialising. Moreover, a return to the camps remained barred. As long as the press
refused to change sides, the government could stare her down.
They had her measure. They had failed to stop her speaking tour,
but that did not matter.

However, Emily had achieved more success than she allowed
herself. She had raised the issue of the camps to national prom-
inence. Information was now systematically collected and news
from the camps was under the political spotlight. This would
soon prove crucial. Other organisations had begun to raise funds
and to make offers to assist the women and children in the camps.
They included the Victoria League, which, as the name hints, was
a women's organisation very much in support of the Empire. It
also offered to send women to the camps, promising they would

take an apolitical approach. Brodrick refused them too.

Emily's report was translated into French and German and circulated on the Continent. Even in the United States, her report attracted comment. This made life more difficult for her as each consequent adverse foreign comment on Britain's conduct of the war was noted in the English press. Some observers began to regard her campaign as traitorous. But in southern Africa, the flow of aid to the camps increased dramatically – from Switzerland, France, Germany and especially the Netherlands and even from Britain. The committee that Emily had started in Cape Town was able to send truck load after truck load of supplies to the camps. Goods and money were also distributed through other channels.

Much of this was invisible to Emily. What she experienced was unremitting attack in the press and in person, the rejection of her bid to return to the camps and the refusal of the government to cease farm destruction, reverse the concentration of civilians and improve the support for the people already concentrated.

Chapter 25

The camps tell
their own story

While Emily was telling one version and the government and its supporters another, the camps were writing their own story, and their version was not what the government wanted or expected.

By the end of June 1901, there were thirty camps for whites.[263] All were situated on the high plateau that occupies the interior of southern Africa except two in Natal and the one at Port Elizabeth. The number of black camps at this date is not known (at least to this researcher), but it is fair to suppose that many of the sixty-four or sixty-six that ultimately existed had already been created, all in the high interior.

The matter of altitude bears dwelling on for a moment. The highest camps (black and white) were at Belfast in the eastern Transvaal at 2,000 metres while the lowest of the interior camps, the still fledgling camp at Orange River Station, was at 1,100 metres. At least twelve of the white camps[264] and at least as many black camps were situated at a greater altitude than the highest point in the British Isles (Ben Nevis in Scotland, 1344 metres). Several camps were at higher altitudes than present-day ski resorts in Australia.

When Emily left southern Africa at the beginning of May, it was autumn and already cold; now it was winter and there were more people in the camps. In this season, the Highveld days are mostly dry, sunny and tolerable, but the night-time temperatures plunge and there is a hard frost. Unprotected water pipes freeze and burst. When the weather changes, the regular downpours of summer become the occasional blizzards of winter. Then a cutting wind turns the mean drizzle to driving snow and everything is blanketed in white. The eastern Highveld, where most of the Transvaal camps were located, is most prone to receive snow; elsewhere it is simply too dry but not necessarily any warmer.

The women and children, inadequately clothed in summer and with little more to wear in winter, were, of course, still living in tents. We know precious little about how they coped with the cold weather. Ironically, the overcrowding probably helped as they huddled together during the icy nights, sharing their body heat. And when the weather was at its worst? Did mothers still go outside to cook their raw food, or did everyone simply go hungry in the meagre shelter that the canvas provided until the weather got better? Or did they make fires inside the tents for heating as well as cooking despite the smoke and fire risk? Whatever they did, whatever they tried, for many it was not enough.

When he met Emily on 4 June, Brodrick could not yet know what the fatality rate for that month would be. He, Kitchener, Milner, Chamberlain, Balfour, Salisbury and others in the cabinet could still entertain their fond expectation that after the initial teething problems the difficulties would be ironed out, the camps would settle down and the fatality rate would fall. They could still dismiss the concerns of the doctors and the hysterics of Emily, the meddler. *We don't want to make them too comfortable*, Alfred Milner had said, himself very comfortable with his new lordship in the delightful English June.

When the June 1901 fatality figures reached England, they put an end to all the hubris. Even now, after more than a century, the information is disturbing: in the Transvaal there were 750 white deaths, a huge increase over the 338 in May. In the Orange River Colony, the fatalities increased from 335 to 395. The total, 1,145, represented a 70 per cent increase on the previous month.[265] These figures are from the official reports collected and printed as Command Paper 819: *Reports &c on the working of the Refugee Camps in the Transvaal, Orange River Colony, Cape Colony and Natal.* There were still no reports of mortality in the black camps.

For the second month in a row, the Bloemfontein camp, on whose behalf Emily had tried so hard, recorded the highest fatality rate in the ORC – 168 people had died in May and 137 in June.

The Times newspaper indicated that the white fatalities in June were 777 in total.[266] It might be forgiven the huge error – this *was* the information supplied in a preliminary government release. The figure is no less concerning; fatalities were rising. The notion that the high fatalities reported in May were a consequence of start-up difficulties and would decline was history. The trend was remorselessly upwards.

The publication of the June statistics was a consequence of Emily's campaign. Her many public talks during July and the constant attempts to counter her message in the press had brought the issue of the camps to national attention. That publicity meant that the troubling June fatality numbers could not be swept under the carpet. They had to be disclosed and reported, and so they were.

If bad news must be acknowledged, it is, of course, better to attribute the responsibility for it to someone else. Who better than the Boers? A common refrain was to blame them for continuing to resist the British conquest. If only they would stop fighting, the inmates could be released and the camp fatalities would cease. Another common line was to accuse them of abandoning women and children on the farms, of refusing to take responsibility for their families. Since the families had been surviving quite well without their husbands and fathers until their homes were destroyed, this charge did not stick very well. Now, with the rising camp fatalities, a much better scapegoat was found: the Boer women themselves.

General Maxwell, the Military Governor of Pretoria, wrote a few lines in a covering note that went with each set of monthly reports from the Transvaal to Kitchener. In May 1901 he highlighted just two issues. The first was a shortage of tents, the second read as follows: *The epidemic of measles has very considerably abated, but the death rate among the children is higher than it should be owing to the crass stupidity and neglect of the mothers themselves. One child suffering from dysentery was given a large raw carrot by its mother at Irene camp; the child died 4 hours afterwards.*[267] Kitchener passed the report on to London without comment.

Modern opinions may differ about the harm that a raw carrot can do, and one isolated case hardly explains hundreds of deaths. Nevertheless, with the alarming June fatalities, Maxwell strengthened his criticism: *Unfortunately, the death-rate amongst the children continues high owing to the prevalence of measles and the extremely cold nights. The Boer mother is greatly to blame, she insists on tending her children, refuses to obey the orders of the doctor, or the advice of the nurse; the Boer remedy for measles, apparently, is a tea made of goats' dung, this is administered with deplorable results. Another favourite remedy appears to be an absolute refusal to wash the children or any attempt at cleanliness.*[268]

Maxwell was the most senior administrator to put views like these on paper, but he was not alone. Elizabeth van Heyningen, a Cape Town academic, writes in her recent book: *Over and over again, in report after report, in casual asides and even, occasionally, in comments from the Boer side, camp officials and others remarked on the insanitary practices of country people.*[269]

It was a convenient deflection of responsibility, responsibility that would otherwise fall on the administration alone. However, the references are so pervasive that they warrant some consideration.

In some degree they were justified. In the second report on the Transvaal camps, the one to which Maxwell attached his 'raw carrot' comment, WK Tucker, the new general superintendent of camps[270], included a more considered remark: *Great attention is paid to the cleanliness of camps, though it must be regretted that the efforts of the Superintendents are not cheerfully assisted by the people themselves as a rule, and a small percentage of refugees whose habits are dirty often entails trouble and sickness on those who are careful.*[271]

Tucker's remark alludes to the diversity that existed among the camp residents, a theme of Van Heyningen's book, and she offers some historical context:

> *The concentration of the Boer families in the camps may be regarded as comparable to the rapid urbanisation experienced in nineteenth-century European and American industrial cities, where large numbers of rural people, with a pre-industrial culture, were concentrated in overcrowded and inadequate accommodation with few sanitary services. The fact that, in South Africa, this process occurred, temporarily, within the space of a few months, in the traumatic conditions of wartime, made the problems particularly acute ... In both cases, the authorities tended to blame the people concerned ...*[272]

Dr Kendal Franks was a medical 'consultant' to the British Army in Pretoria. As the death rate escalated he was sent to make additional inspections of the camps. His visits were invariably brief, and it is doubtful that he fully grasped the difficulties; nevertheless he became an outspoken critic of the Boer women. Yet he, too, recognised a broader context. After an inspection at Nijlstroom where some camp inmates were housed in the town he wrote: *One cottage I visited contained 19 people and a hut near it 10. They were both overcrowded, and the squalor and dirt would equal, if not surpass, some of the residences of the poor in the British Isles such as Whitechapel, St Giles and the Liberties in Dublin.* He added, *These people seemed perfectly happy and contented.*[273]

So, despite the lack of personal hygiene practised by some, the Boers in the camps were not meaningfully different from comparable communities elsewhere at that time. Emily Hobhouse had worked among the farm labourers and miners in her father's parish in Cornwall where she had visited the sick in their cottages. Later she had applied her energies on behalf of industrial workers in the East End of London and may have visited homes where even the children worked in the factories. She understood the context and refrained from hastily judging the people.

However, there is a more patent reason for the personal hygiene practices so criticised by the doctors and administrators: *Of course, it was extremely difficult to maintain a clean family under camp conditions*, wrote Van Heyningen, *especially in the first months when water and soap were in short supply and latrines were rudimentary trenches, up to half a mile from the tents.*[274]

The shortage of water and often simple absence of soap were highlighted by Emily, as we have seen. And, as indicated at the beginning of this chapter, the camps of the interior were at high altitude. In winter, the bucket of water a mother might use to wash herself, her children and everyone's clothes probably had a layer of ice on it in the morning. If she fetched a fresh bucket, the water would not have been much warmer. Heat the water? There was barely enough fuel for cooking. Persuade children to take their scanty clothes off in the bitter weather and submit to a wash in icy water? Many a weary mother would not have tried.

A widespread and serious complaint against the Boers was that they soiled the ground among the tents. Now consider that you are a mother with six children in a tent where even the inside temperature is near or below zero at night. You and your family survive by huddling together, sharing body heat under too few blankets. Someone needs to go to the toilet, someone with inadequate clothing for the temperature outside. There are no lights in the camp. Even candles were often not provided. The toilet facilities are hundreds of metres away, in a primitive and disgusting state and in pitch darkness. What would you tell your child to do? What would you do yourself?

And what about the camps for black people? At this juncture in the war, July 1901, no reports of black camp fatalities had reached London and it seems that no Dr Franks or his counterpart was sent to inspect the circumstances of the people in the black camps. Just about everything in these camps was worse than in the white camps: shelter, food, availability of fuel and sanitary facilities.[275] Yet when inspections did later begin, the familiar refrain was applied to them, too: *Inspector Daller attributed the high death rate among the children 'in a very large measure to the bad nursing of the mothers ... Natives do not seem to care for their children until they reach a useful age'.*[276] If some of the whites could be said to be in transition from a pre-industrial culture, the blacks were even more so. Whatever their difficulties, starvation rations and lack of clothing and effective shelter in very cold weather did not help.

It was also at about this time that the sober but highly critical report of the diplomats in Pretoria was sent confidentially to their governments and to Kitchener and Maxwell. Their concerns had turned out to be all too well justified. A copy would quickly have made its way to London. It had been written by independent, responsible people who had never met Emily Hobhouse. Yet it fully corroborated her report, and worse, it did so with information about camps that she had never seen.

With more than a thousand civilians dying in the camps that

month, the report would be damaging, politically speaking, if it were to become public. The foreign governments were too circumspect to say anything – for the present – but the government could not assume that a report that had received such wide geographical distribution would always remain out of view.

It knew that in the eyes of its peers it had been shown to be incompetent or worse, with appalling human consequences. Brodrick and Milner now probably wished they had paid more attention to Emily, had acted on her advice, had done more for the people in the camps, had called off the press pack persecuting her. A political storm was coming and they needed a response. Attacks on their critics as biased 'pro-Boers' and soothing reassurances that all was under control would no longer be sufficient. They had to *do* something, and Brodrick had quietly been planning for just such an eventuality.

Chapter 26

The government's response

Brodrick's response to the June fatalities in the camps was at once politically clever and a further excuse to delay doing anything, a delay and a strategy that would lead to even worse outcomes. An indication of his line of thinking appeared in a cable he sent to Lord Kitchener on 6 July 1901. It read:

> *Refugee Camps: We are keeping up our wickets against a storm of criticism. The question is being run on political lines and endless organisations want to send out people. We are refusing all but think of sending some half dozen ourselves. I will advise you by telegraph of the names.*[277]

On 22 July, Brodrick revealed the details of his plan: a committee of six women, headed by Mrs Millicent Fawcett, would go to southern Africa to report on the camps. He told the House of Commons that three of them had left for southern Africa that morning and that two were already in South Africa.

The advantages for Brodrick and the government were obvious. While the committee was investigating, it would be premature to act. Procrastination was now justified. The members were hand-picked, and in their report they could surely be relied on to produce the 'right' political result. All of them believed the war was just and that, in war, harsh things sometimes needed to be done. As a committee, it was unique. No commission consisting purely of women had ever been appointed by a British government. And because they were all women, no one would be able to argue that they did not understand the issues faced by women and children. The collective view of these six women would carry more weight than Emily's.

Shortly after the Ladies Committee, as it was soon called, was appointed, the parliament retired for its five-month summer recess. There could be no more scrutiny of the government's policies and no more questioning about events in southern Africa until the ladies had hopefully reported. By then - the cabinet must have hoped - the administration in southern Africa will have mastered the difficulties, and with a bit of luck, that troublesome Miss Hobhouse will have run out of steam. As ministers and MPs left London for their country estates or took their annual holidays in the south of France, Brodrick must have felt reasonably satisfied with himself.

But it was a wholly inadequate response. The situation demanded urgent action and little investigation was needed. The chief superintendents and the chief medical officers already had a reasonably comprehensive knowledge of the circumstances. The doctors in the camps could tell the administration immediately what had to be done; indeed they had largely done so. By instructing Kitchener to act on their advice, St John Brodrick had it in his power greatly to reduce future fatalities. Instead, by choosing the path he did, he must be held responsible for the consequences that ensued.

Emily was deeply dismayed by the delay implied in the appointment of the committee and affronted that she had not been included. In Britain, she knew more about the camps than anyone else and was the pre-eminent spokesperson for the victims. She was aware of the views of some on the committee and knew that they were not well disposed to the Boers or to her.

The leader of the committee, Millicent Garrett Fawcett, was at the time prominent in the campaign for women's rights and in the forefront of the suffrage movement. John Hall, Emily's biographer, gives a useful description of her:

> *Thirteen years Emily's senior, tiny in stature but supremely forceful in nature, this formidable character was a younger sister of Elizabeth Garrett Anderson, the first woman doctor to qualify in Britain, and the widow of a blind Cambridge professor and MP.*[278]

Though her own education had been cut short at the age of fifteen by money troubles in the family business, she was the first woman to be awarded an honorary doctorate by a British university. The award was for her pioneering work for women's higher education. By the time of her appointment she had written a biography of Queen Victoria and a bestseller on economics.

It seems that Emily had made an enemy of Mrs Fawcett before the war began by writing an article on behalf of tenants in an apartment project owned by the Fawcetts. And, says Hall, *Mrs Fawcett made a fearsome foe. She was quite as brimful as Emily of moral certitude and just as given to outbursts of righteous indignation. On the other hand, the frostiness of her demeanour was legendary, with no hint of Emily's excitability in her nature, and stout pillars of the Establishment were known to quail at her glance ... Mrs Fawcett never really tried to be tolerant of people whose opinions differed from her own ... And by the time of the Boer War, no name bore a blacker mark than that of Emily Hobhouse.*[279] *Where Mrs Fawcett parted from Emily irreconcilably was in her fervent Imperialism, grounded in her conviction that the British were a very great people with a mission to rule others.*[280]

Millicent Fawcett had written a letter to the editor of the *Westminster Gazette*, a London paper, disparaging Emily's report on the camps and some historians think this might have put the idea into Brodrick's mind of appointing her the leader of the committee.[281]

The other members of the delegation – Katherine Brereton, Lucy Deane, Lady Alice Knox, Dr Ella Scarlett and Dr Jane Waterston – were hardly more encouraging. Lady Knox was the wife of one of Kitchener's generals. There was no possibility that she would recommend a change in the way the war was being conducted. Dr the Hon Ella Scarlett, a medical doctor of aristocratic background, accepted her appointment with a letter that said, in part: *The refugees are ungrateful, dirty beyond description, and never speak the truth; they have heard something of the pro-Boer agitation at home, and try to be impertinent.*[282]

Dr Waterston was the first female doctor to practise in southern Africa and had already crossed paths with Emily. In Cape Town, she had vetted and appointed nurses for the concentration camps; Emily had found some unsuitable. In a letter that appeared in the *Cape Times* newspaper two days after her appointment was announced, Dr Waterston wrote: *This war has been remarkable for two things – first the small regard that the Boers from the highest to the lowest have for their womenkind, and secondly the great care and consideration the victors have had for the same, very often ungrateful women. Let this be well ground into the minds of our English pro-Boers ... At present there is the danger that the Boers will waken up to have a care for their womenfolk, and will go on fighting for some time, so as to keep them in comfortable winter quarters at our expense, and thus our women and children will lose a few more of their husbands and fathers.*[283]

Katherine Brereton was a nursing sister who had run a hospital for British soldiers in southern Africa and was therefore, like Lady Knox, close to the army. Lucy Deane was an inspector of factories in the United Kingdom and also an expert on infant welfare. Her father, Colonel Bonar Deane, had died in a battle with the Boers in 1881 during the Anglo-Transvaal war.[284] They were capable women and each brought relevant capacities to the mission, but none of the six could be described as independent and open-minded, and the task they had been set did not meet the urgency of the situation. From Emily's point of view, the prospects for the mission were not auspicious.

The team assembled in Cape Town to plan and prepare for their venture. Whatever their politics, they were determined to be systematic and thorough, and they agreed on a list of twenty-two chief points of investigation at each camp. It included water supply and water quality, sanitation, housing, rations and hospital facilities – as might be expected – but it also contained a few items that raise a wry smile: *Kitchens, whether central or private?* and *Are servants allowed, and if so, are they rationed?*[285]

In the introduction to their eventual report, they mention a policy decision they made at the outset: *We endeavoured, as far as circumstances permitted, to make surprise visits to the camps, and with this object we did not invariably pursue the most direct and obvious route from camp to camp. In no case, it is unnecessary to say, did we announce beforehand our proposed visit to the superintendent.*[286]

Caroline Murray and others from Emily's circle of influence in Cape Town met with Mrs Fawcett after she landed, but they found that she and her team were not interested in what they had to say. Offers to accompany the committee on its journey were firmly declined.

In making their plans, they missed other opportunities to become better informed. Had they spoken with Emily in London and, in southern Africa, the chief superintendents of the camps in the Transvaal and the Orange River Colony, they might have adopted a different approach. The chief superintendents would have been made available to brief them, had they requested it. Instead, they elected to start from scratch and do it all on their own. The time it took for them to discover what others already knew would cost many lives.

They were provided with a railway carriage which had a kitchen and dining facilities. Each member had a private compartment and was allowed to bring a servant or assistant. Mrs Fawcett took her adult daughter. They also had interpreters, attendants and guards on board, some of whom would do the cooking. Their travels would be far different from the lonely hardships that Emily had endured.

They set forth, bypassed several camps and arrived for their first inspection at Mafeking on 20 August 1901, a month after their appointment had been announced in the Commons. It was the new camp, closer to town than the one Emily had seen and much larger.[287] Was the choice of this camp a coincidence, or had someone had a word with them? They had arrived at the worst camp of all.

The day before they arrived in Mafeking, *The Times* published the camp statistics for the month of July: white children's fatalities, 1,124; total white deaths 1,412.[288] The accompanying note said: *The corresponding figures for June, 1901, were published in The Times of 25th July.* Since most people would have thrown away that old newspaper long ago and forgotten the previous numbers, few would have realised that these fatalities were 82 per cent higher than the erroneous figures reported the previous month.

The Times again relied on information released by the government (Cd 608, Cd 694). However, the July fatalities were again under-reported. According to the later official reports, 1,694 white people had died that month, nearly one-and-a-half times as many as in June.[289] The situation was completely out of control.

For the first time, *The Times* also reported fatalities in the black camps of the ORC: children 164, total 256.[290] Black deaths in the Transvaal remained unreported.

At about the time that Brodrick announced the Ladies Committee in the Commons in response to the disturbing June fatalities, Lord Kitchener asked Major-General Edward Locke Elliot to take command of a significant new 'drive', this time through the north-western Orange River Colony. Beginning on 28 July 1901, Elliot started at the Vaal River near Klerksdorp and torched and scorched his way south across a 150 kilometre-wide front to the west of the central railway line. He reached his destination, the Modder River, on 10 August.

In military terms, the drive produced insignificant results. Seven thousand Imperial soldiers killed just nine Boers and captured 259, few of whom would have been combatants.[291] The number of women, children, elderly and disabled that were driven into the camps or escaped to fend for themselves in a denuded landscape was never reported and is probably unknown. But the number of people in the ORC camps increased by more than 10,000 in July and August.

A young, English-educated lawyer passed through the region in Elliot's wake. Riding across the veld among burnt houses and destroyed farms, he wrote in his diary: *Dams everywhere full of rotting animals, water undrinkable. Veld covered with slaughtered herds of sheep and goats, cattle and horses. The horror passes description …*[292]

This young Boer was Jan Christiaan Smuts, the former state attorney of the Transvaal and now the newest Boer general. He and Emily Hobhouse were destined to have much to do with each other.

Chapter 27

The ladies investigate

Millicent Fawcett and her fellow committee members steamed back and forth across the Highveld and saw all but one of the white camps. Once they had made up their minds to be thorough and systematic, the outcome was inevitable. Pakenham sums it up well: *If Brodrick expected them to add a ladylike coat of whitewash to the camps, Brodrick was in for a surprise. ... In their criticisms of the camp system, Mrs Fawcett and her Commission confirmed in all essentials the accuracy of Emily Hobhouse's account and the long-overdue nature of her proposed reforms.*[293]

At camp after camp, they cross-examined superintendents, talked to doctors and nurses, inspected the makeshift hospitals, tested water quality, inspected latrines and issued lists of recommendations. In both colonies, the administrations had let it be known that camp superintendents were to implement these recommendations immediately. As a consequence, much had already been accomplished by the time the committee signed their 206-page report in Durban on 12 December 1901.

The document sets the tone on the cover. It is a 'Report on the Concentration Camps in South Africa' – no more talk of 'refugee camps' or 'burgher camps'. *The differences existing between different camps,* they wrote, *are so striking that it would be misleading to attempt any but a very few generalisations concerning them, and the answers to our enquiries must be sought in the separate reports given on each camp.*[294]

They tried to give Brodrick what he wanted – approval of what existed – and they found much to acknowledge and even praise: great efforts had been made, there were ample supplies of 'medical comforts' in camp hospitals and the hospitals themselves reflected credit on the administration. In this respect, it seems that there had been improvements since Emily's departure in May. They also approved of other changes that had been made since Emily had left, such as the schools and shops that were now in every camp. But they could not deny that what they found fell far short of what should have existed.

Many elements were important in making a good camp, they wrote, *but the most important of all is to be found in the character and capacity of the superintendent.* They acknowledged the difficulties that must exist in finding good superintendents, but did not shirk from doing what was needed: *We felt it our duty on more than one occasion to recommend the removal of a superintendent from his post.*[295]

As for the high death rates, they ascribed these to three groups of causes. The first was the insanitary condition of the country caused by war. *It is a truism*, they wrote, *to say that pestilence follows in the track of war* and described how the large number of dead and diseased animals across the land fouled water sources and spread disease. Moreover, *Ordinary industries, such as the production of food stuffs and the rearing of cattle are brought to a standstill all over the theatre of war, with the consequence that in some districts no fresh meat, no fresh milk, and no fruit or vegetables are obtainable for love or money.*[296] The result was predictable: *Wherever a community of little children is found who have to be fed without fresh milk, fresh vegetables, or eggs and sometimes without fresh meat, then a high death-rate will follow as certainly as night will follow day.*[297] But they made no reference to Kitchener's scorched earth policy that in this war was principally responsible for creating the conditions so dangerous to the local population.

The second group of causes were those within the control of the inmates themselves. As shown in Chapter 25, this was a favourite topic of doctors, superintendents and men all the way up the hierarchy to London. The committee described with dismay the fouling of the camp environment with human excreta and the danger this causes, especially of enteric. *It should be remembered that this habit, which is such a source of danger in camp life, where 5,000 or 6,000 people are gathered together in a comparatively small area, is comparatively harmless in the life to which the average Boer is accustomed, where family is separated from family by miles of open country.*[298] They were hardly in a position to speak of the Boer way of life before the war. And they had to concede that the toilet facilities provided by the authorities were often inadequate, especially for children. For example, at Bethulie they wrote: *It is only fair to add that, with the exception of the school latrine, the latrine accommodation was so extremely bad that there is much excuse for fouling the ground.*[299]

The committee reported that the inmates did not trust the hospitals and often declined to commit even seriously ill children. Keeping them in the tents increased the risk and rate of contagion. *Boers, not unlike the more ignorant of the English poor, strongly object to hospital treatment of their children.*[300]

Also dangerous were some of the Boer notions regarding the treatment of disease. *It would be possible to fill pages of this report with accounts of the extraordinary treatment adopted by Boer women for the supposed benefit of their sick children.*[301] Many a child had fallen victim to laudanum poisoning and they recount a litany of misconceived home remedies. In one case, they said, a woman painted the bodies of her two children, ill with measles, with common green paint so that both died of arsenic poisoning.

This [prevalence of misconceived home remedies] *is also a difficulty with which every doctor in England is familiar, and with regard to the character of the Boer domestic pharmacopoeia, no doubt parallel horrors could be found in old-fashioned English family receipt [sic] books of 150 or 200 years ago. But whatever parallels can be found, or excuses made, for these practices, in estimating the causes of the high death rate in the camps, we are bound to take them into account.*[302]

The third set of causes contained those within the control of the administration. *There can be little doubt*, they wrote, *that in the first instance the military did not take sufficiently into account the difference necessary between the treatment of women and children and that of soldiers.*[303] They mention overcrowding as an example, selection of sites as another. While the water supply and sanitation was admirable in some camps, ... *in others either water supply, or sanitation, and in some cases both of these, are distinctly bad; we would single out as among the worst examples, as we saw them on our first visit, Mafeking, Aliwal North, Middelburg, Belfast, Kroonstad and Standerton, while for an ill-chosen site Merebank has an unenviable priority. ... In some camps we found extremely impure water being used even in the dispensary, unboiled and unfiltered.*[304]

They continue:

It ought to have been foreseen that a dietary without fresh milk, vegetables, or meat would be followed by a lowering of vitality and that scurvy would almost certainly result, and earlier precautions ought to have been taken to prevent it.

And:

Again, when once the formidable character of the measles epidemic, followed as it was by pneumonia and kindred diseases, made itself evident, more strenuous and earlier exertions ought to have been made to secure the services of an adequate supply of efficient doctors and nurses to cope with the outbreak.[305]

Not much here to cheer Brodrick.

During their travels, Mrs Fawcett and her committee returned to some camps to review progress. Some of their recommendations addressed deficiencies Emily had highlighted months earlier: there should be, they recommended, boilers for sterilising drinking water, more food and better diets, more fuel, beds so that people would not have to sleep on the ground, more nurses and doctors and camp matrons. They went much further: public bake ovens to be run by the camp administration, water engineers to secure an adequate volume of water of suitable quality for each camp, more teachers (at least 100 more for the ORC alone), an increased allocation of rail trucks to carry supplies to the camps, adequate local transport for the removal of refuse and bringing in of water and fuel where this was needed, and mandatory work by all male inhabitants *for the good of the camp*.[306] They met both Kitchener and Milner and impressed upon them the urgency of action and the importance of making resources available.

There were, of course, things the Ladies Committee did not include in their report. They did not, like Emily, question the whole policy of concentration. Nor did they recommend that farm burning should stop. This was not their business. If the soldiers chose to clear the land, then that was not for them to discuss.

They did not report on the black camps — this was outside their terms of reference — but Van Heyningen cites evidence that Deane and Waterston, members of the committee, did visit some of them.[307]

There was something else they did not mention. The name 'Emily Hobhouse' appeared nowhere in their report despite the congruence of their findings with hers.

Despite the committee's efforts, the fatalities in the camps rose further and remained at an alarmingly high level. The figures for the white camps were: August, 2,665 (an increase of nearly 1,000 over July); September 2,548; October 3,217; November 2,951; December 2,437.[308] In every month of their visit, the fatalities were higher than in any month before their arrival.

In the black camps the fatality rates also climbed relentlessly: August, 575 (the first month for which full statistics were purportedly available); September, 728; October, 1,327; November, 2,312; December, 2,831.[309] In that December, the month in which the Ladies Committee delivered their report, the camp population – white and black – exceeded 200,000 and 5,268 people died in them.

The unfortunate Mafeking camp set the record for the monthly fatality rate in the white camps. In October 1901, 406 people perished there, 8.5 per cent of the camp population. If that number of people had died there every month, everyone would have been dead in less than a year.

Alfred Milner returned to southern Africa in August 1901. After the peerage that had been bestowed upon him and the approving social life he had enjoyed in consequence, it was back to grim reality. The camps were ultimately his responsibility. The situation had deteriorated badly in his absence and was still deteriorating. His superior, Joseph Chamberlain, the Colonial Secretary, was now aware of the high mortality and was soon in correspondence with him. At first Chamberlain was supportive, helping, for example, to arrange for additional nurses and doctors as recommended by Millicent Fawcett's team.[310] But when the September reports arrived in early November and it was clear that the death rate was not declining, he sent a lengthy and pointed telegram to Milner.[311]

You are now ... in a position to exercise full control of the
arrangements for all camps, it began, making it clear where
he considered the responsibility resided, and continued:
It is necessary, in view of your responsibility that I should be
satisfied that all possible steps are being taken to reduce the
rate of mortality, especially among children, and that full and
early reports of the state of the camps should be sent to me.
He set out in detail the information he wanted and asked
multiple questions.

Milner got the message. Within days he issued comprehensive
instructions to the camp administrators. The most important part
of this missal was his reference to costs: *It is clearly the desire of His*
Majesty's Government that expense should not be allowed to stand
in the way, when it is a question of providing anything necessary to
improve the health of the camps.[312] Later Chamberlain reinforced
that point.[313]

Finally, what needed to be done could be done. The tide turned
and the mortality rate declined quite rapidly. By April 1902 the
camp population was higher than ever, but the total fatalities in
that month – black and white – were down to 891.

The war ended the following month, on 31 May 1902, but
that was not the end of the camps or the camp fatalities. Most
of the residents had nowhere to go, and the camp population
increased still further as guerrillas who had laid down their arms
joined their families in the tents. They, too, were homeless. Then
the slow process of rebuilding the devastated country and empty-
ing the camps began.

Inevitably, the credit for the reduction in camp fatalities went
mostly to the Ladies Committee. Emily Hobhouse never received
any recognition for her role. Though Millicent Fawcett would
have hated to admit it, the work of the Ladies Committee was

merely a continuation of the process Emily had begun. The questions that her supporters had asked in the parliament using the information she had supplied, had caused Brodrick to ask for routine reports on the camps from Kitchener. It was due to her public campaign that the government could not keep the distressing fatalities secret when the information arrived, nor could the papers avoid publishing them. Without that information, the seriousness of the concentration camp situation might have taken longer to register, the Ladies Committee would not have been appointed when it was and Chamberlain might not have realised what was happening until months later.

There are other reasons why the fatalities declined. For a start, the weather, though it took until mid-summer before the grim reaper's harvesting abated. Not only did the temperature become more benign, the spring and summer rains also led to the gradual improvement in the availability, quality and variety of food.

Kitchener applied a new twist which also made a difference. In December 1901 he gave orders that no more people were to be brought into the camps.[314] As the camp populations stabilised, the superintendents were able to get on top of the situation and no further disease was introduced by the arrival of sick and contagious people. However, the destruction of homes and burning of farms did not cease. Just as the camps were becoming safer, the new victims were simply abandoned in the vastness of the veld without shelter and often without food. Kitchener thought this would put more pressure on the guerrillas to surrender. It eventually did. The Boers feared not only for the lack of shelter and food that their families were made to endure, but also for their security in a country where racial animosities were very much alive.

There is another, disturbing reason why the camp mortality

declined – the children, especially the small children, were mostly dead. An early indication of this reached Emily in August 1901 in a letter from Mrs Krause, one of the women who had worked with her in the Bloemfontein camp. Mrs Krause wrote from Germany where she had joined her husband in exile, that she had learnt that in one part of the camp nearly all the children were dead.[315]

The officials knew it, too. On 4 December 1901, Milner wrote to Goold-Adams to express his disappointment that the fatalities in the Orange River Colony had risen again in the second half of November. He said: *The theory that all the weakly children being dead, the rate would fall off, is not so far borne out by the facts. I take it the strong ones must be dying now, and that they will all be dead by the spring of 1903![316]* The exclamation mark is Milner's.

Two weeks later, on 19 December, WK Tucker, the General Superintendent of Camps in the Transvaal, reported that there had been a marked improvement in the death rate in that colony. He predicted that this improvement would continue and gave several reasons. The first reads, *The weak and emaciated have largely died out.[317]* Tucker was too circumspect to explain who the 'weak' were.

Today the best-preserved Boer War concentration camp site in South Africa is probably the one located on the farm Doornbult, a kilometre or so from the Orange River railway station where the Orange River Camp once stood. The camp was established later than most as an overflow for Kimberley. The land is now private property and there is no town at this isolated railway station. After the war, the site was simply abandoned and forgotten. The low rainfall makes the region unsuitable for ploughing and growing crops. The farmers keep sheep and cattle, but the stocking ratio is very low and over the last 110 years there has been little to disturb the site.

When the farm changed hands twenty years ago, the site's significance was rediscovered by the new owners. Today one can still discern circular bare patches where some of the bell tents once stood. Relics abound – empty condensed milk cans (still clearly dated), broken and makeshift cooking utensils, children's toys improvised from bones, wire and cans, and much more. The rectangle where the hospital marquee was located is clear and a mound identifies the position of the hospital kitchen's rubbish tip. A pre-war, two-roomed, stone building near the railway line is intact. It accommodated the camp doctor for a while, then served as home for the Canadian nurses who worked there.

A disused windmill of later vintage marks the well that was for a time the sole, inadequate water supply. In this dry country-side its yield was so low that water could only be drawn for an hour in the morning and an hour in the evening. It is a considerable distance from the tents and its location brings home the difficulties the residents faced. They had to fetch and carry their own water.

The owners of the farm, Lemmer and Rina Wiid, have worked hard to obtain recognition for the historical significance of this place and they have had some success. It now has a degree of protection and a large padlock on the gate discourages unaccompanied visitors. Through assiduous research, Rina and a co-author have established the names of all 268 people who died there. The list appears in their book, together with a few details on each person.[318] Two hundred and sixteen were children. Not all the ages at death are shown, but the ages that are known indicate that more than half of all those who died in this camp were children below the age of four.

Rina and Lemmer fenced and restored the camp cemetery at their own expense. She has been able to determine who lies in each grave. Often it is more than one little corpse. After Rina had shown us around the cemetery, she said quietly, in Afrikaans, *Teen die einde het die sterftes afgeneem. Daar was nie meer kindertjies nie.*

226

[Towards the end the deaths declined. There were no more little children.][319]

One comes away with a lump in the throat, bereft of words. For the children of the camps, especially the little ones, Brodrick's Ladies Committee was too late.

Cemetry of the Orange River Camp

Chapter 28

Torment

While Brodrick's ladies were travelling from camp to camp along the railway lines of southern Africa, Emily was experiencing a difficult time in England. She was exhausted from her campaigning and deeply frustrated that she had been sidelined by the government. Through July, August and September, the news from the veld was all dire. Her correspondents told her so and *The Times* published the rising fatality figures. And she was powerless to do anything about it. By August, the parliament was in recess, so no one could hold the government to account for the deterioration.

Her story was no longer current. People preferred to wait for reports from the new camp visitors, visitors who could inspect all the camps, not just the few that Emily had been allowed to see, and who would provide up-to-date information.

Emily wished she could return. Since leaving Cape Town she had asked repeatedly for permission to visit the camps again, to see for herself how things stood and to make herself useful. But that avenue, too, was closed. The government had succeeded in one of their objectives – making Emily ineffective. The realisation of this added to her frustration and she kept searching for a way around the barriers.

When in late September the camp statistics for the month of August were published showing another large increase in the number of people who had died,[320] Emily could contain her frustration no more. She wrote a lengthy open letter to the Secretary for War.[321] It was published in *The Times* and said, in part:

Sept. 29, 1901

Dear Mr Brodrick,

Three months have passed since I approached you on the subject of the Concentration Camps in South Africa, three terrible months in the history of those camps. Can the appalling figures just shown in the Government returns for August and the preceding month pass unnoticed by the Government and the great mass of the English people? Will you bear with me for a moment if I approach you again on this sad topic ...

Will nothing be done? Will no prompt measures be taken to deal with this terrible evil? Three months ago I tried to put this matter strongly before you, and begged permission to organise immediately alleviatory measures, based on the experience I had acquired, in order thus to avert a mortality I had plainly seen as increasing. My request was refused, and thus experience which I could not pass on to others rendered useless. The repulse to myself would have mattered nothing, had only a large band of kindly workers been instantly despatched with full powers to deal with each individual camp as its needs required. The necessity was instant if innocent human lives were to be saved.

She excoriated Brodrick for the three months lost while the Ladies Committee was selected, appointed, travelled to southern Africa and began its enquiries, and she went on: *Will you not now, with the thought before you of those 3,245 children who have closed their eyes forever since I last saw you, on their behalf, will you not now take instant action, and endeavour thus to avert the evil results of facts patent to all, and suspend inquiry into the truth of what the whole world knows?* She urged that her proposals be implemented instead and then asked:

> *Yet is it not conceivable that we might go further? The men cannot end the war. The women will not end the war. Cannot children help to bring about that peace that both sides so earnestly desire? Thousands have given their innocent lives. Thousands more are sick and like[ly] to die. Is it not enough? What the children need of proper food, clothing, and shelter cannot be brought to them; transport is too difficult, supplies too scarce. They must die, die where we have placed them, in their hundreds and their thousands, unless the war ends and sets them free. 'The cry of the children' comes to us now not from our own mines and factories, but from across the seas. Will it be heard and answered?*

Brodrick, she insisted, must end the war by offering the Boers terms they could accept.

The rhetoric was soaring, the logic undeniable, the politics disastrous. Brodrick did not respond; he did not have to.

Of this letter Emily wrote years later, *I wrote it in a white heat of feeling consequent upon the last issue of the death-rate of those months.*[322] This was an admission that acting in the white heat of the moment is usually not the wisest thing to do. Even friends and supporters wondered what Emily hoped to achieve by this open letter.

The Times published a response a few days later in the form of a letter to the editor.[323] It read:

Sir, In a letter published in to-day's issue of The Times *Miss Emily Hobhouse makes an impassioned appeal to Mr Brodrick on the subject of the mortality and suffering among the Boer children now congregated in the concentration camps provided by the English Government. As to the accuracy of her facts and figures, or the extent to which the suffering, great as it may be, has been mitigated by the humane efforts of our people, I have nothing to say which you would think worthy of place in your columns, where the matter has been debated and elucidated with more knowledge than I can pretend to. But I must confess that among the many amazing utterances which the war in South Africa has inspired, not one seems to me more amazing than Miss Hobhouse's assumption that, although the Boer men – and I understand her to add the Boer women also – are not moved one hair's-breadth in the direction of surrender by the sickness and death of their children, yet it is very barbarous on the part of the British Empire not to end the war at all costs because there is sickness and death among the offspring of these people! She clearly has not the slightest hope that the fathers of these children will give up a losing cause to save the little ones, but we – we British – are not to be 'deaf to the cry,' &c! A more severe indictment against the Boers, male and female (from Miss Hobhouse's point of view) could scarcely be framed. I am glad the accusation comes from so enthusiastic an advocate of their side, and is not brought by any prejudiced patriot in these islands. A charge of inhumanity such as this is perhaps deserved, but would certainly be passionately denied and vehemently resented if made by,*

Sir, your obedient servant,
An Insignificant Englishwoman.

The letter is typical of the attacks Emily endured. To many readers it would have seemed a telling response and it must have had some political effect. But there is another way of looking at it. The number of children condemned to die in the camps each month was now much greater than the number of burghers the Imperial forces could hope to kill or capture in combat. The letter was tantamount to justifying warfare in which the enemy is brought to surrender by inflicting hardship and death on their children. Whether intentional or otherwise, the consequences were the same. Not too many in Britain would have been comfortable had they understood the equation that was being drawn.

Many Boers *were* troubled by the dilemma they were in and were contemplating surrender for the sake of their families.

By the time her open letter to Brodrick appeared in print, Emily had already decided what her next move would be. The government's refusal to give her permission to return to southern Africa applied only to the war zone as demarcated by districts under martial law. As a law-abiding citizen, there was nothing to prohibit her from travelling to Cape Town. At risk of becoming irrelevant in England, and feeling frustrated and impotent, she had made up her mind. She would go there.

Chapter 29

At sea again

Emily arranged for a nurse, Elizabeth Phillips, to accompany her on the new voyage to Cape Town.[324] Her health had deteriorated under the stress of the speaking campaign and subsequent events, and she felt she could well do with some assistance. After their arrival, Nurse Phillips would stay in southern Africa and work there, possibly in the camps if that could be arranged.

Their departure was booked for 5 October 1901 on the *Avondale Castle*. When Emily made her reservation, she asked the shipping company, the Union Castle Line, to omit her name from the passenger list and they agreed. She said she needed rest on the voyage, rest that only anonymity could bring.

Her family and supporters were not sure what Emily hoped to achieve by undertaking this journey. The answer she gave was that she wished to investigate the circumstances of the British refugees in the port cities. These were people who had fled the republics when war was declared but lacked the means to travel home to Britain or who wished to return to the former republican territories when the war was over. Many of them were miners from the Transvaal gold fields and they and their families were said to be struggling in Cape Town, Port Elizabeth, East London and Durban.

The cause was valid but hardly in the same league as her previous endeavours, and no one quite believed that this was all that Emily had in mind. Her commitment was, after all, to the women and children in the concentration camps. Perhaps the attraction was that in Cape Town she would have access to information about the camps that she could not get in Britain, possibly even firsthand accounts.

Her brother, Leonard, came to see her off at Southampton and he repeated the concern he had expressed earlier: the port cities could be placed under martial law. If this happened, it could spell trouble for Emily. She would then be under the direct control of the military authorities who had wide powers. Large areas of the Cape Colony and Natal were already under martial law – as were the former republics – and there was talk that the port cities would follow.

Emily travelled first class, dined at the Captain's table and soon recovered something of her old spirit. Safely at sea, she disclosed her identity to all who cared to know; anonymity was no longer important. When other passengers found out who she was, many turned their backs. But a few took an interest in her. One sceptic, Miss Steedman, was on her way to become the headmistress of a girls' school in Bloemfontein and wished to learn all she could about the place, the country and its people. Emily had relevant knowledge. They talked, Steedman was converted and they became enduring friends.

The name 'Anonymous' on the passenger list had attracted the attention of a sniffing journalist who succeeded in discovering the identity of the passenger behind the intriguing designation. As a consequence, the Colonial Office became aware that Miss Hobhouse was again on her way to southern Africa and the telegraph lines informed Milner and Kitchener that she was heading in their direction. Aboard the *Avondale Castle* on the high Atlantic, Emily had no way of knowing of this development.

Meanwhile, events in the war had taken a turn that would have a far-reaching influence on Emily.

A month before Emily's departure, Jan Smuts, the former State Attorney of the Transvaal, had led a new invasion of the Cape Colony. This young man already had a history that set him apart from the ordinary. He was born in the Cape Colony and his family still lived there. After topping his law class at Cambridge and being admitted to the Bar in London, he returned to practise law in Cape Town. But his political sympathies lay with the emerging Afrikaner nation, he was a republican at heart and he went to Pretoria where the cause was most clearly crystallised and he became a republican citizen. The ageing President Paul Kruger recognised his abilities and appointed him to be his legal advisor and state attorney.

When, during the war, Kruger left the country to go into voluntary exile in Europe, Smuts sought and received his permission to turn his hand to soldiering. He admired General de la Rey, a skilful strategist, and asked to join him in the western Transvaal. There Smuts showed he was as tough as he was smart. After campaigning for a time in the Transvaal, learning his new business quickly, he persuaded the Boer leaders to allow him to launch a new invasion of the Cape Colony.

His prospects looked slim. He took just two hundred men. They had adequate horses but were poorly equipped in almost every other respect. After a year of guerrilla fighting, some of the men had just a handful of bullets for ammunition, their clothing was reduced to rags, and they used makeshift sandals for shoes. Smuts chose especially high country near Basutoland to cross the Orange River and they endured extreme cold, riding miserably through sleet and rain.

Kitchener assigned General French to stop Smuts's invasion and, as anticipated, they rushed thousands of troops to the region. But the audacious Smuts and his men evaded capture, sometimes narrowly, and advanced far into the Colony. They raided British encampments for supplies and attracted volunteers to their cause as they went. By early October they were better equipped, stronger in number and near enough to Port Elizabeth to see the city lights at night.

Smuts was too sensible to tackle a large, heavily defended city like Port Elizabeth. He split his commando in two to make pursuit more difficult and the getting of supplies off the land less onerous on the resident population. He turned his men to the north-west, the two detachments going by different routes. But his brief sojourn in the proximity of Port Elizabeth gave Kitchener an opportunity he had been looking for and he again urged the Cape Colonial Government to agree to the declaration of martial law in the coastal cities. Now that Smuts had demonstrated the threat, they reluctantly agreed. On 9 October 1901, while Emily was still at sea, martial law was declared in all the Cape ports. The event foreshadowed in Leonard's warning had materialised.

By the time Smuts reached the north-western Cape Colony, a remarkable 1,600 kilometres from his entry point, he was in command of two thousand burghers, all much better equipped than the small band with whom he had launched his invasion. He now had sufficient strength to take control of a substantial region and he remained in control of it until the war ended. In the light of the effort and resources committed to stopping and capturing him, it was a remarkable achievement, all the more so for a man just thirty-one years old in a society that looked to older men for leadership.

Smuts went on to great things. After the war, he became reconciled to British colonisation, taking the view that further resistance was futile and a better outcome for his people could be achieved through co-operation. When Britain restored self-government to the new colonies, he played a key role in unifying southern Africa. He became prime minister of the united South Africa during both world wars. Concurrently, he commanded Allied troops during those wars and was a member of the small

Imperial War Cabinet in London on both occasions. His international status is indicated by the fact that he is the only person whose signature appears on the peace treaties that ended both world wars. He worked with President Woodrow Wilson on the founding of the League of Nations and was later also directly involved in the establishment of the United Nations. By then, he and Winston Churchill were good friends. His election as chancellor of Cambridge University, a position he held to his death, was just one of the many honours bestowed upon him. A statue of Jan Smuts stands in Parliament Square in London not far from the statue of Winston Churchill.

This busy man became a friend and supporter of Emily Hobhouse and they corresponded to the end of her life. In later years, Emily began her letters to him with 'Dear Oom Jannie', 'oom' being an Afrikaans term of familiarity, endearment and respect.

But all that lay in the future. On board the *Avondale Castle* steaming towards Cape Town, Emily had not yet heard the name of Jan Smuts and she had no way of knowing that her life was about to be cast into new and deeper turmoil.

Chapter 30

Troubled endings

Kitchener and Milner agreed that Emily Hobhouse should not be allowed to land when the ship reached Cape Town. Under martial law, Kitchener had the authority to prevent her and he issued orders that she be turned back.

When the *Avondale Castle* arrived on 27 October 1901, there was, once again, no berth immediately available and she dropped anchor in the bay. A steam tug soon drew alongside bearing a Lieutenant Lingham. He ordered that no passengers be allowed to disembark and proceeded to interview every one of them, more than four hundred in all. When Emily's turn came, he sent her to the back of the queue, saying he wanted to see her last. Being singled out in this way was ominous, so when he finally turned to her, she asked to see him in the captain's cabin. She later wrote to Leonard:

> *I took him to the Captain's cabin for I had an instinctive turning to the Captain at that moment, as the only man to stand by me. He welcomed us in and was himself withdrawing when the officer stopped him saying the matter concerned him also. He, Lingham, then turned to me and informed me I was placed under arrest, that I should not be allowed*

to land in South Africa anywhere and that I was to have no
communication with anyone on shore by word or letter.
I drew up and asked him from whom he had received
such an order and he replied from Colonel Cooper, Military
Commander of Cape Town. I further asked from whom did
the Colonel receive such instructions and he replied he could
say no more. Then he turned to Captain who looked horribly
miserable, for we are very good friends, and said I was placed
in his charge and he would be held responsible for me. He
was to see I did not leave the ship nor hold with anyone.
Next he gave me the alternative of returning home by the
Carisbrook[e] on the Wednesday or of remaining where I was.
I replied to return by the Carisbrook[e] was out of the question
for I felt wholly unfit for another long voyage.[325]

Emily asked if Lingham would take letters to the commandant
and the governor for her. He agreed to do so and to collect them
the next morning. She kept her head through dinner, then poured
herself out to Miss Steedman, who was taken aback at the action
taken against her new, shipboard friend. Together they composed
letters to Milner, Kitchener, Hely-Hutchinson (Governor of the
Cape Colony) and Colonel Cooper. Emily resolved to stay and
fight. Her letter to Leonard continued:

All night I lay awake shuddering from head to foot with
the effects of the shock for oddly enough it was a shock and
unexpected in that form. Then I began to see my way and brace
myself to the battle. I shall be very polite, very dignified, but
in every way I possibly can a thorn in the flesh to them. I see
already many ways of being a thorn.[326]

To embarrass the authorities, she would ensure that her arrest
would be much talked about in Cape Town; if she could not com-
municate with people ashore, others could do so on her behalf.

She would demand a guard to relieve the ship's captain of the burden of retaining her on board; the presence of the guard would make her more conspicuous. She would refuse to return to England until it suited her. She would insist on being held on land – in prison if the authorities insisted.

So ended day one of the melodrama that unfolded over the next five days. Lingham and Cooper were nervous – this was a responsibility unknown in their experience – and they documented every step they took. It created a convenient record so that we have more than Emily's word for what happened next.

The next day, the ship berthed and Colonel Cooper went on board himself to persuade Emily to accept a passage home on the *Carisbrooke Castle*. She again declined and asked to be put ashore, even if it meant imprisonment. She found the ship noisy, cold and uncomfortable and complained of being unwell. Cooper refused and, after leaving her, made enquiries about the *Avondale Castle*'s schedule. He learnt that she would need six or seven days to complete the discharging of her cargo. He was not prepared to allow the impasse to continue that long and resolved to put Emily on the next ship to sail for England. He sent Lingham to inform Emily of this.[327]

Ashore, Emily's friends had anticipated her arrival and made their own enquiries.

> *Dearest Miss Hobhouse,* wrote Caroline Murray in a note passed to Emily, *Mrs Currey and I have come into town to meet you – We have just been to the Union Castle Office where we have heard that your ship came in yesterday afternoon but that no passengers have yet been able to land nor will be for some time yet. We shall probably have to go back without seeing you this morning but I hope that you and your friend will come out to us at Kenilworth as soon as you can.*[328]

Later in the day, as the other passengers disembarked, it became known that Emily would not be allowed ashore. Mrs Engela Botha, the mother of two of the girls for whom Emily had arranged schooling in Bloemfontein, wrote on the same day:

My dear Miss Hobhouse! With much regret I learned this afternoon that you are so close to land, and not allowed to come ashore, how disappointed I do feel as I anticipated to see you and now all hope is vanished, and I am indeed very sorry to learn from Miss Steedman who called on me, that your health is undesirable. Oh! I wish I could show you some kindness. If I may I will send you some fruit and flowers that is to say if the Military will allow me the great pleasure, yes this is a world of trouble and sorrow![329]

On day three, General Wynne, the commanding officer at Cape Town and Colonel Cooper's superior, received a telegram from Lord Kitchener that said simply: *High Commissioner and I are agreed that Miss Hobhouse should not be allowed to land.*[330] It appears to have been in response to a question from Wynne. Perhaps he had asked for authority to detain Emily on land. The reply left Wynne and Cooper no flexibility at all.

On the fourth day, Cooper sent Lingham to see Emily again. He put his instructions in writing:

Will you impress upon her the inadvisability of remaining on the Avondale Castle … Miss Hobhouse gives as her reason that she is unable to go to sea again so soon after a rough passage, and complains of not being well. In these circumstances I shall probably have to place her on another ship and I would much prefer if she went voluntarily. In the meantime she is not to land and visitors will not be allowed to see her without a special pass from this office. Please give strict orders to ensure that she does not attempt to escape.[331]

Lingham replied:

I interviewed Miss Hobhouse last evening, immediately on receipt of above instructions. Miss Hobhouse decides to remain on board the Avondale Castle as she knows the Captain and stewards, and because it is warmer at the South Arm than in a ship in the Bay. She has given me her word that she will not attempt to leave the ship until she has received replies to her letters to Lord Kitchener and the High Commissioner when she will reconsider her position.[332]

Cooper then asked Lingham to inform Emily of the message General Wynne had received from Kitchener and to ask her to hold herself in readiness for transfer to another vessel, the *Roslin Castle*, whose departure for England was imminent. The *Roslin Castle* was a military transport taking invalid soldiers back to England. It would be less comfortable than the *Carisbrooke Castle*, which had by then departed.

Lingham to Cooper, in a note clearly written for the record:

On Thursday evening, October 31st, acting on your orders by telephone, I informed Miss Hobhouse that she must embark on board H.M. Transport Roslin Castle that same afternoon, to which she replied that it was quite impossible as she was much too ill.

The usual Embarkation Order was handed to Miss Hobhouse …

I then wrote to you submitting that some Medical man be requested to come and see her, in answer to which I received a telephone message from you saying that the P.M.O. is sending a Senior Medical Officer to Miss Hobhouse, but the transfer of Miss Hobhouse from the Avondale Castle to the Roslin Castle need not be delayed.

I then went back and requested Miss Hobhouse to have her

luggage packed up by her attendant. Miss Hobhouse forbade
her attendant to do anything in the matter and I then ordered
two of the stewardesses of the ship (through the Chief Officer)
to pack up Miss Hobhouse's luggage, which was done in the
presence of the lady's attendant.[333]

Evidently the loyal Nurse Phillips was still with Emily.

Cooper had in the meantime relented somewhat and allowed some of Emily's friends to visit her on board the ship. One of them, Betty Molteno, was on board and witnessed the exchange between Emily and Lingham. She recognised that Emily needed all the support she could get, remained on board and later wrote a full account of the afternoon's events.

Elizabeth Molteno was Caroline Murray's sister and no light-weight. It will be recalled that their father had been prime minister of the Cape Colony and that their sister-in-law's family controlled the shipping line that owned the vessel on which she and Emily found themselves. She herself was a headmistress.

A medical officer, Colonel JF Williamson arrived. He, too, kept a record of the meeting:

... Miss Hobhouse was then sitting in a deck chair on the
upper deck with some friends, I sent my card to her but she
returned it and refused to see me. I was therefore obliged
to introduce myself and inform her of the reason for my
visit. After repeated refusals and great delay I induced Miss
Hobhouse to allow herself to be moved into the smoking room
of the ship which was the nearest available room and quite
suitable for the purpose. I, there, in the presence of one of her
friends, a Miss Molteno, and also of a nurse, a Miss Phillips,
who had come out with Miss Hobhouse on the Avondale
Castle, satisfied myself that Miss Hobhouse was quite fit to
return to England at once and that the voyage would in no
way endanger or shorten her life.[334]

When he received Williamson's opinion, Cooper ordered Lingham to remove Emily's luggage to the *Roslin Castle* and Williamson to transfer Emily – by force if necessary. Her bags were trans-shipped immediately, but Emily still refused to move.[335]

Williamson went to the *Roslin Castle* and fetched two stout nurses to move Emily. Emily was equal to the challenge:

I spoke quietly to the women asking them to lay no violent hands upon me. They answered they were under military orders, and this I said I understood, but I put before them that the laws of humanity and nature are, or should be, higher than military laws, and appealed to them not to mar their sacred office as nurses by molesting a sick woman. I had appealed in vain to the men, but I hoped I should not appeal in vain to my own sex.[336]

The nurses turned and left.

Later, about 7 pm, Williamson reappeared with two male orderlies. She still refused to budge. *Madam*, said the doctor, *do you wish to be taken like a lunatic? Sir*, she replied, *the lunacy is on your side and with those whose commands you obey. If you have any manhood in you, you will go and leave me.*[337]

Williamson and the orderlies then picked Emily up and, despite her protests, carried her in a chair with as much care as they could off the *Avondale Castle* and on to a carriage ashore. She was conveyed to the quay where the *Roslin Castle* lay and carried aboard that vessel. Nurse Phillips came too, believing Emily to be too unwell to make the voyage home on her own. Betty Molteno witnessed it all, recording even the derisory hoots of the dock workers as Emily and her bearers passed by.

On the following morning, 1 November 1901, Caroline Murray and her husband, Dr Charles Murray, were allowed to visit Emily on board. Then the ship sailed for England.

Emily wrote four angry letters dated the day of the ship's

departure. They were not well written and even less well considered; this was another heat-of-the-moment reaction. She excoriated the Governor, Sir Walter Hely-Hutchinson, for failing to respond to her pleas for help and Colonel Cooper for brutally carrying out brutal orders. She told both that she would make the affair widely known in England, mentioning their names and those of Williamson and Lingham, too.[338]

Her letter to Milner made no concessions for his high office. It read:

> Your brutal orders have been carried out and thus I hope you will be satisfied.
>
> Your narrow incompetency to see the real issues of this great struggle is leading you to such acts as this and many others, staining your own name and the reputation of England.
>
> I liked you at first and would have helped you. But now I see you more clearly as you really are and can believe it is true what a man once said to me: that you have 'the soul of a spy.' Perhaps that is necessary in a despot ...
>
> You have lost us the heart of a fine people; beware lest that is but the prelude to the loss of their country also.

Kitchener's letter was the shortest. It said, in part[339]:

> Your brutality has triumphed over my weakness and sickness ...
>
> I hope in future you will exercise greater width of judgement in the exercise of your high office. To carry out orders such as these is a degradation both to the office and manhood of your soldiers. I feel ashamed to own you as a fellow-countryman.[340]

Emily recognised that behind this melodrama were men of power who had blindly stumbled into a shameful system, one that they had refused to recognise for what it was when she had pointed it out and one that they could not now – with two hundred thousand people in detention – abandon or change overnight. They must have realised that for them personally, for Kitchener and Milner and also for Brodrick, it meant disaster if the British public came to understand what they had wrought in the camps. Their only defence at this point was to hide the facts as best they could and above all to keep them from the eyes and ears of the articulate Emily Hobhouse who would lay out, once again, for all to see, in painful detail, the scale and severity of the suffering they were still inflicting. She was not afraid of them; they were very much afraid of this lone, frail, feisty woman.

After Emily arrived in Britain, Lord Hobhouse and other legal friends expressed the view that her forcible return was illegal. With their assistance, she sought to take action against the government, but it came to nothing. They had to serve papers on Lord Kitchener, the man principally responsible for her arrest, but he was far out of their reach waging war in Pretoria.

Emily could now see no practical way of assisting the camp occupants. Deeply depressed by their ongoing suffering, in poor health and badly needing a rest, she withdrew from the public arena.

She found peace at the Old Convent Inn on the shores of Lake Annecy in the small French town of Talloires. In this beautiful place, with the lake at her feet and the towering mountain at her back, she worked on her book, *The Brunt of the War and Where it Fell*.[341] It is a well-documented account of the suffering in the camps and an impassioned defence of what she had done.

She was at Talloires when she learnt from a newspaper that the war was over. The report said that the Boers had surrendered and that the Treaty of Vereeniging, as the peace agreement was called, had been signed on 31 May 1902 in Pretoria. *Till that moment, she wrote, … I had hardly realized the strain which the war had been. The sudden release from that tension seemed too much and I remember how I sat there by the waterside and cried my heart out.*[342]

PART 4

Conclusion

Chapter 31

Postscript on the camps

The number of camps that eventually existed is not precisely documented. The British Concentration Camp Database (BCCD) lists 94 camps, black and white.[343] However, Otto has 45 white camps[344] and Warwick says there were 66 black camps[345] (but he shows only 64 on his map), a total of 111 (or 109). Maps prepared by the Boer War Museum in Bloemfontein show a total of 112 camps – camps for whites at 47 locations (page 252–3) and camps for blacks at 65 places (page 254-5). Among these sources, there is evidently some variation in the definition of 'concentration camp'. Some camps were created only to be evacuated shortly afterwards or created only once the war was virtually over and their short-lived nature apparently accounts for some of the differences; they are included in some counts, not in others.

The number of fatalities in the camps is also not known exactly. According to the most commonly quoted figures, more than 42,000 people died: 27, 927 whites[346] and 14,154 blacks.[347] Of these white deaths, 22,074 were children, 4,177 were women and 1,676 men. Similarly, more than 80 per cent of the black deaths were those of children.[348]

1. Uitenhage
2. Port Elizabeth
3. East London
4. Kabusi
5. Aliwal North
6. Norvalspont
7. Orange River Station
8. Kimberley
9. Vryburg
10. Mafeking
11. Bethulie
12. Springfontein
13. Bloemfontein
14. Brandfort
15. Winburg
16. Ladybrand
17. Kroonstad
18. Vredefort Road
19. Heilbron
20. Vereeniging
21. Krugersdorp
22. Potchefstroom
23. Klerksdorp
24. Kromellenboog
25. Irene
26. Meintjeskop
27. Vanderhovensdrift
28. Nylstroom
29. Pietersburg
30. Balmoral

31. Belfast
32. Middelburg
33. Barberton
34. Heidelberg
35. Johannesburg
36. Standerton
37. Volksrust
38. Ladysmith
39. Harrismith
40. Eshowe
41. Howick
42. Pietermaritzburg
43. Pinetown
44. Merebank
45. Wentworth
46. Jacobs
47. Isipingo

CAPE COLONY

Orange R

Cape Town

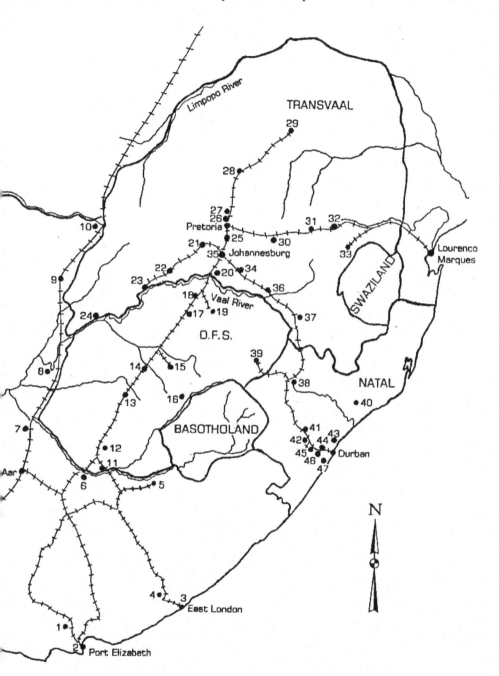

Locations of concentration camps for whites.

Courtesy of Anglo Boer War Museum

253

1. Oranje
2. Kimberley
3. Taungs
4. Dryharts
5. Thaba Nchu
6. Bloemfontein
7. Allemans-Siding
8. Houtenbek
9. Eensgevonden
10. Vetrivier-Road
11. Holfontein
12. Winburg
13. Welgelegen
14. Virginia
15. Rietspruit
16. Ventersburg-Road
17. Holfontein
18. Geneva
19. Bosrand
20. America-Siding
21. Honingspruit
22. Serfontein
23. Roodewal
24. Koppies
25. Vredefort-Road
26. Heilbron
27. Wolwehoek
28. Taaibosch
29. Vereeniging
30. Meyerton
31. Witkop
32. Kliprivier
33. Klipriviersberg
34. Natalspruit

35. Bezuidenhoutvallei
36. Boksburg
37. Rietfontein-West
38. Bantjes
39. Brakpan
40. Springs
41. Nigel
42. Krugersdorp
43. Frederikstad
44. Koekemoer
45. Klerksdorp
46. Irene
47. Olifantsfontein
48. Van der Merwe-Station
49. Elandsrivier
50. Bronkhorstspruit
51. Wilgerivier
52. Balmoral
53. Brugspruit
54. Groot Olifantsrivier
55. Belfast
56. Middelburg
57. Elandshoek
58. Nelspruit
59. Heidelberg
60. Greylingstad
61. Standerton
62. Platrand
63. Paardekop
64. Volksrust
65. Harrismith

CAPE COLON

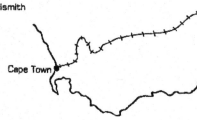

Cape Town

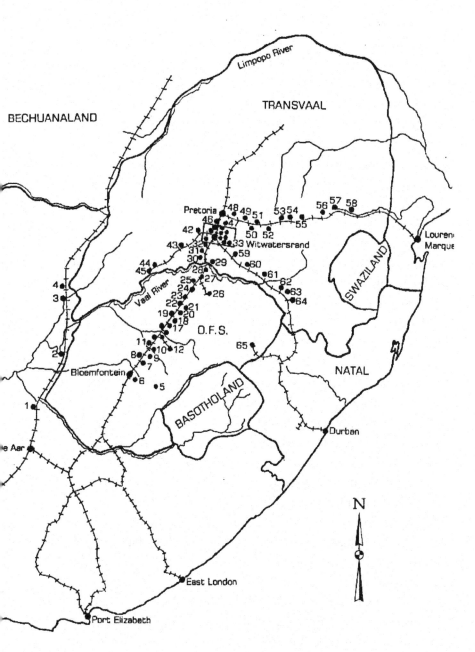

Locations of concentration camps for blacks.

Courtesy of Anglo Boer War Museum

The first comprehensive effort to determine the number of deaths in the white camps was undertaken by PLA Goldman, a South African government official, during an investigation that lasted from 1906 to 1914. His work led to the numbers cited above. In addition to official reports, Goldman solicited information from NGK church ministers, magistrates and other local sources across the country. (NGK, 'Nederduitse Gereformeered Kerk', usually translated as the 'Dutch Reformed Church', the largest but by no means the only church of the Boers during and after the war.)

More recently, Liz Stanley, a British sociologist, and Helen Dampier, a British historian, examined Goldman's papers and concluded that he had probably under-recorded the number of deaths by a considerable margin. They point to a number of shortcomings and omissions.[349]

This opinion is not supported by work still underway at the University of Cape Town on the British Concentration Camp Database, a project that aims to make available on the web the names of all the people who were in the white camps. The project is far advanced – see <www2.lib.uct.ac.za/mss/bccd/> – and indicates, name by name, which individuals survived or perished along with other information. A short examination of the data base illustrates the difficulties involved in arriving at a definitive fatality count: names were often recorded inconsistently – Ellen was sometimes Ella, Eagar was sometimes Eager or even Edgar. The opportunities for error are legion. Dr Elizabeth van Heyningen, who is in charge of the project, is of the view that Goldman's fatality count is 'probably about right' with duplications offsetting omissions.[350]

As for the black fatalities, besides the BCCD, only one study is known to this writer, the book by the Cambridge-based historian Peter Warwick. Dr Warwick's numbers rely on the official reports and, as he points out, the quoted figure of 14,154 'certainly underestimates' the real number since no records are available for the early period of the camps' existence and because many deaths probably occurred within the camps that were not officially recorded.[351]

The total Boer population of the two republics at the start of the war was estimated to be just 195,000.[352] This means that about 14 per cent of that population died in the concentration camps. The proportion of children that succumbed was much higher although specific numbers were not found. Van Heyningen believes that 'just under half' the children (0–15 years) died[353], but for the younger children the fatality rate was greater still. In the Orange River Camp, for example, as mentioned in Chapter 27, Wiid and West found that hardly any children in the first years of life survived.[354] A whole cohort of the Boer population was virtually extinguished.

In the white camps, the highest mortality rate occurred during Emily's ill-fated second voyage to Cape Town on the *Avondale Castle*. In that awful month of October 1901, 2.9 per cent of the camp occupants died, an annualised fatality rate of more than one third. The worst month in the black camps was even worse. In December 1901, in mid-summer, 3.2 per cent of the camp residents died.[355] More details appear in the Appendix at the back of this book.

When the mortality is dissected by time, something interesting emerges. Of the many thousands of recorded fatalities, only 913 white deaths had been reported by the end of May 1901 and no black deaths. It is clear that by far the majority of the people who died, died later. Why is the end of May 1901 relevant? Because it is then that Emily Hobhouse arrived back in England and raised the alarm. If the immediate action that she and others demanded had been taken, tens of thousands of lives might have been saved. That is where the deepest tragedy lies and from which the greatest culpability arises.

The responsibility belongs to just a handful of men in power: Lord Roberts who burnt the first farms and created the first camps; Lord Kitchener who took his cue from those beginnings and turned the suffering of civilians into a general instrument of war; Lord Lansdowne and St John Brodrick, successive Secretaries for War, who supported and defended these methods, even encouraged them, and, in Brodrick's case, refused to take action when Emily told him what she had found; and Lord Milner, duplicitous, revelling in his own importance, equally deaf to what he should have heard, blind to the inconvenient facts before him. And let's not forget the Prime Minister, Lord Salisbury, who should have asked harder questions, should not have defended the camps, should have intervened; nor the Colonial Secretary, Joseph Chamberlain, eloquent spokesperson for the war and defender of Kitchener's tactics. It is only a slight amelioration of his culpability to acknowledge that he was the first of these men to intervene decisively to reduce the fatality rate in the camps. It was very late when he did so. Arthur Balfour, Deputy Prime Minister and leader of the governing Unionists in the House of Commons, was another man of great eloquence and defender of the policies that the government applied in South Africa. These few are the most important, the most culpable. There are others of course, many others, but they were followers.

It is equally necessary to recognise those who emerged from this with honour: Henry Campbell-Bannerman, the leader of the opposition and subsequent prime minister; David Lloyd George, the most outspoken government critic and also a future prime minister; the blind Leonard Courtney MP, Emily's initial mentor and source of inspiration; John Ellis MP, John Morley MP, Sir William Harcourt MP, Herbert Lewis MP, all men of great intelligence and willing to make their voices heard in the parliament; and the Bishop of Hereford, who backed Emily's British campaign. Then, of course, there were the less visible people who supported Emily directly: first and foremost the Hobhouses, brother Leonard, uncle Arthur and aunt Mary. Courtney's wife, Kate, was always closely engaged, as was Joshua Rowntree and the Bradby sisters, Dorothy and Barbara, who, as volunteers, tirelessly administered the collection of money and clothes through a large number of volunteers working for the Distress Fund. Caroline Murray was the kingpin of the supporters in Africa and Caroline Fichardt did not flinch from taking personal risks to accommodate and support Emily in Bloemfontein.

Perhaps the last word on the concentration camps of the Boer War should be granted to Alfred Milner. Once he had sniffed the change in the wind, once his superior, Joseph Chamberlain, had begun to insist on urgent action to reduce the death rates in the camps, then he, too, found it expedient to deny the reality no longer. On 7 December 1901, he wrote to Chamberlain:

> *The black spot – the one very black spot – in the picture is the frightful mortality in the Concentration Camps. I entirely agree with you in thinking, that while a hundred explanations may be offered and a hundred excuses made, they do not really amount to an adequate defence. I should much prefer to say at once, so far as the Civil authorities are concerned, that we were suddenly confronted with a problem not of our making, with which it was beyond our power properly to grapple. And no doubt its vastness was not realised soon enough. It was not till six weeks or two months ago that it dawned on me personally, (I cannot speak for others) that the enormous mortality was not merely incidental to the first formation of the camps and the sudden inrush of thousands of people already sick and starving, but was going to continue. The fact that it continues is no doubt a condemnation of the Camp system. The whole thing, I think now, has been a mistake.[356]*

Chapter 32

After the Boer War

Emily Hobhouse returned to South Africa a year after peace was made and toured the devastated countries for five months. During this period she made two notable new friends, the novelist, Olive Schreiner and Jan Smuts.

Schreiner was famous, having written *The Story of an African Farm*, a pre-Boer War novel that, remarkably, is still in print. She was as opinionated as Emily and was also a friend of Smuts's. Emily stayed for a week with her at her modest house in De Aar, and later she visited and stayed with Emily in England.

Jan Smuts had returned to legal practice, but his mind was on the future of his people. Emily met him in Pretoria; their connection would continue beyond her death.

Emily now conceived a plan to assist in the post-war recovery of the former republics. Her concept was to establish trade schools to teach industrial textile skills to Boer women so that they could earn cash incomes for their impoverished communities. After her tour, she raised funds, bought equipment and learnt all she could about textile manufacturing, much of this in Continental Europe. In the process she acquired an able partner, Margaret Clark, a member of the well-known shoe manufacturing family.

Emily Hobhouse after the Boer War

During this period, a small event occurred that had a far-reaching influence. The background is this: when the war ended, the deposed Free State President, Marthinus Steyn, was gravely ill. His wife, Tibbie, accompanied him to Europe to seek treatment for a condition that was not well understood in South Africa. He was so ill that she was not sure he would survive the voyage. Meanwhile, Emily quietly raised money to assist them in obtaining the treatment he required. He recovered and, while he was recuperating in the south of France, Emily called on them during one of her trips to the Continent. The grateful Steyns welcomed her, Emily met the ex-president for the first time and renewed her contact with Tibbie. So began a deep friendship that endured for the rest of their lives.

Emily and Margaret Clark returned to South Africa, worked much too hard given Emily's poor state of health and after three years had established twenty-six textile schools. At this point the venture became too big for them and they handed it over to government boards – one in the Transvaal and another in the Orange River Colony. It was one of the most constructive things Emily achieved.

By 1908 she was back in Europe. Feeling estranged from Britain and with limited financial resources, she settled in Rome where the cost of living was lower. Her contacts still played their part in this new existence, for she was the guest of the Marchesa de Viti de Marco at social occasions and, at some of these gatherings, fraternised with Baron Gottlieb von Jagow, the German ambassador. However, her health was poor and for the most part she lived an isolated life, sustained by her correspondence, much of it with Olive Schreiner, Jan Smuts and Tibbie Steyn.

Henry Campbell-Bannerman had by this time won a post-war election. Partly as an act of contrition for what had happened in the concentration camps, his government granted self-government to the two new colonies. In the first elections, the Afrikaners won government in both former republics. A little more than five years after the war, they were again ruling their countries. The war had largely been pointless.

The Boers now referred to themselves as Afrikaners; they were no longer just farmers, no longer Dutch but a new nation forged in the bitter defeat of war.

Smuts, now deputy leader of the new government in the Transvaal, busied himself with the unification of the British colonies in southern Africa. This objective was achieved in 1910 when the Union of South Africa came into being as a dominion within the British Empire – the modern South Africa. The constitution was largely written by Smuts himself and skilfully negotiated with the various interests. It was thus not Milner, but his avowed enemies, the former Boers, who achieved unification by democratic means. In Milner's vision, Rhodesia and Bechuanaland would join as well, but they chose to stay out of it. The Afrikaners were in the majority in the former Cape Colony, and with their strongholds in the Transvaal and the former Orange River Colony, they dominated the government of the new country. Effective Boer control now extended over a much greater area than before the war!

Despite a demanding public life, Smuts continued to correspond with Emily and began to administer her financial affairs for her. When she was in a pinch, he advanced a loan or made a gift to help her out.

During the war, Marthinus Steyn had conceived the idea of establishing a significant monument to commemorate the women and children who had died in the camps. By 1911, he judged the time had arrived to put the idea into action and led a fundraising campaign. A year later, sufficient funds were available to complete the project. A site was selected on the outskirts of Bloemfontein and a design was adopted that called for a towering obelisk, visible from afar, with a sculpted group of figures on a plinth at its foot. The South African sculptor, Anton van Wouw was appointed to create the group.

South Africa did not possess facilities or expertise to make a bronze casting of the dimensions required and Van Wouw based himself in Rome to undertake his commission. He was advised to consult Emily – then conveniently in Rome – about the work. She, opinionated as always, rejected his initial concept and persuaded him to adopt her idea instead.

When the construction was complete, Steyn invited Emily to come to South Africa to inaugurate the monument. By this time, Louis Botha, the wartime Boer commander, was the prime minister of the united South Africa, and he, Smuts, Steyn and other leaders were working for conciliation between English and Afrikaans speakers. There was a danger that the inauguration could degenerate into an anti-English demonstration, something they were anxious to avoid. One can surmise that they wanted Emily to do the opening, not just because of what she had done, but also because she was an Englishwoman. Because of her humanitarian work for the Afrikaners, she was beyond reproach and her presence would mute anger against the British.

Emily accepted the invitation and left Italy against medical advice. After arriving in South Africa, she took the train from Cape Town but got only half way to Bloemfontein. Still well short of the altitude at her destination, and feeling unwell, she stopped at Beaufort West where she accepted the advice of a local doctor to proceed no further. With a weak heart, the thinning air would endanger her life.

At the inauguration of the memorial, extracts of her speech were read by the former mayor of Bloemfontein, Charles Fichardt[357], the man who had suggested that Emily stay with his mother Caroline. Amid pomp and ceremony, Tibbie Steyn unveiled the more than life-sized sculpture Van Wouw had created in Rome and Emily's part in its creation was at once evident. Standing before it today, one is confronted with the tragic young mother of Springfontein. She gazes, numb with grief, into the distance, the limp body of her only child, a little child, lying dead on her lap. The friend standing by her shoulder calls on heaven to

Monument to the women and children who died in the camps

witness the tragedy. It is troubling to behold, hard to digest.

Printed copies of Emily's speech were distributed among the crowd in both English and Afrikaans. It excoriated the men who created and ran the camps but urged the audience not to judge the British people by those individuals. It urged reconciliation and forgiveness and pointed out that she represented thousands of English people who had been deeply concerned for the Boer women and children, who had worked for them and who had campaigned with her to bring change. It said that black people had also suffered in the war and urged the Afrikaners to recognise their suffering, too.

The message fell on stony ground. The audience had come to remember their dead, dead wives, dead children, dead mothers and fathers, dead grandfathers and grandmothers, dead brothers and sisters, dead neighbours and friends. The emotional scars were still too fresh. They were not yet ready for forgiveness, not yet able to recognise the pain and grief of others. For many, everything that they had once owned had been taken, including their pride as independent nations. Before them lay a bleak, impoverished, uncertain future.

After failing to reach Bloemfontein, Emily retreated to Cape Town where she became the guest of the prime minister and Mrs Annie Botha at Groote Schuur, the grand house on the slopes of Table Mountain. There Betty Molteno introduced her to the Indian lawyer, Mohandas Gandhi, who campaigned against the discrimination that he and his fellow Indians suffered in South Africa. Gandhi was about to call a strike, a strike he believe could be averted if Botha and Smuts would meet and negotiate with him. They had refused. He appealed to Emily for assistance. She asked him to defer the strike for two weeks, wrote a carefully worded plea to Smuts and managed to arrange a gathering of Mr and Mrs Botha, Gandhi and herself at Groote Schuur. Negotiations ensued and the strike was averted.

When Emily sailed for England, it was Gandhi who fare-welled her at the dockside. Gandhi's twenty-odd years in South Africa straddled the Boer War. He was well informed about Emily, greatly admired her humanitarian work in the camps and knew of the political difficulties she had endured in England. He was inspired by her textile enterprise and its underlying philosophy of self-help, so much so that he learnt to spin himself. Later, back in his homeland and recognised as the great Mahatma that he was, he led his nation to independence. His house in Mumbai is now a museum and his spinning wheel is still there.

When the First World War began in 1914, Botha and Smuts persuaded a divided nation to join forces with Britain. Many of their former compatriots could not countenance military action on the side of the former enemy and rebelled. The government had to put down the rebellion by force. Christiaan de Wet, who was among the rebels, was imprisoned. Both Botha and Smuts resumed military roles and led South African forces into German South-West Africa. They conquered the territory for the Allies, Botha returned to govern South Africa while Smuts went to eastern Africa to lead the Imperial troops against the German occupation in that region. When David Lloyd George became British prime minister in 1916, he invited Smuts to join an Imperial War Cabinet of just five members. Smuts moved to London and took his seat alongside an old adversary, Alfred Milner. Then Botha died suddenly of natural causes and Smuts became the wartime prime minister of South Africa.

Meanwhile, Emily was somewhat rejuvenated by her trip to South Africa and sought to regain relevance during the First World War. She remained a determined pacifist, opposed Britain's entry into the war and refused throughout the conflict to demonise Germans. She recognised that pacifism could not co-exist with chauvinism, jingoism and xenophobia. These views were shared by few in Britain and she alienated more people than ever. Even her brother Leonard disagreed with her now and her nephew Oliver signed up for war service.

In the midst of the conflict, Emily once again succeeded in doing something quite remarkable. She made contact with the German Government through the embassy in neutral Switzerland and, citing Von Jagow, obtained permission to secretly visit occupied Belgium and a camp at Ruhleben near Berlin where British civilians were interned.

Once in Berlin, she made contact with Baron von Jagow, now the German Foreign Minister. Von Jagow welcomed her cordially and they met for an hour in his office, reminiscing about happy times at Marchesa de Viti de Marco's in Rome. The day after the meeting and still in Berlin, she wrote to Von Jagow suggesting a role for herself in bringing about a meeting between Von Jagow or his delegate and a prominent Englishman as a prelude to peace negotiations. Von Jagow indicated a willingness to talk but suggested it was up to the British to make the first move. Emily was encouraged and saw an opportunity for herself to play a catalytic role in ending the war.

The British through their embassy in Switzerland were meanwhile observing Emily's movements and were suspicious of her contact with the German Embassy. On her return to Berne, her passport was confiscated and she was given a one-way travel document to the United Kingdom. Knowledge of her contact with the enemy preceded her and she had difficulty arranging a meeting with anyone at the right level to indicate that the Germans could be enticed to talk if approached in the right way. When she did, her suggestion was met with scorn. Her visit to Germany became public knowledge and once again she was the subject of heated debate in the parliament. Forceful suggestions that she should be tried for treason were averted only by the alternative view that she was a harmless but slightly dotty old woman.

The ideological gulf between her and Smuts could now not be greater. Although they lived near each other, he would not accept her invitations to call but did occasionally see her at his hotel in the presence of others. He tolerated her pacifist activities and did not terminate their correspondence.

When the war ended, Emily was nearly sixty and in poor health. Her reputation was in shreds, at a new low.

Smuts participated in the Versailles Peace Conference where he found himself in a minority of delegates opposed to the imposition of harsh terms on Germany, arguing that this could lead to future instability in Europe. When the terms became publicly known, Emily was indignant. She was especially outraged by the requirement that Germany hand over 140,000 milk cows, a blow, in her view, that would land especially heavily on children. In their disapproval of the terms, she and Smuts were once again of similar opinions.

Much of Europe was in ruins and difficult social conditions prevailed. This was just the sort of crisis to get Emily Hobhouse going. A Swiss charity had been started to bring starving Austrian children to live in Swiss households until conditions improved. They struggled to find the necessary funds and appealed to Emily for assistance. She swung into action, became the secretary of the fund and succeeded in extending the scheme to include children from famine-stricken parts of Germany, Czechoslovakia and Hungary. Next she became chairman of a fund for babies in the Russian city of Petrograd. When the international charity, Save the Children, was founded, both of these funds were absorbed under its umbrella and Emily took a prominent role in this new organisation.

In Berne she heard of difficult social conditions in Leipzig and went to see for herself. Once again her organising skills and fundraising abilities came to the fore and before long she had a local committee at work providing extra food for 11,000 children in thirty-four schools. She won many plaudits for her work on the Continent. It mattered to her that she was assisting the children of former enemies. Her mission had a twofold intent. On the one hand it was relieving distress and hardship; on the other it was a gesture of reconciliation and an assertion of the common humanity that all share.

During this post-war activity, Emily sold many of her treasured possessions to raise money, depleting her already thin financial resources. The activity was more than her frail heart could bear and she was obliged, at intervals, to take rest periods, sometimes in hospital. By 1921, she was staying with her brother Leonard in London.

Tibbie Steyn remained in touch, and when she realised that Emily had fallen on hard times she raised funds in South Africa to present Emily with a gift that enabled her to buy a home in St Ives, Cornwall. There, at Tibbie's suggestion, Emily began writing an autobiography that was never completed.[358]

St Ives was an attractive place but not a sensible choice for someone like her. With her intense interest in affairs of the day and her desire to remain engaged, she soon felt isolated there. She sold the house and bought a place in London instead.

Emily Hobhouse died on 8 June 1926. Her funeral service was conducted at St Mary Abbots, the local church near the nursing home where she died and near her last home in Kensington. Just a handful of friends and relatives attended the service, which was conducted not by the vicar but by an assistant curate of the parish. The curate happened to be Canadian.[359]

Her brother ensured that the *Manchester Guardian* carried a substantial obituary, highlighting her humanitarian work in South Africa. But *The Times* had learnt nothing, understood nothing. Its obituary said that during the Boer War she had gone out to report on the concentration camps that had to be established when the Boers *refused to recognise their responsibility for the care of their women and children … The deficiencies which she found there were largely unavoidable owing to the conditions in which the camps were formed while the mortality was in part at least due to the occupants' ignorance of nursing and their primitive ideas of medicine and sanitation. Unfortunately her report was eagerly seized on for purposes of agitation not only by the Boer propagandists but by those whose sympathy with the Boers was less than their hostility to Britain.*[360] Thus dismissed, Emily Hobhouse was soon forgotten in Britain.

Her body was cremated and the government of South Africa applied to take custody of her ashes. They were taken to Bloem-

Right Groote Kerk in Bloemfontein where Emily Hobhouse's commemoration service was conducted in 1926

fontein to be laid to rest. A grateful nation wished to pay homage and an organising committee was created to arrange an appropriate commemoration. Mrs Tibbie Steyn was invited to chair the committee and she accepted.

On the day of the commemoration, the main church in the city, a stone's throw from Kya Lami where Emily had stayed with

the Fichardts, was too small to accommodate the mourners. After the service, the cortege made its way to the outskirts of the town, to the memorial for the women and children who had died in the camps. A brass band played and girls in white dresses, every one with first names 'Emily Hobhouse', escorted the ornate hearse drawn by plumed horses mounted by soldiers in dress uniform. They were followed by another two hundred girls bearing palm fronds and the rest of the mourners. Caroline Murray thought there were more than 20,000 people present.

Field Marshall Jan Christiaan Smuts, now a distinguished international statesman and ex-prime minster of South Africa, delivered one of several eulogies. He spoke of what Emily Hobhouse had done in the name of common humanity.

As suggested by Tibbie Steyn, her ashes were interred in a niche in the plinth at the base of the obelisk that is the centrepiece of the National Women's Memorial. She rests there below

Plaque on Women's Monument marking the location of
Emily Hobhouse's ashes

the traumatised, grieving mother of Springfontein and her dead child.

After the ceremony, Smuts wrote to Emily's nephew Oliver, who was managing her affairs in England. He said simply, *We buried her like a princess.*[361]

Only five people have been buried at the Women's Monument in Bloemfontein. Emily shares the honour with President and Mrs Steyn, Commandant-General Christiaan de Wet and the Reverend John Daniël Kestell, spiritual leader of the Free State Boers during and after the Boer War. Kestell had presided at her commemoration service.

Appendix

Boer War concentration camp occupation and fatalities

1901	April 01		May 01		June 01		July 01		August 01		September 01	
	Internees	Deaths	Internees	Deaths	Internees	Deaths	Internees	Deaths	Internees	Deaths	Internees	Deaths
WHITES[i]												
Transvaal	23,812	240	38,573	338	45,426	750	53,717	1,067	58,114	1,477	58,883	1,369
%		1.0		0.9		1.7		2.0		2.5		2.3
ORC	20,412	?	24,887	335	31,694	395	36,146	642	42,107	1,164	44,572	1,127
%				1.3		1.2		1.8		2.8		2.5
Natal	2,524	?	?	?	2,614	7	2,751	6	2,848	24	6,044	52
%						0.3		0.2		0.8		0.9
Total	46,748		?		79,734	1,152	92,614	1,715	103,069	2665	109,499	2,548
%						1.4		1.9		2.6		2.3
BLACKS[ii]												
Transvaal					11,570		14,759		22,795	145	28,491	441
%										0.6		1.5
ORC					20,790		22,713	256	30,359	430	37,098	287
%								1.1		1.4		0.8
Total					32,360		37,472		53,154	575	65,589	728
%										1.1		1.1
BLACK AND WHITE TOTAL[iii]												
Transvaal					56,996		68,476		80,909	1,622	87,374	1,810
%										2.0		2.1
ORC					52,484		58,859		72,466	1,594	81,670	1,414
%										2.2		1.7
Natal					2,614		2,751		2,848	24	6,044	52
%										0.8		0.9
Total					112,094		130,086		156,223	3,240	175,088	3,276
%										2.1		1.9

(*Footnotes*)

i   White statistics are from Otto, JC Die Konsentrasiekampe, Protea Boekhuis, Pretoria, 2005, ISBN 1-919825-22-3, pp 159–61. Otto's sources are the official British reports (Command Papers or 'Blue books'). Otto's numbers have been compared with individual official reports in selected cases (ref Cds). There are minor differences in some months, just as there are differences between official documents.

	October 01		November 01		December 01		January 02		February 02		March 02		April 02	
	Internees	Deaths	Internees	Deaths	Internees	Deaths	Internees	Deaths	Internees	Deaths	Internees	Deaths	Internees	Deaths
WHITES														
	57,905	1,616	56,883	1,521	56,821	1,040	55,297	639	48,728	287	47,021	174	44,744	106
		2.8		2.7		1.8		1.2		0.6		0.4		0.2
	45,306	1,514	44,384	1,340	43,755	1,250	42,404	755	41,138	289	37,939	179	40,340	109
		3.3		3.0		2.9		1.8		0.7		0.5		0.3
	8,988	87	10,367	90	11,164	147	12,206	85	19,175	52	20,715	70	24,022	46
		1.0		0.9		1.3		0.7		0.3		0.3		0.2
	112,199	3,217	111,634	2,951	111,740	2,437	109,907	1,479	109,041	628	105,675	423	109,106	261
		2.9		2.6		2.2		1.3		0.6		0.4		0.2
BLACKS														
	32,006	687	39,323	956	43,420	1,160	48,932	992	52,139	530	52,606	417	53,198	297
		2.1		2.4		2.7		2.0		1.0		0.8		0.6
	43,944	640	45,791	1,356	45,987	1,671	49,054	1,542	49,205	936	48,693	555	55,188	333
		1.5		3.0		3.6		3.1		1.9		1.1		0.6
	75,950	1,327	85,114	2,312	89,407	2,831	97,986	2,534	101,344	1,466	101,299	972	108,386	630
		1.7		2.7		3.2		2.6		1.4		1.0		0.6
BLACK AND WHITE TOTAL														
	89,911	2,303	96,206	2,477	100,241	2,200	104,229	1,631	100,867	817	99,627	591	97,942	403
		2.6		2.6		2.2		1.6		0.8		0.6		0.4
	89,250	2,154	90,175	2,696	89,742	2,921	91,458	2,297	90,343	1,225	86,632	734	95,528	442
		2.4		3.0		3.3		2.5		1.4		0.8		0.5
	8,988	87	10,367	90	11,164	147	12,206	85	19,175	52	20,715	70	24,022	46
		1.0		0.9		1.3		0.7		0.3		0.3		0.2
	88,149	4,544	196,748	5,263	201,147	5,268	207,893	4,013	210,385	2,094	206,974	1,395	217,492	891
		2.4		2.7		2.6		1.9		1.0		0.7		0.4

ii   Black statistics are from Warwick, Peter, Black People and the South African War 1899–1902 Cambridge University Press 2004, ISBN 0 521 27224 6, p 151. In addition to those above, Warwick also provides the data for May 1902 when the occupation of the black camps reached a total of 115,700 with 523 fatalities. Warwick likewise cites official reports as his sources.

iii   Camps in the Cape Colony were administered either from the ORC or Transvaal and are included under the corresponding colony. The camps could not be emptied when the war ended on 31 May 1902. Most internees had no homes to which to return. Camp occupation continued and so did the fatalities.

Endnotes

The abbreviations used in these endnotes refer to the sources listed from p 282 onwards.

1   EH3, RvR p 32
2   EH3, JHB p 71, RvR p 42
3   RvR p 441
4   EH3, RvR p 34, JHB p 65
5   EH3, RvR p 33
6   RvR p 35, JHB p 66
7   EH3, RvR p 35, JHB p 66
8   EH3, RvR p 37, JHB p 68
9   EH3, RvR p 38
10 RvR p 39
11 JH p 11
12 AT p 33
13 JH p 5
14 EH3, RvR p 38
15 EH3, RvR p 41
16 JHB p 73, RvR p 43
17 EH3, JHB p 75, RvR p 43
18 EH3, RvR p 45
19 EH3, RvR p 45, JHB p 79
20 EH3, RvR p 45, JHB p 79
21 MP Dep 184, 21.v11.15
22 RvR p 57
23 EH3, RvR p 57
24 EH3, RvR p 47
25 RvR p 47, JHB p 81
26 RvR p 47
27 RvR p 48, JHB p 86
28 RvR p 525
29 JHB p 86
30 HJO p 8
31 ACD p 195
32 Cd 426, p 2 I (Feb 1900)
33 EH1 p 10
34 JHB p 37 (Farms in the republics usually had rifles. All men between sixteen and sixty were liable for military service at short notice and had to bring their own horses and rifles. They also used rifles to hunt and protect stock as carnivores still roamed the veld.)
35 Cd 426, p 7 XIII (31 May 1900)
36 Cd 426 p 10, XIX (16 June 1900)
37 Cd 426 p 11 XX (19 June 1900)
38 TP p 463
39 P-C pp 159–63
40 Cd 524 p 9
41 EH1 p 17
42 TP p 505
43 P-C p 175
44 RD p 233
45 Cd 524
46 LMP p 187
47 A box made of fir or pine planks
48 RvR p 49, see also JHB p 87
49 EH1 p 118
50 Cd 819 p 37. These rations were for the people in the white camps visited by Emily. Trollope notes in his report that the rations for the inmates of the 'native' camps cost

less than half as much per person per day. (p 36)

51 RvR p 89, JHB p 146

52 EH1 p 117, quoted in JHB p 90

53 JC Otto investigated camp food more extensively (see JCO pp 83–101). Variations in amounts occurred over time, in different parts of the country and by category of inmate. But the list of ingredients is almost always the same and the variations are small.

54 JCO p 85

55 RvR p 50, JHB p 89

56 RvR p 51, JHB p 89

57 RvR p 48, JHB p 88

58 RvR p 51, JHB p 90

59 RvR p 52, JHB p 90

60 RvR p 52, JHB p 92

61 EH1 p 119

62 RvR p 53, JHB p 93

63 EH3, RvR p 54, JHB p 94

64 EH3, RvR p 54, JHB p 94

65 RvR p 55, JHB p 95

66 Milner Papers, dep 173 p 121; also JHB pp 96–97

67 The background to these comments is that Milner had suggested to Kitchener that Boers who had surrendered should be used as peace emissaries to their former compatriots. JJ Morgendaal and A Wessels volunteered to do so and carried a circular from Kitchener on the treatment of surrendered Boers to the men in the field in an attempt to induce more burghers to lay down their arms. They were detained at first contact and taken to Commandant-General Christiaan De Wet's commando where they were court martialled but detained pending an appeal to a higher court. While they were in detention, the commando was warned of the approach of a British force and had to move quickly. Morgendaal either impeded the commando's mobility or was unfortunate enough to give the impression of deliberately doing so and was summarily shot. Wessels had received a death sentence at his court martial for being a traitor but was reprieved and survived. (PT pp 196–97, TP p 488, JHB p 97)

68 RvR p 59, JHB p 104

69 EH3, RvR p 61, JHB p 107

70 MP 173, 2 Jan 1901

71 RvR p 58

72 Bartholomew's reduced survey map of South Africa.

73 HJO p 8

74 CdW, p 202, FP p 30, TP p 495, RK p 402

75 CdW, p 201

76 FP p 30

77 Cd 522 p 10

78 TP p 495

79 J&S p 214, TP p 537

80 RK p 407

81 TP p 497

82 Examples: FP p 32, TP p 497, T&F p 178, DR p 147

83 Examples: J&S p 192 (two accounts), T&F eg pp 139, 148, 149, 181, DR p 148

84 Cd 522 p 7

85 Cd 522 p 8 (FP p 32 suggests only 132 burghers were eliminated from the battlefield, mostly by voluntary surrender.)

86 RvR p 66, JHB p 111

87 JHB p 120, RvR p 68

88 JHB p 113

89 JHB p 114

90 JHB p 125

91 JHB p 120, RvR p 68

92 RvR p 451

93 JHB p 111, RvR p 65

94 JHB p 109, RvR p 63

95 JHB p 122

96   RvR p 75, JHB p 129
97   EH3, JHB p 128, RvR p 75
98   JHB p 109, RvR p 63
99   JHB p 120, RvR p 68
100 JHB p 123, RvR p 71
101 JHB p 121
102 JHB p127, RvR p 74 (RvR indicates this letter was to 'Correspondent not identified', JHB that it was to Leonard Hobhouse)
103 RvR p 454, JHB p 124
104 RvR p 80, JHB p 136
105 RvR p 81, JHB p 136
106 RvR p 81, JHB p 136
107 JHB p 137, RvR p 82
108 EH3
109 RvR p 86, JHB p 143
110 JH p 86
111 JHB p 144, RvR p 87
112 JHB p 144, RvR p 87
113 RvR 87, JHB p 144
114 RvR p 89
115 RvR p 90, JHB p 147
116 RvR p 90, JHB p 147
117 RvR p 92, JHB p 149
118 RvR p 97, JHB p 155
119 RvR p 101
120 RvR p 102
121 JCO p 159
122 RvR p 103
123 RvR p 104
124 JHB p 139
125 Cd 522 p 11
126 Cd 819 p 16
127 Cd 819 p 113
128 Cd 819 p 16
129 Cd 819 p 51
130 Warwick (PW p 149) says: 'In the Transvaal little is known about the number of black refugees before the end of June 1901 when 11,570 had been concentrated.' However, when Boer farms were destroyed, the blacks living on those farms as sharecroppers or labour tenants were generally also removed – see PW p 147, for example.
131 RvR p 107
132 RvR p 108
133 RvR p 108
134 JHB p 176
135 RvR p 111
136 RvR p 112
137 Cd 522 p 11
138 Cd 819 p 4
139 See JHB p 189
140 Cd 819 p 5–35
141 Cd 819 p 8 and p 6
142 Cd 819 p 16
143 Cd 819 p 16
144 Cd 819 p 21
145 Cd 819 p 21
146 Cd 819 p 23
147 Cd 819 p 23
148 ibid.
149 ibid.
150 Cd 819 p 24
151 Cd 819 p 25
152 JCO p 82
153 Cd 819 p 26
154 Cd 819 p 28
155 Cd 819 p 36
156 Elizabeth v Heyningen, the Cape Town based historian, points out that reports on individual camps in the ORC were prepared as indicated by correspondence registers. But they did not appear in the published papers and have not been found in archives (personal communication). It is therefore unknown if they support Trollope's assertions or whether they reached Kitchener or London
157 CO p 13
158 CO p 13
159 RvR p 92
160 Cd 819 p 6
161 TP p 495
162 JHB p 173, RvR p 109
163 EH1 p 139, also quoted in JCO p 66

164 JB
165 JB Chs XII and XIII
166 ConsR
167 US Arch. (See Sources of information, p 284, for more details)
168 US Arch.
169 RvR p 226
170 Cd 819 p 111
171 Cd 819 p 61
172 JB Ch XIV
173 JHB p 189
174 JHB p 163
175 JHB p 191 citing WO 32/22
176 JHB p 194
177 JHB p 194
178 The passenger list and log of the voyage are in the Milner Papers, MS 185
179 JHB p 180
180 TP p 501
181 RvR p 116, JH p 90
182 RvR p 448
183 RvR p 115
184 TP p 502
185 TP p 502
186 According to JHB p 189, the committee members in April 1901 were Sir Thomas Dyke Acland (chairman), WFH Alexander, CE Maurice, Miss ED Bradby, H Nevison, Mrs James Bryce, R Oliver, Mrs Leonard Courtney (Kate), Joshua Rowntree, Lady Davey, the Marchioness of Ripon, Lady Hobhouse, JS Trotter, PA Molteno, Lady Farrer (Hon Treasurer), FW Lawrence (Hon Secretary) and Emily.
187 RvR p 127
188 Cd 819 p 93. The report is dated 1 June 1901.
189 RvR p 128. The version of this letter reproduced in JHB p 214 does not contain the last comment on Brodrick.

190 See RvR p 464
191 JH p 93
192 JHB p 216
193 JH p 93–94, JHB 216
194 TP p 508; *The Times*, 15 June 1901 p 12
195 *The Times*, 18 June 1901 p 9 (Other sources differ slightly, giving a fatality figure of 338 – see e.g. JCO.)
196 TP p 509 citing Hansard
197 TP p 509 citing Hansard
198 *The Times*, 18 June 1901 p 9
199 EH1 p 127
200 *The Times*, 18 June 1901 p 9
201 EH2
202 RvR p 460
203 EH2 p 14
204 *The Times*, 19 June 1901 p 9
205 *The Times*, 19 June 1901 p 9
206 *The Times*, 20 June 1901 p 6
207 *The Times*, 20 June 1901 p 5
208 *The Times*, 20 June 1901 p 9
209 *The Times*, 20 June 1901 p 5
210 *The Times*, 20 June 1901 p 9
211 Cd 819 p 92
212 Cd 819 p 94
213 Cd 819 p 84
214 Cd 819 p 82
215 Cd 819 p 78
216 Cd 819 p 77
217 Cd 819 p113
218 Cd 819 p 63
219 JH p97
220 JH p 97
221 *The Times*, 26 June 1901 p 14
222 RvR p 448
223 Three Balliol graduates became prime ministers – Asquith, Macmillan and Heath.
224 *The Times*, 26 June 1901 p 14, JHB p 241–47
225 *The Times*, 26 June 1901 p 14
226 JH p 105, JHB p 262
227 *The Times*, 26 June 1901 p 14
228 *The Times*, 1 July 1901 p 8

229 *The Times*, 1 July 1901 p 8
230 *The Times*, 1 July 1901 p 8
231 *The Times*, 2 July 1901 p 11
232 *The Times*, 4 July 1901 p 10, also 6 July p 6
233 JHB p 270
234 MG 8 July 1901 p 7
235 *The Times*, 9 July 1901 p 11
236 JHB p 275
237 *The Times*, 12 July 1901 p 11, JHB p 276
238 *The Times*, 9 July 1901, JH p 105
239 MG, 15 July 1901
240 *The Times*, 18 July 1901 p 6
241 JHB p 277, 278
242 *The Times*, 20 July 1901 p 13
243 JHB p 280
244 MG 23 July 1901 p 12
245 JHB p 285
246 JHB p 286
247 JHB p 286
248 RvR p 130, JHB p 307, MG 15 Aug 1901 p 9
249 RvR p 130, JHB p 307, MG 16 Aug 1901 p 9
250 RvR p 130, JHB p 307
251 RvR p 131 (EH refers to the Sunday before 29 Aug, which was 25 Aug)
252 JH p 105
253 JHB p 275
254 *The Times*, 20 July 1901 p 13
255 RvR p 130
256 RvR p 123
257 RvR p 124, JHB p 276
258 JHB p 285
259 JHB p 286
260 *The Times*, 1 Aug 1901, also EH1 p 135
261 *The Times*, 2 July 1901
262 *The Times*, 5 July 1901
263 See JCO pp 159, 160, 161
264 The possibly incomplete list is Balmoral, Belfast, Bloemfontein, Harrismith, Heidelberg, Heilbron, Johannesburg, Kroonstad, Middelburg (TVL), Springfontein, Standerton and Volksrust.
265 Cd 819 p 113 and p 107, JCO p 159,160
266 *The Times*, 25 July 1901 p10.
267 Cd 819 p 45
268 Cd 819 p 50
269 EvH1 p 190
270 Tucker, in the Transvaal, was called the 'General Superintendent' while his counterpart in the Orange River Colony, Trollope, had the title of 'Chief Superintendent'.
271 Cd 819 p 46
272 EvH1 p 191
273 Cd 819 p 216
274 EvH1 p 190
275 Van Heyningen has a chapter on the black camps, see EvH1 pp 150–78
276 EvH1 p 156
277 JHB p 271 citing WO 32/8061 8145
278 JH p 109
279 JH p 111
280 JH p 112
281 JH p 113
282 JH p 113
283 RvR p 452
284 EvH1 p 192
285 Cd 893 p 1
286 Cd 893 p 1
287 Cd 893 p 169
288 *The Times*, 19 Aug 1901 p 8, JHB p 309
289 According to Cd 819, the fatalities in the white camps for June were: TVL 750, ORC 359, Natal 7, Total **1,116**; for July: TVL 1,067, ORC 621, Natal 6, Total **1,694.** See pages 107, 113, 203, 209, 223.
290 *The Times*, 19 Aug 1901 p 8, JHB p 309
291 CW p 216
292 TP p 519
293 TP p 515

294 Cd 893 p 1
295 Cd 893 p 7
296 Cd 893 p 14
297 Cd 893 p 15
298 Cd 893 p 16
299 Cd 893 p 57
300 Cd 893 p 16
301 Cd 893 p 16
302 Cd 893 p 17
303 Cd 893 p 17
304 Cd 893 p 18
305 Cd 893 p 18
306 Cd 893 pp 9–14
307 EvH1 pp 172, 193
308 JCO pp 159, 160, 161
309 PW p 151
310 Cd 853 from p 1
311 Cd 853 p 22, CO p 49
312 Cd 902 p 8
313 Cd 853 p 128
314 J&S pp 215, 271
315 JHB p 287
316 JHB p 401 citing the Milner Papers dep 185 ff 277–82
317 Cd 934 p 50
318 W&W p 111
319 Personal communication, 2006
320 *The Times*, 27 Sept 1901 p 5
321 EH1 p 137, *The Times*, 3 Oct 1901 p 5
322 RvR p 125
323 *The Times*, 5 Oct 1901 p 12
324 JH p 123
325 JHB p 335, RvR p 139
326 JHB p 336, RvR p 140
327 JHB p 340, citing Milner Papers, Miss Hobhouse, 8ii p 233
328 JHB p 342

329 JHB p 342
330 JHB p 343
331 JHB p 343
332 JHB p 343
333 JHB p 344
334 JHB p 345
335 JHB p 346
336 RvR p 148, JHB p 346
337 RvR p 148, JHB p 348
338 RvR p 151, JHB p 351
339 RvR p 151, JHB p 351
340 RvR p 151, JHB p 351
341 EH1
342 JHB p 474, RvR p 164
343 BCCD
344 JCO pp 159–61
345 PW p 145
346 FP p 57, JCO p 156, JHB p 474, JH p 153
347 PW p 151
348 PW p 152
349 S&D 2009 p 14
350 EvH personal correspondence
351 PW p 151
352 HJO p 8
353 EvH, personal correspondence
354 W&W and personal communication with Rina Wiid
355 PW pp 151, 152, JH p 153
356 JHB p 403
357 JH p 213, p 215
358 The incomplete draft was sent to Tibbie Steyn and now resides among the Steyn papers in the Free State Archives.
359 JH p 289
360 JF p 270
361 JH p 296, JHB p 587

Sources of information cited in the text

ABP	Paterson, AB (Banjo) – see RD below
ACD	Doyle, Arthur Conan, *The Great Boer War*, George Bell & Sons, London, 1900.
AM	Sir Alfred Milner, correspondence cited in TC (see TC below)
AT	Terreblance, Annette, *Emily Hobhouse*, Afrikaanse Pers Boekhandel, Johannesburg, 1948 (in Afrikaans)
BCCD	A database entitled British Concentration Camps of the South African War 1900–1902 <www2.lib.uct.ac.za/mss/bccd/> This database is managed at the University of Cape Town and additions were still being made at the time of writing.
BF	Farwell, Byron, *The Great Boer War*, Allen Lane, Penguin Books Ltd, London, 1977, ISBN 0 7139 0820 3
BN	Nasson, Bill, *The War for South Africa: The Anglo-Boer War 1899–1902*, Tafelberg, an imprint of NB Publishers, Cape Town, 2010, ISBN 978-0-624-04809-1
Cd 426	*Proclamations issued by Field Marshall Lord Roberts in South Africa*, Report to Parliament, 1900
Cd 522	*South Africa Despatches, Despatch by General Lord Kitchener, dated 8th March, 1901, relative to Military Operations in South Africa*, Report to Parliament, 1901
Cd 524	*Return of Buildings burnt in each Month from June 1900 to January 1901*, Report to Parliament, 1901
Cd 819	*Reports, &c., on the working of the Refugee Camps in the Transvaal, Orange River Colony, Cape Colony, and Natal*, Report to Parliament, November 1901
Cd 893	*Report on the Concentration Camps in South Africa by the Committee of Ladies*, Report to Parliament, 1902
CdW	De Wet, Commandant-General Christiaan Rudolf, *Three Years War*, Galago Books, Alberton, South Africa, 2005, ISBN

1-919854-09-6 (originally published by Archibald Constable and Co, 1902)

CO Colonial Office Papers, *Correspondence relating to Refugee Camps in South Africa*, African (South) No 687, printed for the Colonial Office, July 1902.

ConsR Consular report. The National Archives of the United States, *Despatches from United States Consuls in Pretoria, 1898–1906*, Microcopy No T-660, roll 2 Volume 2, January 1, 1901 – December 28, 1903.

CW Wilcox, Craig, *Australia's Boer War: The War in South Africa 1899–1902*, Oxford University Press, Oxford, 2002, ISBN 0 19 551637 0

DR Reitz, Deneys, *Commando: A Boer Journal of the Boer War*, Faber and Faber Limited, London, 1929

EH1 Hobhouse, Emily, *The Brunt of the War and Where it Fell*, Kessinger Publishing's Legacy Reprint. (first published by Methuen & Co, London, 1902)

EH2 Hobhouse, Emily, *Report on a visit to the Camps of Women and Children in the Cape and Orange River Colonies*, printed and published by The Friars Printing Association Limited, London, 1901

EH3 Hobhouse, Emily, Unpublished draft autobiography in the Free State Archives, Bloemfontein. In the draft, Emily reproduced many of her own letters to her brother Leonard and aunt Mary, Lady Hobhouse. (They had been kept by her aunt and were returned to Emily.) Steyn Collection, A 156/3/11 and 12

EvH1 Van Heyningen, Elizabeth, *The Concentration Camps of the Anglo-Boer War: A Social History*, Jacana Media Pty Ltd, Johannesburg, 2013, ISBN 978-1-4314-0542-8

EvH2 Van Heyningen, Elizabeth, 'Women and disease: The clash of medical cultures in the concentration camps of the South African War', in Cuthbertson, Grundlingh and Suttie, *Writing a Wider War*, Ohio University Press, Athens, OH, 2002. ISBN 0-8214-1462-3 (also published by David Philip Publishers, Cape Town, ISBN 0-86486-607-0)

FP Pretorius, Fransjohan, *The Anglo-Boer War 1899–1902*, Struik Publishers, Cape Town, 1998, ISBN 1 86872 179 5

HJO Ogden, HJ, *The War against the Dutch Republics in South Africa, its origin, progress and results*, National Reform Union, Manchester, 1901

J&S Judd, Denis & Surridge, Keith, *The Boer War*, John Murray, London, 2002, ISBN 0-7195-6169 8

JB Brandt, Johanna, *The Petticoat Commando*, Mills & Boon, London, 1913 (This publisher might cause raised eyebrows. However, Johanna van Warmelo Brandt became a prominent writer and member of the post-war Afrikaner community.

The book carries an introduction by Sir Patrick Duncan, cabinet minister and later Governor-General of South Africa. It was first published, in Afrikaans, initially in serial form in *Die Brandwag*, a magazine, and later as a book, *Die Kappiekommando*.)

JCO   Otto, JC, *Die Konsentrasiekampe [The Concentration Camps]*, first published in 1954, republished by Protea Boekhuis, Pretoria, 2005, ISBN 1-919825-22-3

JF   Fisher, John, *That Miss Hobhouse: The Life of a Great Feminist*, Secker and Warburg, London, 1971

JH   Hall, John, *That Bloody Woman: The Turbulent Life of Emily Hobhouse*, Truran, Truro, Cornwall, 2008, ISBN 978 185022 217 0

JHB   Balme, Jennifer Hobhouse, *To Love One's Enemies*, Hobhouse Trust, Cobble Hill, BC, Canada, 1994, ISBN 0-9697133-0-4

LMP   Phillipps, Capt L March, *With Rimmington*, Edward Arnold, London, 1901

MG   *Manchester Guardian*, a newspaper published in Manchester, UK, forerunner of *The Guardian* now published in London

MP   Milner Papers, New College, Oxford, on permanent loan to the Bodleian Library, Oxford

P-C   Pine-Coffin, John Edward, *One Man's Boer War 1900: The Diary of John Edward Pine-Coffin*, edited by Susan Pine-Coffin, Edward Gaskell Publishers, Devon UK, 1999, ISBN 1-898546-34-7 ('With thanks to Edward Gaskell publishers (Devon UK) for permission to quote from *One Man's Boer War 1900*.' The publisher insisted on this form of acknowledgement, and we gladly comply.)

PT   Trew, Peter, *The Boer War Generals*, Wrens Park Publishing, 2001, ISBN 0 905 778 677

PW   Warwick, Peter, *Black People and the South African War 1899–1902*, Cambridge University Press, 1983, ISBN 0 521 27224 6

RD   Droogleever, Robin WF (ed.), *From the Front: A.B. (Banjo) Paterson's Dispatches from the Boer War*, Pan Macmillan Australia Pty Limited, Sydney, 2000, ISBN 0 7329 1062 5

RG&D   Extract from Robinson, Ronald; Gallagher, John and Denny, Alice, *Africa and the Victorians: The Official Mind of Imperialism*, MacMillan & Co, London, 1965, reprinted in TC (see below).

RK   Kruger, Rayne, *Good-bye Dolly Gray: The Story of the Boer War*, Cassell & Company Ltd, London, 1959

RvR   Rykie van Reenen (ed.), *Emily Hobhouse: Boer War Letters*, Human & Rousseau, Cape Town, 1984, ISBN 0 7981 1823 7 (based on the Steyn Collection, Bloemfontein, see EH3 above)

S&D 2009   Stanley, Liz & Dampier, Helen, *The number of the South African War (1899–1902) Concentration Camp Dead: Standard Stories,*

	Superior Stories and a Forgotten Proto-nationalist Research Investigation, Social Research Online 14(5)13, 3 Nov 2009, <www.socresonline.org.uk/14/5/13.html>
TC	Caldwell, Theodore C (ed.), *The Anglo-Boer War: Why Was It fought? Who Was Responsible?* DC Heath and Company, Boston, 1965
T&F	Todd, Pamela & Fordham, David, *Private Tucker's Boer War Diary*, Elm Tree Books, London, 1980, ISBN 0 241 10272 3
The Times	*The Times*, a newspaper published in London.
TP	Pakenham, Thomas, *The Boer War*, Weidenfeld and Nicholson Limited, London, 1979 ISBN 0 297 77395 X
US Arch	The National Archives of the United States, *Despatches from United States Consuls in Pretoria, 1898–1906,* Microcopy No T-660, roll 2 Volume 2, January 1, 1901 – December 28, 1903.
VAR 153/3/11	Free State Archives, Bloemfontein. Steyn Collection: Draft Autobiography of Emily Hobhouse – Part 1.
W&W	Wiid, Rina & West, Winnie, *Die Oranjerivierkampe tydens die Anglo-Boereoorlog [The Orange River camps during the Anglo Boer War] 1899–1902*, Protea Boekhuis, Pretoria, 2002, ISBN 1-919825-77-0

Acknowledgments

The writing of this work would have been much more difficult without the books of Rykie van Reenen (RvR) and Jennifer Hobhouse Balme (JHB). Van Reenen's contains Emily Hobhouse's Boer War letters in full, and Balme's contains the same letters either fully or in substantial extract. Although the letters are also available at the Free State Archives in Bloemfontein, and were consulted there, the convenient reproduction of those letters in these books, and the contextualising provided in these two sources were invaluable.

Mrs Balme also kindly read this manuscript, made suggestions and provided additional information and photographs not otherwise available. Elizabeth van Heyningen, an historian with deep knowledge of the camps, also read the manuscript, corrected many errors, filled omissions and provided substantial commentary.

I am especially grateful to Prof Marilyn Lake, Professor in History at the University of Melbourne and until recently the President of the Australian Historical Association; Prof Dorothy Driver, Professor in the Department of English and Creative Writing, University of Adelaide; Dr Robin Derricourt, friend, archaeologist, academic and former CEO of the University of NSW Press and Dr Robin Droogleever, President of the Australian Anglo-Boer War Study Group, all of whom graciously consented to read the draft. Their helpful comments led to improvements and they provided much-needed encouragement to proceed to publication. Other friends also read the manuscript and made useful suggestions, notably Frances le Roux.

At an earlier stage of development, the manuscript was independently reviewed by Helen Barnes-Bulley (through Varuna, The Writers House, Katoomba, NSW) and Stuart MacDonald (through the NSW Writers' Centre). Their assistance and encouragement were also very valuable.

Archivists and librarians in the UK, South Africa and Australia guided and assisted me in retrieving materials and opened gates to hidden online resources. Their assistance was and is greatly appreciated. Marie-Louise Taylor undertook the pre-publication edit and I am most thankful for her diligent input.

The final acknowledgement goes to my wife, Jane, who lived tolerantly through the process of creation, graciously travelled to locations she would otherwise not have visited, read the draft and remained encouraging all the way through. She wrote a completely different book of her own during the gestation of this one. It preceded this book into publication.

Photographic credits

Jennifer Hobhouse Balme: Cover image of Emily Hobhouse and page 261

Anglo-Boer War Museum, Bloemfontein: Also cover images of Emily Hobhouse and concentration camp, and pages 69, 111, 116, 131, 252–3, 254–5

Robert Eales: pages 28, 227, 265, 271, 272

Jane R Eales: page 289

Naming convention

Throughout this book, as the reader will have seen, Emily Hobhouse is mentioned frequently by her first name only while others (mainly men) are often mentioned by their last or full names. To avoid giving an unintended impression, a word of explanation is offered on the naming convention that was adopted.

It seemed that calling EH by her first name would be appropriate as this is a popular rather than an academic account. *She* is the main character in the book and it is about her. For a book aimed at a general market, using only her full name or last name seemed unnecessarily formal. On the other hand, it is conventional that historically important figures are referred to by their last names or full names but not their first names. Hence: Milner, Alfred Milner, Sir Alfred Milner, Lord Milner; Kitchener, Herbert Kitchener, Lord Kitchener; Mrs Fawcett, Millicent Fawcett – but not Alfred, Herbert or Millicent. Books published in the last few decades on Emily Hobhouse, whether by women or men, all follow this convention (except Van Reenen who uses the abbreviation 'E.H.').

If the principal character in the book were male, the same rule would apply. Thus, if this were a book about Deneys Reitz, (a young Boer who fought in and wrote a well-known book about the war) his first name would mostly be used. But if it were about Jan Smuts, it would mostly be 'Smuts'.

About the author

DR ROBERT EALES went to high school in the South African city of Bloemfontein where much of this book is set. Subsequently, he studied at the University of the Witwatersrand in Johannesburg and Balliol College, Oxford.

His career was in management consulting and banking and he worked in Johannesburg, Sydney, London and, briefly, in San Francisco. He retired from the business world in 2005 and has been researching the South African War of 1899-1902 ever since. He has delivered many talks on this war, presented papers at conferences and been published in historical journals.

Index

Lightning Source UK Ltd.
Milton Keynes UK
UKOW01f2302180118
316422UK00015B/481/P